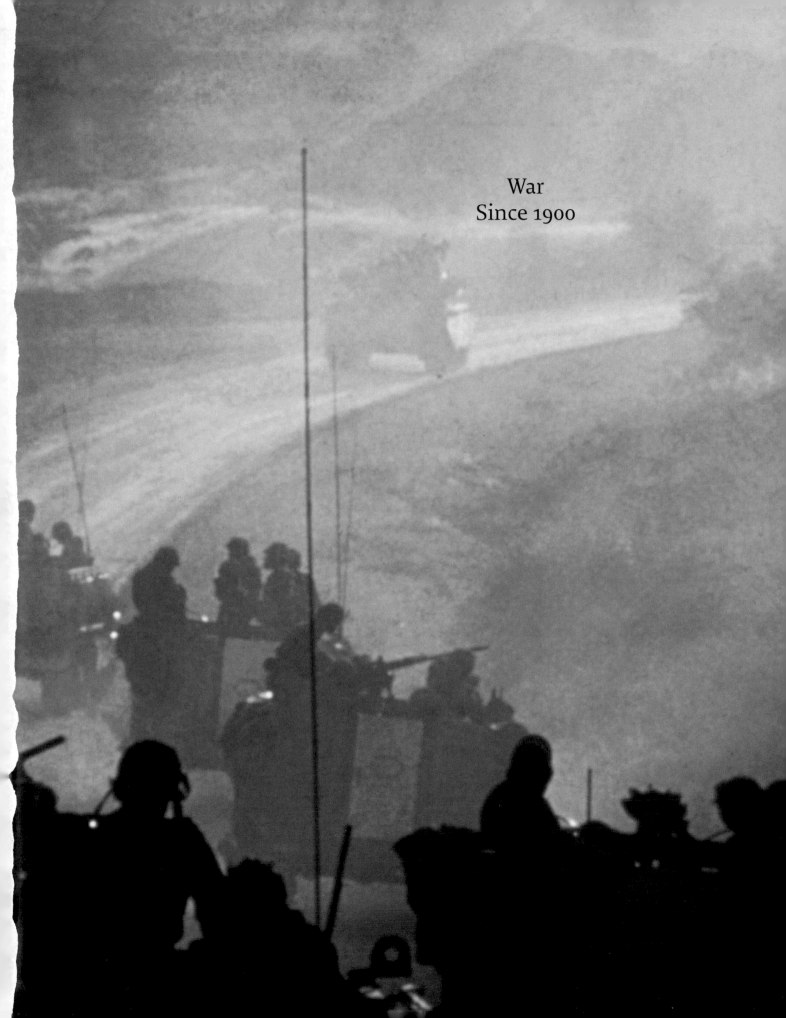

War
Since 1900

War
Since 1900

EDITED BY JEREMY BLACK

With 294 illustrations, 177 in color

p. 1 An Israeli armoured brigade makes its way up to the Golan Heights at dawn of Day 2 of the Yom Kippur War, 1973.

pp. 2–3 South Vietnamese army rangers, supported by helicopters, make their way through long grass during an assault into the Plaine des Joncs, Vietnam, *c.* 1965.

These pages A young man holding his Kalashnikov rifle looks over the remote Omo Valley, Ethiopia, 2009.

Chapter 10: 'End of Empire' was translated from the French by David H. Wilson.

First published in 2010 in hardcover in the United States of America by Thames & Hudson Inc., 500 Fifth Avenue, New York, New York 10110

thamesandhudsonusa.com

Library of Congress Catalog Card Number 2010923316

ISBN 978-0-500-25163-8

Printed and bound in China by Toppan Printing

Contents

Introduction

The Changing Nature of Modern War

The fundamental character of conflict does not change. Killing and risking being killed, for the sake of forcing others to accept one's will, remain the basic condition of warfare, and also pose the lasting problem of the contrast between output, in the shape of military activity, and outcome, in the form of an accepted political solution. The theme of continuity has also been pushed hard by combatants in some of the conflicts discussed in this volume, whether Nazis pursuing a supposed German destiny in terms of European living space, Russians seeking warm-water ports, or al-Qaeda arguing that Islam should regain control of lands once under Muslim sway, notably southern Spain and Israel.

Right Mars attacks, from a 1906 edition of H. G. Wells's *War of the Worlds*. As the 20th century progressed, Wells's terrifying vision of warfare waged with an utter disregard for human life began to seem increasingly prescient. Indeed, in World War II the terrorizing of civilian populations and annihilation of cities were actively pursued as strategies.

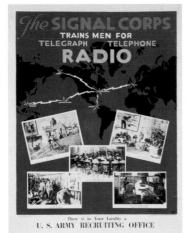

Above A World War I recruitment poster for the US Army Signal Corps. World War I was a testing ground for new technologies, although tactics were slow to adapt.

Opposite A German Fokker D.VII in the air over the Western Front in 1918. As part of the armistice agreement at the end of World War I, all Fokker D.VIIs were signed over to the Allies – a reflection of the increasing importance of air superiority.

Yet there have also been fundamental discontinuities in the nature and context of warfare, as the chapters that follow amply demonstrate. A chapter on sea power in a book on 17th-century warfare would hardly discuss submarines or aircraft carriers, while aerial capability in the 19th century was restricted to balloons without engines and also primitive rockets. These spheres of conflict were to be very different in the 20th century. By 1909, American battleships were being designed with larger coal bunkers, allowing a steaming radius of 18,500 km (10,000 nautical miles), which was a major increase on the situation in the 1890s. Major naval powers were responding to the transforming potential offered by radio, while aircraft were of increased interest to armies and navies. In 1900, the American navy commissioned the USS *Holland*, its first submarine; in 1912, the American Eugene Ely piloted the first plane off a ship; and the British army integrated air power into manoeuvres in the early 1910s. Interest in the future of warfare gripped the literary imagination, public debate, and government discussion and planning. Air power very much suggested new possibilities, and a sense of unlimited boundaries was revealed in H. G. Wells's 1897 serial *The War of the Worlds* – in which Martian missiles convey war machines that

overrun England and destroy London, only to fall victim to bacteria. Wells captured an awareness that war might not conform to rules or limits, and this anxiety was to be fully vindicated in the two world wars of the 20th century.

New technologies were tested in World War I, a key conflict that is justifiably the subject of two chapters, as well as being discussed in those on air and sea warfare. These technologies became more potent in World War II, so that, by the time of the Combined (Anglo-American) Bomber Offensive against Germany in 1942–45, air power was seen as a strategic tool, a capability that was to be amply demonstrated with the dropping of the American atomic bombs on Japan in 1945. The nature of naval conflict was also transformed by air power. Although Britain, the United States and Japan developed a significant carrier capability in the 1930s, they continued to emphasize battleship construction, whereas Hitler and Stalin also sought to acquire battleships. This reflected a reluctance to embrace change, but there was too a concern about the vulnerability of carriers and a lack of experience of the effectiveness of air power.

This situation was transformed during World War II. Air power not only proved highly effective in the struggle by Britain, Canada and the United States against German submarines in the Battle of the Atlantic, helping turn the tide against them in 1943, but also played the key role in the struggle between Japan and the United States for dominance of the Western Pacific. In the Battle of the Coral Sea in 1942, surface units did not see each other, and the fighting was a matter of air attacks; this pattern was the dominant, although not sole, one thereafter.

Technology on land was also very different by 1945 from what it had been in 1914. Large-scale advances, such as those made by the Americans across southern Germany and by Soviet forces into Manchuria, were highly mechanized and rapid-moving as a result. Tanks were supported by mechanized infantry and artillery.

Nevertheless, any stress on change has also to take note of important continuities. The prime killer of men in World War II was neither aircraft nor tanks but, as in World War I, artillery. Troops were deployed in different formations from those used in Napoleonic warfare at the start of the 19th century, but there were important similarities between the conscript armies in both periods, not least in terms of tactics and operations based on the availability of large numbers of troops.

Above The nuclear bombs dropped on the Japanese cities of Hiroshima and Nagasaki in August 1945 killed as many as 250,000 people, the overwhelming majority civilians. The horrifying destructive potential of this new type of weapon would define global relations for decades to come.

'The harder the fighting and the longer the war, the more the infantry, and in fact all the arms, lean on the gunners.'
Field Marshal Bernard Montgomery, 1945

Opposite A unit of Soviet tanks on their way to the front at the Battle of Kursk, 1943. It remains the largest ever armoured clash, and the resulting decisive Soviet victory gave the Red Army the strategic initiative for the rest of the war.

The world wars were long seen as the definition of modern warfare: 'large-scale', 'industrial', 'total' and 'deadly' were key adjectives. The arithmetic of threatened nuclear destruction during the Cold War between the US-led West and the Soviet-led Communist bloc from 1946 to 1989 appeared to keep this description valid. Indeed, there was sufficient nuclear potential to destroy all human life, and the catastrophe of nuclear conflict appeared imminent on a number of occasions, in 1962 and 1983 for example.

Yet the experience of conflict for the major powers after 1945 was in practice very different. Wars for survival were replaced by expeditionary warfare, such as the Americans in Vietnam from the early 1960s to 1975 and the Soviets in Afghanistan in 1979–88; conscription ceased (in the early 1970s in the United States); and there was no total mobilization of society's resources. Indeed, spending on the military

An American Marine in Somalia meets local children as he guards food aid distribution during 'Operation Restore Hope', 1993.

as a percentage of total national expenditure fell in most major states, while the share devoted to social welfare rose.

At the same time, however, war was devastating many parts of the Third World, notably, but not only, because it was linked to famine and disease, as well as to more deliberate policies of attack on civilian society. This warfare was frequently waged in pursuit of ethnic or social strategies aimed at the reduction, if not the extirpation, of groups that were judged a threat, most graphically with the massacres in Rwanda in 1994, but also in Congo and Sudan. Much of the conflict lacked the regularity sought by the professional forces of the major powers, and this absence served to underline the diversity of the nature of warfare. There was often a pronounced overlap with political struggles for control within states, notably in Africa, the continent where conflict was most insistent from the 1980s.

When in turn such forces came into conflict with the regular militaries of major states – for example Afghans against Soviet units in the 1980s and against NATO units in the 2000s – there was an asymmetrical warfare that raised major, and continuing, questions about the nature of military capability and the pursuit

'In the end, no amount of American forces can solve the political differences that lie at the heart of somebody else's civil war.'

Barack Obama, US Senator, 2007

of effectiveness in war. This situation is not a new one. Across the 20th century, Western military superiority on land was more conditional and less secure than is generally presumed. This was especially so in the Middle East, for example in Egypt and Iraq after World War I, when the Western forces found it difficult to do better than their Ottoman predecessors. Yet despite the limitations, it was a case of Western troops in Beijing (1900) and Baghdad (1917/2003), and not vice versa.

The problems faced by the Americans after conquering Iraq in 2003 and by NATO in Afghanistan in the mid-2000s have forced the leading powers to rethink tactics and doctrine, notably leading to a greater emphasis on counter-insurgency, and they have also raised issues about the nature of domestic support for long-term military commitments. The last indicates a major shift from the situation in 1900. Imperialism no longer enjoys support, while militarist values are publicly displayed in very few societies. There has been a revolution in attitudes to the military that represents a profound change in the context of conflict.

Taliban fighters load a multiple rocket launcher. The purpose of the US-led invasion of Afghanistan was to capture Osama Bin Laden, destroy al-Qaeda and remove the Taliban regime; only the last has been achieved to date, although the Taliban have still not been defeated.

1 The Prelude to War, 1900–1914

LAWRENCE SONDHAUS

KEY DATES

20 May 1882 Triple Alliance formed by Germany, Austria-Hungary and Italy

18 August 1892 Military convention concluded between France and Russia

11 October 1899 Boers invade Cape Colony, initiating Anglo-Boer War

31 May 1902 Treaty of Vereeniging signed, ending Anglo-Boer War

8 February 1904 Japanese attack on Port Arthur: outbreak of Russo-Japanese War

8 April 1904 Entente Cordiale concluded between Britain and France

5 September 1905 Treaty of Portsmouth signed, ending Russo-Japanese War

2 December 1906 HMS *Dreadnought* commissioned

31 August 1907 Anglo-Russian convention concluded, completing Triple Entente

18 October 1912 Balkan League initiates First Balkan War against Ottoman Empire

30 May 1913 Treaty of London signed, ending First Balkan War

29 June 1913 Bulgaria turns on Balkan allies: outbreak of Second Balkan War

10 August 1913 Treaty of Bucharest concluded, ending Second Balkan War

Opposite Admiral Togo's fleet sortie against Port Arthur, 9 February 1904 – the day after Japanese torpedo boats surprised the Russian Pacific squadron.

Warfare in the fourteen years preceding the outbreak of World War I was motivated by conflicts spilling over from the 19th century that also foreshadowed the bloodier struggles of the 20th. Three of these wars rose above the rest in scope and broader significance. The Anglo-Boer War of 1899–1902, essentially a colonial conflict, matched Britain against a determined foe of European stock armed with late-model European weapons. The Russo-Japanese War of 1904–5, like the Crimean War a half-century earlier, exposed Russia's relative weakness vis-à-vis the other great powers, and served notice that Japan had emerged as the leading power in the Far East. Finally, the Balkan Wars of 1912–13 engulfed Europe's most volatile region without, for the moment, igniting the continent as a whole.

Since the end of the Thirty Years War (1648), Europe's most powerful states had coexisted in an often uneasy balance, making and breaking alliances among themselves in pursuit of their own interests. By 1900 five of the six leading European states had joined peacetime alliances: Germany, Austria-Hungary and Italy, united in the Triple Alliance (1882), and France and Russia, linked by an alliance and military convention (1892–94). Britain, still the world's leading industrial nation as well as its leading naval and colonial power, remained unattached at the turn of the century, as did the emerging non-European powers, the United States and Japan.

THE ANGLO-BOER WAR

Britain's conflict with the white South Africans known as Boers, or Afrikaners, dated from its appropriation of the Dutch colony at the Cape of Good Hope in 1806. Boers migrating inland from the Cape eventually established the Orange Free State and South African Republic (Transvaal), agrarian countries left alone by the British until the discovery of diamonds and gold made them targets for annexation. Transvaal reasserted its independence in a brief war with Britain (1880–81), but tensions escalated after the Witwatersrand gold rush of 1886 saw it become swamped with immigrants (*uitlanders*), mostly English-speaking, who were denied political rights. Ten years later, feelings flared after L. S. Jameson invaded Transvaal on behalf of the uitlanders. The incident assumed a greater importance internationally when Kaiser Wilhelm II sent a telegram congratulating the Transvaal president Paul Kruger on Jameson's defeat, signalling the onset of the pre-1914 deterioration in Anglo-German relations. In September 1899 Britain formally demanded equal rights for Transvaal's uitlanders, an action threatening enough to activate a 1897 defence treaty between the two Boer republics. On 11 October 1899 the Orange Free State and Transvaal initiated hostilities with a pre-emptive strike into the Cape Colony.

Throughout the war British forces performed poorly in the field. Auxiliaries were far less reliable than regulars and remained prone to panic under fire even late in the war. Most British officers emphasized volley fire by tight formations of infantry, a tactic effective in colonial warfare against non-Europeans but disastrous against the Boers. Like most militias since antiquity, the Boer armies were led by amateurs. Each commando elected its own officers, and senior commanders were drawn from the political leaders of the two republics. Few Boer generals had knowledge of strategy or tactics, and command-and-control issues plagued the Boer war effort, especially when their troops were amalgamated into larger formations. The loose militia structure of the commandos made them most effective in smaller actions, where individual initiative, ingenuity and bravery mattered most.

The Boer armies proved incapable of executing the decisive opening offensive that President Kruger hoped would win the war before the British could bring their considerable strength to bear. Their initial moves included besieging British garrisons at Mafeking and Kimberley, on the western border of the Orange Free State, and at Ladysmith in Natal. An uncoordinated offensive across the Orange river to seize three railway junctions in the Cape Colony captured only the one at Stormberg. The British commander, General Sir Redvers Buller, focused on rescuing the besieged garrisons. All three were relieved, but only after Buller had given way to Field Marshal Lord Roberts. The change came in the wake of Britain's 'Black Week' of 10–15 December 1899, when the Boers blocked drives to retake Kimberley, Ladysmith and Stormberg, in each case beating back unimaginative frontal assaults by British infantry.

Under Roberts the British exploited their growing numerical superiority to push back the Boers on all fronts. After abandoning Kimberley to Roberts, General Piet Cronjé inexplicably circled his wagons at Paardeberg in the western Orange Free State, allowing his army to be surrounded there by Roberts's superior force. The Battle of Paardeberg (February 1900) ended in the surrender of Cronjé and his 4,000 troops. Thereafter British forces advanced through the Boer republics, occupying all the cities and larger towns, and finally took Pretoria on 5 June. Boer commandos resorted to guerrilla tactics, prompting Roberts to authorize the retaliatory burning of farms and houses adjacent to railway and telegraph lines destroyed by saboteurs. Roberts left South Africa in November 1900, believing the war to be won, but after Paardeberg the British did not manage to capture or destroy a significant body of Boer commandos. Boer leaders formalized the guerrilla strategy and supplemented it with incursions into the Cape Colony to revolutionize the large Afrikaner population living there. These raids were all beaten back, and just 6,000 of the Cape Colony's 260,000 Afrikaners rebelled against the British. Under Roberts's successor, General Lord Kitchener, anti-sabotage measures stripped the occupied Boer countryside of anyone and anything of use to the commandos. Kitchener's men imprisoned Afrikaner women and children in concentration camps (where thousands of their black African servants and labourers also languished), destroyed crops, confiscated livestock, and built 10,000 blockhouses to guard railway and telegraph lines. The brutal campaign deprived the Boers of the means to continue resistance and also, psychologically, caused more of them to give up the cause as lost.

In the end, it was through the draconian measures normally associated with Kitchener (though begun by Roberts), backed by the sheer force of their numbers,

Above For the most part farmers and hunters, the Boer commandos proved able marksmen, most effective when engaged in guerrilla warfare.

Right French lithograph depicting a British concentration camp in the occupied Boer republics, 1901.

Opposite Paul Kruger, the Transvaal president, in a *Vanity Fair* cartoon of 1899.

In the Anglo-Boer War, the British found themselves under fire from guns of their own manufacture. Here, uniformed Transvaal State Artillery operate the Maxim gun known as the 'Pom-Pom'.

that the British forced the Boers to the peace table. British and imperial casualties included 21,000 dead (13,000 from disease). On the Boer side, where combatants were more difficult to differentiate from civilians, at least 30,000 died, of whom 4,000 to 8,000 were men under arms. The peace terms provided for a general amnesty for Boer combatants, including their leaders.

In the military realm a consensus quickly developed that the conditions in South Africa had been unusual enough to limit the broader applicability of any macro-level strategic or operational lessons learned there. Thus the lessons taken from the war were limited to the micro-level of weaponry, tactics and training. It was the first war in which the infantrymen of both sides were armed primarily with magazine rifles, and infantry firepower had clearly been decisive. Quick-firing artillery and smokeless powder, which had revolutionized naval combat in the 1880s, likewise had made their first appearance in land warfare. Sceptics countered that much of the conflict had occurred in treeless, barren terrain, and the thin atmosphere of the veldt had exaggerated the range of both firearms and artillery. Tactically, British infantry had been most successful when deploying in extended order

'Perhaps it is God's will to lead the people of South Africa through defeat and humiliation to a better future and a brighter day.'

Jan Smuts, to Boer delegates at the Vereeniging peace conference, South Africa, 31 May 1902

BRITISH ENTRY INTO PRETORIA—JUNE 5, 1900.

British lithograph depicting Field Marshal Lord Roberts and General Lord Kitchener reviewing troops following the capitulation of Pretoria on 5 June 1900.

and advancing in small groups under cover. There had not been a single successful bayonet charge in the entire war. British cavalrymen had been most useful when they fought dismounted with rifles, like the Boer commandos. Important organizational lessons transformed the British army's reserve formations, culminating in the creation of the Territorial Force in 1908. Most other great powers took notice and adopted measures to close the gap in fighting ability between their reserves and regular troops.

THE RUSSO-JAPANESE WAR

Tensions between Russia and Japan had their immediate origins in the Sino-Japanese War of 1894–95, after which Russian diplomatic pressure (supported by France and Germany) forced the Japanese to return the Liaodong Peninsula, with Port Arthur, to China. The Russians then persuaded the Chinese to lease these same territories to them, and to allow Port Arthur to be linked to Russia via the Chinese Eastern Railway and the South Manchurian Railway. As work on the railways progressed, the Russian Pacific squadron moved from Vladivostok to Port Arthur, which was ice-free year-round. Thereafter the rivals strengthened their forces on land and at sea, until their competition for spheres of influence in Manchuria and Korea led to a breakdown of relations. On 8 February 1904 Japan initiated hostilities in a surprise attack against the Russian squadron at Port Arthur.

The Russian army of 1904 included 1.1 million conscripts on active service backed by 2.4 million reserves. At the start of 1904 the Japanese army included 380,000 conscripts on active duty and 470,000 reserves. The active force grew steadily during the war, and by its end included 900,000 troops deployed on the East Asian mainland. The deployment of Japanese troops began the day after the navy's raid on Port Arthur, with the landing of the First Army at Chemulpo (Inchon). These troops met no resistance until they reached the Yalu river, and crossed into Manchuria on 1 May 1904. Days later the navy landed the Second Army on the Liaodong Peninsula, 100 km (60 miles) north-east of Port Arthur. Foreshadowing the bloody action to come, on 25–26 May these troops overcame an entrenched Russian force at Nanshan with a series of frontal assaults that resulted in 4,300 casualties, more men than Japan had lost in the entire Sino-Japanese War a decade earlier. The defeat forced the Russian

On 13 April 1904 a Japanese mine sank the Russian battleship *Petropavlovsk* during a sortie against the blockade at Port Arthur.

Above General Aleksei Kuropatkin, commander-in-chief of the Russian armies, fighting at the Battle of Liaoyang (24 August – 4 September 1904).

Above right A woodblock print showing the Japanese attacking the walled town of Chinchou during a violent thunderstorm, 24 May 1905. In the subsequent Battle of Nanshan, the Japanese were victorious but suffered heavy losses.

army on the Liaodong Peninsula to withdraw to Port Arthur, leaving the Japanese in control of the nearby seaport of Dalny (Darien) and astride the railway leading north to Harbin. The Japanese navy then landed General Maresuke Nogi's Third Army at Dalny and the Fourth Army west of the mouth of the Yalu. While Nogi assumed responsibility for the siege of Port Arthur, the Fourth Army joined the First and Second in moving north into central Manchuria to meet the steady stream of troops from European Russia arriving via rail to reinforce General Aleksei Kuropatkin's Russian army.

The deployment of Nogi's Third Army caused a crisis for the Russians, who lacked the strength either on land or at sea to relieve the pressure on Port Arthur. The Japanese navy's victories in the battles of the Yellow Sea (10 August) and Sea of Japan (14 August), combined with its successful blockade of Port Arthur, left Russia with no usable sea power in the war zone. The question then became one of whether Port Arthur could hold out until Russia's Baltic Fleet reached the Far East to break the blockade. On the land side Nogi used the same tactics that had worked at Nanshan, with the same staggering losses. In addition to minefields, barbed wire and machine guns, the siege also featured the use of electric fences and searchlights, wireless radio and artillery barrages of enemy trenches. Meanwhile the Russian warships bottled up in the harbour were either sunk by shellfire or scuttled. With the Baltic Fleet still months away, Port Arthur capitulated on 2 January 1905. The five-month siege cost the Japanese at least 58,000 casualties, the Russians 31,000. News of the surrender sparked unrest on the home front, and in St Petersburg the Bloody Sunday massacre (22 January) marked the onset of the Revolution of 1905.

While Nogi besieged Port Arthur the main campaign unfolded in central Manchuria, where Field Marshal Iwao Oyama held overall command of the Japanese forces facing the main Russian army under Kuropatkin. As reinforcements swelled

> '*From a hill in front of us we saw white smoke rising and spreading a strange odor far and wide; that was the cremation of our brave dead, the altar on which the sacrifice to the country was being burnt.*'
>
> Lieutenant Tadayoshi Sakurai, after the Battle of Nanshan, 26 May 1904

Right From 5 December 1904 the Japanese army at Port Arthur turned their 11-inch howitzers against the Russian Pacific Fleet blockaded in the harbour below, thus hastening the Russian surrender.

Opposite At the Battle of Tsushima (27–28 May 1905), the Russian Baltic Fleet suffered almost total defeat at the hands of Admiral Togo.

the size of the opposing armies, trenches became more extensive and the Japanese advance slowed amid escalating losses on both sides. The battles of Liaoyang and Shaho resulted in 100,000 casualties between them. Nogi joined Oyama from Port Arthur in time for the decisive Battle of Mukden (20 February to 10 March 1905), in which each side deployed just over 270,000 men. Presaging the continuous fronts of World War I, the opposing trench lines grew to a length of 145 km (90 miles) at Mukden, the largest and bloodiest battle in history up to that time. Kuropatkin avoided encirclement at Mukden and withdrew to be reinforced behind a new front farther north, but not before suffering losses of nearly 90,000 men (including 20,000 captured), compared with over 75,000 killed and wounded in Oyama's armies.

Mukden was the last significant land battle of the war, but even as the Revolution of 1905 swept the Russian home front, the tsar refused to sue for peace until after Admiral Zinovy Rozhestvensky's fleet, arriving from the Baltic too late to save Port Arthur, met Admiral Heihachiro Togo's fleet at Tsushima (27–28 May 1905). Togo won a decisive victory over Rozhestvensky's larger but older fleet, which was sunk or captured in its entirety, save three small escort ships, while the Japanese lost just three torpedo boats of their own. In addition to driving Russia to seek terms, Japan's stunning victory at Tsushima attracted world attention for another reason: the efficiency of their largest-calibre guns decided the battle. Naval architects had already produced designs for all-big-gun battleships, but the tactical verdict of Tsushima vindicated the concept and opened the way for a revolution in naval warfare.

Peace negotiations hosted by US President Theodore Roosevelt at Portsmouth, New Hampshire, resulted in a treaty (5 September 1905) giving Japan the southern half of Sakhalin Island and the Russian lease of Port Arthur and the Liaodong Peninsula, along with control over the South Manchurian Railway. Russia and Japan agreed to evacuate the rest of Manchuria and respect Chinese sovereignty there. Russia acknowledged a Japanese sphere of influence in Korea, which Japan annexed in 1910.

Command of the sea in the war zone enabled Japan to deploy over 1 million men to the East Asian mainland at a loss of just three transport vessels. The Russian navy's inability to disrupt the deployment negated the impact of the Russian army's achievement of shipping over 1 million men to the Far East via an 8,000-km (5,000-mile) single-track railway, and also foiled Kuropatkin's strategy of standing on the defensive until Russia's superior numbers could be brought to bear. The operations of both armies were hamstrung by logistical problems, since Kuropatkin had to stay close to his railway lifeline, and Oyama repeatedly won victories

'The fate of the empire rests upon this one battle; let every man do his utmost.'

Admiral Heihachiro Togo, signal flown from flagship *Mikasa* at outbreak of Battle of Tsushima, 27 May 1905

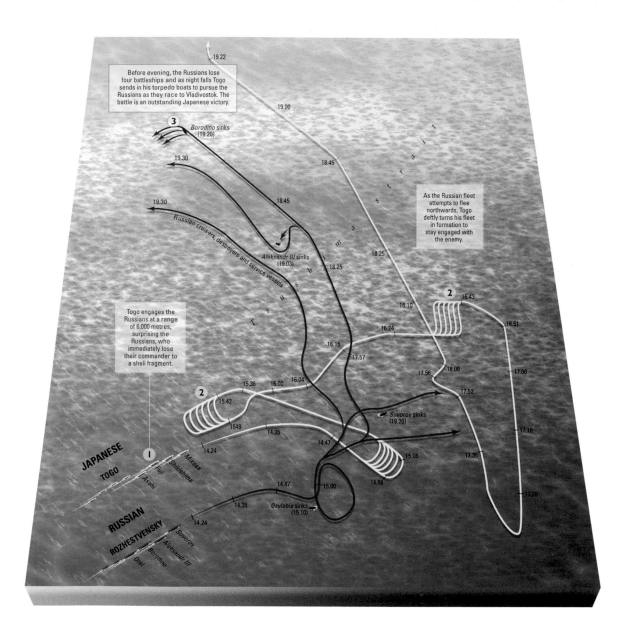

21

that were unexpectedly costly in men and materiel. The Japanese could reinforce and resupply their armies more quickly than the Russians, but not fast enough to exploit their successes. They also benefited from more efficient communications and better execution of their plans, while the Russians suffered from command-and-control problems and debilitating personal rivalries among their generals. Kuropatkin enjoyed a great advantage in cavalry, but his mounted troops did little to provide him with intelligence or to disrupt Japanese operations. There are no definitive figures on the human cost of the war. Japan probably suffered at least 200,000 casualties, including as many as 80,000 dead. Total Russian losses were at least 335,000 and perhaps as high as 435,000, including at least 60,000 dead. Relatively low civilian casualties (estimated at 20,000) reflect Japan's benign attitude towards Chinese civilians, a sharp contrast with its brutal policies in World War II. The Japanese also treated prisoners of war humanely, likewise in sharp contrast to their future practices.

In the Russo-Japanese War, as in the Anglo-Boer War, infantry on both sides operated most successfully in extended order and when advancing in small groups under cover, but open-field bayonet charges had been pursued successfully by both armies, albeit at horrific costs, invalidating (at least for many observers) the lessons from South Africa concerning the decisive nature of firepower by dispersed infantry. Machine guns had been employed extensively for the first time, but commentators criticized both sides for using them strictly as defensive weapons. The limited use of heavy artillery, mostly in the siege of Port Arthur, allowed for a wide range of speculation concerning its future utility. Ultimately the outcome supported the conventional wisdom of the prevailing 'cult of the offensive': attackers won wars and defenders lost them (see box opposite). The Japanese had demonstrated that an attacking force with the morale to absorb losses of 35 to 40 per cent could still prevail, even on a battlefield where modern technology favoured the defender.

Stereoscopic photograph of Russian troops standing over a trench filled with Japanese dead, Port Arthur, 1904.

The Cult of the Offensive

The 'cult of the offensive' emerged from a German way of war rooted in the military reforms enacted by Prussia following its humiliating defeat at the hands of Napoleon in 1806. Carl von Clausewitz (1780–1831) served as the prophet for this faith, his posthumous *On War* (1832) functioning as its holy scripture, and Field Marshal Helmuth von Moltke the Elder (1800–1891) its delivering messiah. Following Moltke's triumphs against Austria (1866) and France (1870–71) in the Wars of German Unification, Clausewitz's *On War* was translated and studied throughout Europe. Moltke, like Napoleon, sought the destruction of enemy armies in decisive battles. Those seeking to emulate the Prussian–German example likewise embraced the offensive and overlooked the longest section of *On War*, which concerned defensive warfare. The German general and military writer Colmar von der Goltz, the leading Social Darwinist interpreter of Clausewitz, accelerated the trend with his international bestseller *The Nation in Arms* (1883).

The cult of the offensive persisted despite evidence from the Anglo-Boer War and the Russo-Japanese War that emerging technologies favoured defensive warfare. Paradoxically, it offered the greatest hope to two of the weaker military powers of Europe, Austria-Hungary and France. Franz Conrad von Hötzendorf, instructor at the War School in Vienna and, later, chief of the Austro-Hungarian general staff, and Ferdinand Foch, instructor and later commandant at the War School in Paris before becoming supreme allied commander in 1918, both advocated offensive strategies that proved to be completely inappropriate for the situations their countries faced in World War I. The results were fatal for Austria-Hungary and nearly so for France.

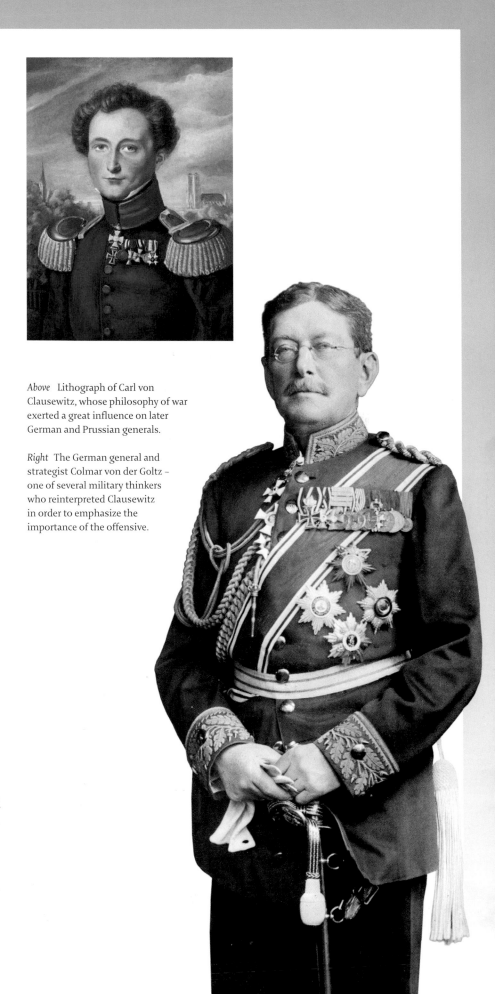

Above Lithograph of Carl von Clausewitz, whose philosophy of war exerted a great influence on later German and Prussian generals.

Right The German general and strategist Colmar von der Goltz – one of several military thinkers who reinterpreted Clausewitz in order to emphasize the importance of the offensive.

THE BALKAN WARS

The short-term causes of the Balkan Wars (1912–13) dated from the Russo-Turkish War of 1877–78, which had weakened Ottoman Turkey's grip on the Balkans. The Congress of Berlin (1878) left Serbia, Montenegro and Romania independent, Bulgaria autonomous but still under Ottoman suzerainty, and Bosnia and Herzegovina still technically Ottoman but occupied by Austria-Hungary. The Young Turk Revolution (1908) prompted Austria-Hungary to annex Bosnia-Herzegovina and Bulgaria to declare its independence, but left a revitalized Ottoman government determined to retain its remaining Balkan territories – Albania, Macedonia and Thrace – which were coveted in whole or in part by Bulgaria, Serbia, Montenegro and Greece. After the Turks became embroiled in the Italo-Turkish War (1911–12), these four states formed the Balkan League and mobilized for war. On 18 October 1912, the same day the Italians and Turks formally ended their war, the armies of the Balkan League invaded the Ottoman Empire.

The Balkan League mobilized just over 1 million troops (600,000 Bulgarians, 230,000 Serbs, 200,000 Greeks and 35,000 Montenegrins), of whom roughly 700,000 saw action against the Turks. Greece's modest navy sufficed to control the Aegean, hampering the Turks' efforts to deploy and supply their troops. Only Serbia and

Bulgarian troops deployed at Kartal Teji during the siege of Adrianople, First Balkan War, 1912–13.

Montenegro coordinated their military operations, reflecting the league's character as a loose alliance among rivals united only in their mutual hatred of the Turks. Of the 850,000 men in the Ottoman army, around 400,000 were engaged in the Balkans. Aside from Montenegro, the Balkan states were better armed than the Turks, with more artillery of more recent vintage.

As the war unfolded, Serbia, Montenegro and Greece attacked Turkey's Albanian provinces, while Serbia, Bulgaria and Greece invaded Macedonia, and Bulgaria attacked Thrace. In size or severity none of the ensuing battles approached the largest engagements of the Russo-Japanese War. Nevertheless, the Battle of Lyule Burgas (29 October to 2 November 1912), matching 130,000 Turks against 110,000 Bulgarians, generated over 42,000 casualties. The Turks then fell back on the Çatalca line, 32 km (20 miles) from Constantinople, where they supplemented a series of existing forts by digging a 24-km (15-mile) continuous front of trenches from the Black Sea to the Sea of Marmara. The Çatalca trenches resembled the Western Front of World War I more than did anything in Manchuria during the Russo-Japanese War, as there were no flanks to turn and frontal assaults became the only option for the attackers. After Bulgaria rejected an Ottoman appeal for an armistice, on 17 November General Radko Ruskov Dimitriev began his assault on the Çatalca line with 176,000 troops, just as

Right Turkish troops during the First Balkan War, 1912–13.

Below Siege gun at Adrianople, 1912–13. The Balkan armies shelled the Turkish stronghold with artillery such as this Bulgarian Krupp 150-mm (6-inch) gun (Model 1895), supplemented by more modern Serbian Schneider-Canet guns.

a cholera epidemic swept the Bulgarian ranks; five days later heavy losses in killed, wounded and sick left Dimitriev with only 86,000 still fit for action. In early December Bulgaria, Serbia and Montenegro agreed to an armistice, and peace talks opened in London. Even though they had already achieved their principal war aim of taking Salonica (Thessaloniki) on 8 November, the Greeks fought on in the hope of also acquiring Janina (Ioannina), just south of Albania. During the truce the Montenegrin siege of Scutari (Shkodër) and the Bulgarian siege of Adrianople (Edirne) continued. After negotiations broke down on 16 February 1913, the action focused on the fate of these isolated Ottoman garrisons, with the Greeks taking Janina (3 March); the Bulgarians, Adrianople (26 March); and the Montenegrins, Scutari (23 April). At Adrianople the Bulgarian army became the first in history to employ a creeping barrage to prepare the way for infantry attacks. The Bulgarians also used aircraft to drop grenades on Turkish trenches.

By the Treaty of London (30 May 1913) the great powers of Europe allowed Serbia to keep Kosovo and Greece to retain Epirus with Janina, but assigned most Albanian territory (including Scutari) to a new independent state. Greece and Serbia partitioned Macedonia, limiting Bulgaria's gains to Thrace. The treaty pleased none of the victors but left the Bulgarians most dissatisfied; on 29–30 June they attacked Serbian and Greek positions in Macedonia, initiating the brief Second Balkan War. The Turks resumed hostilities against the Bulgarians, and Montenegro also intervened, but the entry of Romania (neutral in the First Balkan War) proved decisive, adding 300,000 fresh troops to the 400,000 deployed by Bulgaria's other enemies. Bulgaria held its own against Serbia and Greece but abandoned Adrianople to the Turks in order to defend its capital, Sofia, against Romanians invading from the north. Bulgaria sued for peace on 31 July and in the Treaty of Bucharest (10 August 1913) ceded Eastern Thrace to the Ottoman Empire and Southern Dobruja to Romania.

The human toll suffered in the two Balkan wars was high, considering the populations of the states involved. Bulgaria sustained 83,000 casualties in the First Balkan War and 93,000 in the Second, followed by Serbia (82,000 and 50,000), Greece (29,000 and 22,000) and Montenegro (9,500 and 1,200). After losing 100,000 men in the First Balkan War the Turks suffered very few casualties in the Second; Romania likewise sustained only light casualties in the march on Sofia that forced an end to the war. Medical care and sanitation were far worse than they had been in South Africa or Manchuria; death and incapacitation from cholera and dysentery accounted for perhaps half of all casualties.

A year after the end of the Balkan Wars most of Europe would be engulfed in World War I, and the intervening time did not allow for much reflection on what lessons could be learned. Like the Japanese in Manchuria, the Bulgarians were praised for their willingness to assault entrenched positions and for their use of the bayonet. Few commentators noticed that the Bulgarian army learned from the bloodbath at the Çatalca line that infantry assaults required robust artillery support, and acted on the lesson with the innovative creeping barrage in taking Adrianople.

ALLIANCES, ALIGNMENTS AND ARMS RACES, 1900–1914

The landscape of great-power relationships grew increasingly inflexible over the years 1900 to 1914. The mutual fear of Germany that had motivated the Franco-Russian alliance also infected Britain, prompting rapprochements with France in 1904 and Russia in 1907. While these three powers collectively became known as the Triple Entente, they did not conclude a military convention until after World War I had already begun. Meanwhile, by 1914 the Triple Alliance ranked as the longest-running peacetime alliance in European history, enduring despite the mutual animosity of Austria-Hungary and Italy and, after 1900, Italian unease over the rising Anglo-German antagonism. On the eve of the Balkan Wars, the Italo-Turkish War had damaged Italy's relations with all three members of the Triple Entente and resulted in the renewal of the Triple Alliance in 1912, but when the assassination of Franz Ferdinand at Sarajevo triggered commitments that embroiled the rest of the great powers, Italy proved unable to side with Austria-Hungary and against Britain. Beyond Europe, Japan was linked to the Triple Entente by virtue of an alliance with Britain, concluded in 1902, leaving only the United States unattached.

The years immediately preceding World War I witnessed an unprecedented increase in military and naval expenditure, with the six great powers of Europe collectively spending 50 per cent more in 1913 than in 1908. The Anglo-German naval race served as centrepiece to the general pre-war competition in armaments. Germany's quest to rival Britain at sea began in 1897, with the appointment of Admiral Alfred von Tirpitz as state secretary in the Imperial Navy Office. Reichstag approval of the goals of Tirpitz's initial fleet programme was secured in 1898, after a speech to the legislators in which the admiral used ominous Darwinian language to

> *'For Germany the most dangerous enemy at the present time is England. It is also the enemy against which we most urgently require a certain measure of naval force as a political power factor.'*
> Admiral Alfred von Tirpitz, to Kaiser Wilhelm II, 6 June 1897

27

1. und 2. Geschwader und kleine Kreuzer im Kieler Hafen.

The Imperial German navy's First and Second squadrons, passing in review in Kiel harbour, 1911.

characterize the expansion of the fleet as a 'question of survival' for Germany. The Tirpitz plan quickly moved Germany from fifth place to second among Europe's naval powers.

The oldest of the existing battleships counted in Tirpitz's 1898 plan reached the end of their prescribed service lives in 1906, just as Britain introduced its two new revolutionary warship designs: the dreadnought battleship and the battlecruiser (see box overleaf). Because the new designs rendered all existing larger warships obsolete, the British negated their own considerable advantage in pre-dreadnought battleships and armoured cruisers, and gave the Germans the opportunity to catch up with them in battle-fleet strength. Tirpitz subsequently built all new German battleships as dreadnoughts, and large cruisers as battlecruisers. Despite the acceleration of German naval construction, the British continued to out-build the Germans on an annual basis, and by the end of July 1914 Britain had 29 capital ships in service and 13 under construction, while Germany had 18 in service and 8 under construction. The British advantage would suffice to keep the German fleet in port for most of World War I.

'Our only probable enemy is Germany. Germany keeps her whole fleet always concentrated within a few hours of England. We must therefore keep a fleet twice as powerful as that of Germany always concentrated within a few hours of Germany.'

Admiral Sir John Fisher, to the Prince of Wales, 23 October 1906

Meanwhile, for their armies, most of the great powers reduced their service requirement to mirror the German model of two years of active duty, while following the British lead in upgrading the calibre of reserve formations. In Germany concern that the army had been neglected during the naval build-up led to legislation in 1913 for a peacetime active-duty force of 890,000. The prospect of so many more Germans actually serving their two years of active duty rather than being exempted prompted France, with its much smaller population, to counter by increasing its term of active duty from two years to three, effective immediately, and a new recruiting class was added without the release of the class due to return to civilian life. This Franco-German competition to improve the capabilities of the two armies, like the Anglo-German naval race, heightened existing tensions and contributed to the sense that a general war was inevitable.

ON THE EVE OF WORLD WAR I

Internationally, the years 1900 to 1914 created the conditions in which World War I began and escalated. The Anglo-Boer War underscored the isolation of Britain and led to its partnerships with Japan, France and Russia. The Russo-Japanese War confirmed Japan's emergence as a great power and exposed Russia's weaknesses; in 1914 an emboldened Japan would use its British tie as a pretext for intervening in World War I, while Russia would demonstrate that it had recovered from the debacle of 1904–5 much faster than expected. Finally, the warfare of 1912–13 had rendered the Balkans more volatile than ever, as each of the Balkan countries emerged with more territory and larger populations but still harboured grander ambitions. The outcome alarmed Austria-Hungary in particular, as Serbia had doubled in size but still coveted Bosnia-Herzegovina and an outlet to the sea. Militarily, the fighting in South Africa, Manchuria and the Balkans provided glimpses of the horrors to come, but strategists and tacticians refused to abandon their faith in offensive warfare. They went to war in 1914 knowing it would be bloody (though underestimating just how bloody) and expecting it to be brief. Perhaps most important of all, the three major wars of 1900–14 served notice that a successful modern war effort required the wholehearted support of the home front. The anti-peace riots in Japan that greeted the Treaty of Portsmouth (1905) and the Bulgarian public's rejection of the Treaty of London (1913) served as reminders that when civilian populations gave such support, they would accept nothing less than total victory.

> 'Not one of these Balkan nations has succeeded in gathering together all of its scattered fragments. And, at the same time, every one. . .now includes within its borders a compact minority that is hostile to it.'
>
> Leon Trotsky, war correspondent in the Balkans, after the Treaty of Bucharest, 10 August 1913

The *Dreadnought* and the Battlecruiser

The revolution touched off by HMS *Dreadnought* came more by accident than by design. In drafting a programme of capital ships for 1905–6, Britain's first Sea Lord, Admiral Sir John Fisher, appeased battleship advocates by including the battleship *Dreadnought* (18,110 tons, ten 12-inch [305-mm] guns, 11 inches [280 mm] of armour, with a speed of 21 knots [39 kph]) along with the units he considered more important, the three battleship-sized cruisers or 'battlecruisers' of the Invincible class (17,370 tons, eight 12-inch guns, 6 inches [152 mm] of armour, with a speed of 25 knots [46 kph]). The *Dreadnought* was to be built first, as a test platform for the unprecedented size, all big-gun armament and the turbine engines that would also be features of the three battlecruisers.

Above Admiral Sir John Fisher (1841–1920), whose naval reforms brought the British fleet into the modern age.

Right HMS *Dreadnought*.

Opposite above A pair of 12-inch (305 mm) guns on the broadside ('wing') turret of HMS *Dreadnought*.

A PAIR OF 12 INCH GUNS BROADSIDE OF H.M.S "DREADNOUGHT" "THE ALL BIG GUN WARSHIP"

Far from seeking to reinvent the battleship, Fisher wanted the *Dreadnought* to be Britain's last battleship and for all subsequent capital ships to be built as battlecruisers – ships with the global reach needed to defend Britain's overseas interests against its traditional rivals, France and Russia. But changes in the international situation soon undermined his strategic vision. Britain maintained its entente with France (1904) and concluded another with Russia (1907), while Germany emerged as its primary naval rival. Thus the dreadnought battleship, better suited for a war against Germany in the North Sea, won out over the battlecruiser. Fisher had never intended to replicate the *Dreadnought*, yet it became the new model capital ship for the world's navies.

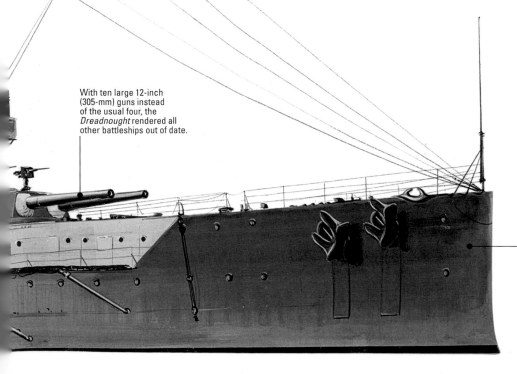

With ten large 12-inch (305-mm) guns instead of the usual four, the *Dreadnought* rendered all other battleships out of date.

Powered by new steam turbines, the *Dreadnought* had a top speed of 21 knots (39 kph), 3 knots faster than battleships with traditional piston engines. Its displacement was 18,110 tons.

2 World War I: An Unwinnable Conflict, 1914–1916

MICHAEL NEIBERG

Opposite French soldiers at Verdun, one of the longest and deadliest battles of the war, 1916. Even after hundreds of thousands of casualties, the lines had barely moved.

When hostilities began in 1914, even the most pessimistic of generals expected a relatively short war. Conventional wisdom held that neither the economic nor the social structures of Europe were durable enough to survive a long war. Confident generals planned offensive wars on the enemy's territory in order to make the enemy pay the costs of war and, of course, to spare their own people the terrors of an occupation. Many of the key French and German decision-makers remembered all too well the Franco-Prussian War of 1870–71 and the horrors of the Paris Commune that followed. They drew the lesson that armies must begin a war aggressively or risk ceding potentially decisive initiative to the enemy. They also saw clearly the impact of allowing an enemy to invade one's homeland.

PLANNING FOR WAR

War planning was thus aggressive and counted on the conflict lasting one or two campaigns. This optimism, which seemed warranted to most military professionals, helps to explain the resulting mental shock of the war's early years. Armies went off to battle in 1914 expecting a war of movement appropriate to their pre-war doctrine and weapons. Most infantrymen went to war expecting to close with the enemy using their bayonets, clearing the way for the traditional decisive arm of the European battlefield, the cavalry. Artillery pieces (except for a small number of very large pieces used to destroy fortifications) were consequently light, in accord with a doctrine of offensive warfare. The main French gun fired a 75-mm (3-inch) shell; its German counterpart fired a 77-mm shell. Both relied heavily on pre-war stocks

> '*Whatever you do,*
> *you lose a lot of men.*'
> French General
> Charles Mangin, 1917

of shrapnel shells, designed to kill men in the open field. The French in particular disdained heavier guns because of their expense and their limited mobility. Moreover, few professional soldiers sought careers with the heavy artillery, because they expected the big guns to be left behind as the infantry and cavalry attacked.

A few officers saw a different picture when they looked forward to the next war, but they were in a clear minority. Among them was the British general Sir Ian Hamilton, who had seen the power of Russian machine guns against attacking Japanese infantry in his role as an observer in Manchuria in 1905; he told a parliamentary committee that the only role of cavalry in that war had been to prepare rice for the infantry. Also in this group was the French artillery officer Philippe Pétain, who believed that even light artillery pieces were powerful enough to break up attacking infantry formations at enormous human cost; his views found little favour in the pre-war French army and his maxim *le feu tue* ('firepower kills') went largely unheeded in an army that clung to a belief in *offensive à outrance* ('offensive to the utmost'). That doctrine preached the power of will and elan to overcome the material dangers of the modern battlefield. The Japanese, offensively minded French officers were fond of saying, had won the Russo-Japanese War despite their losses, and had done so by acting aggressively. The French were unusually strident in their adherence to the offensive, but they were representative of all armies in 1914. Thus as soon as they had sufficient manpower, all the major armies were on the march. They did so according to carefully prepared war plans that had been years in the making. All of them depended on audacity, rapid movement and aggressive field command.

INITIAL TACTICS AND OPERATIONS

The French army's first test of its aggressive tactics occurred in the difficult terrain of Alsace-Lorraine. Two French field armies entered the 'lost provinces' hoping to erase the sting of their humiliating loss to the Germans in 1871. Eager French soldiers liberated Alsatian towns to ecstatic reception from the locals until they reached the main German defensive lines. On 14 August the French, clad in their pre-war uniform of bright red trousers and blue tunics, began their main move towards Metz and Strasbourg. Near Morhange they became the first men on the Western Front to learn

German soldiers advance across Belgium before the beginning of trench warfare, August 1914. Fatigue caused by marches such as this contributed to the German failure at the First Battle of the Marne.

the bloody lesson of failure when uncoordinated infantry attacked established enemy positions defended by machine guns. French soldiers died in waves, in what were the highest casualty rates the French army suffered in the entire war. The liberation of Alsace-Lorraine would have to wait four deadly years.

If the French were the most aggressive in their tactics, the Germans were the most aggressive in their operations. Long before war was declared, the German army had been planning for an invasion of France as well as neutral Belgium and Luxembourg. The army would have to move as quickly as possible because the war plan was risky and depended on speed. No matter what the diplomatic crisis leading to war, seven-eighths of the German army would head west through Belgium and the Ardennes with the ultimate goal of seizing Paris before the respected French army could respond effectively. Paris had to fall in six weeks in order for the German army to redeploy its forces east to meet the Russians, who were allied to France. The Germans presumed that the Russians would mobilize slowly because of the great distances of the Russian Empire and their generally ineffective bureaucracy. As the Franco-German frontier was heavily fortified, the Germans planned to outflank the French with an advance through

> *'What is perhaps most terrible of all is the complete and necessary banishment of peace from the scene of Europe. Hereafter there may be a time for such a word, but not now.'*
> Irish nationalist Tom Kettle, 8 August 1914

Right Crowds gather in the Place Rogier, Brussels, to watch German troops enter the capital, August 1914. The Germans subjected Belgians and many Frenchmen to an intense and punishing occupation.

Below Helmuth von Moltke, nephew and namesake of the hero of the Wars of German Unification. He suffered a nervous breakdown when his plan to take Paris failed.

> *'Things are going badly, the battles east of Paris will not be decided in our favour . . . We shall be crushed in the fight against East and West. Our campaign is a cruel disillusion. And we shall have to pay for all the destruction which we have done.'*
>
> Helmuth von Moltke to his wife, 9 September 1914

Belgium, a nation whose neutrality was guaranteed by an international treaty to which the Germans were a signatory.

The German war plan, known to history as the Schlieffen plan, was breathtaking in its audacity and its demands on German soldiers. It required that the Germans find enough soldiers to simultaneously invade Belgium, defend Alsace and provide a minimal guard against the Russians. The plan therefore put thousands of inexperienced and recently recalled reservists into the front lines, a risk no other continental army was willing to take. The decision put sufficient numbers of men into battle (or so the Germans thought), but it asked much more of the reservists than most of them were able to give. The plan also largely discounted two important variables, the British and the Belgians. The British army was small by European standards, comprising just 100,000 officers and men, but its soldiers were long-serving professionals who knew their craft well. The decision of the British government to deploy the British Expeditionary Force to Belgium in response to Germany's invasion placed a formidable obstacle in the way of the German army's rash war plans.

The Germans had largely discounted the Belgians as well. They expected that their new artillery pieces would destroy the Belgian fortification belts with a level of firepower never before seen in history. The big guns, custom-designed to demolish the modern Belgian fortifications, did their work, and the Belgians generally retreated as expected in the face of superior German forces. The Belgian army, chronically underfunded and technologically far behind those of its more powerful neighbours, could offer little sustained resistance. The Germans did not, however, expect an unremitting guerrilla war against Belgian partisans called *francs-tireurs* ('irregular sharpshooters'). That war was not terribly bloody, but it did have two important consequences. First, it forced the Germans to devote soldiers to guard supply lines, thereby slowing down the German timetables. Second, brutal German reprisals against defenceless Belgian civilians tarnished the Germans in the eyes of neutral nations, and gave the British and French additional motivation to fight.

The German plan to capture the French capital in six weeks had no chance of succeeding under any circumstances, but the unexpected resistance of the British and Belgians, combined with the tough opposition of three French armies, undermined the plan before German soldiers reached Paris. Exhausted from their difficult march through Belgium, short on supplies and with armies beginning to march in diverging directions, the Germans regrouped. On 30 August, with his men 100 km (60 miles) north-east of the French capital, the German First Army commander

> '*Few of this nation's regimental officers show much concern for a funny little country like Belgium, although most of them may be buried there before they are much older.*'
>
> Sir Henry Wilson, 1912

General Alexander von Kluck decided to change his axis of attack. Instead of moving south-west as part of an effort to encircle Paris from the west, he would move south-east as part of a gigantic pincer movement designed to bag the French and British armies along a massive 560-km (350-mile) front from Montdidier to Belfort.

The decision was an admission that all of Germany's pre-war planning had to be thrown away. It also set up the titanic Battle of the Marne between the worn-out men of the German, French and British armies (see box overleaf). The French stole the first step when aviators detected the German turn to the south-east, allowing the French to put strong forces on the German right wing. In the most famous episode of the battle, the French rushed thousands of newly arrived soldiers from the train stations of their arrival to the front line in taxis. In the centre of this massive battlefield, tired British troops, who had been fighting a tactical retreat since first encountering German forces in Belgium, contributed to the attack, forcing the Germans to retreat. At the extreme right, French defences in and around the fortress of Verdun held, meaning that Paris was safe. The 'miracle of the Marne' saved Paris, and maybe the war, for the Allies.

Fully aware that the German war plan he had spent so much of his life preparing was failing, Moltke knew he faced a crisis. He dispatched a trusted staff officer, Lieutenant Colonel Richard Hentsch, to the front with broad powers to make whatever changes he thought necessary. Hentsch met the commanders of the German First and Second armies and understood the military significance of the gap that had opened between them. He issued orders under Moltke's name for the two armies to close the gap by conducting a strategic withdrawal. Unable to take Paris and too tired to try again, the German commanders, though put out at taking orders from an officer well below them in rank, had little choice but to agree. They retreated to the heights north of the Aisne river, resumed contact between their flanks and began to dig in to prepare for a possible Allied counter-attack.

That counter-attack, known as the First Battle of the Aisne, lacked the strength to dislodge the Germans from their positions. Two processes then began that set the tone for much of the remainder of the war. The first, known as the race to the sea, involved each side stretching its lines north to avoid being outflanked. This

The First Battle of the Marne, September 1914

At the time, the First Battle of the Marne was the largest battle ever fought. The armies were extended from the outskirts of Paris to the eastern fortifications of Verdun. Soldiers in all the armies were exhausted, short of supplies and still stunned from the level of casualties the first few weeks of the war had inflicted. Several key decisions carried the day for the Allies and made heroes out of senior officers. Douglas Haig and Ferdinand Foch both pushed their forces forward to close gaps and put unexpected pressure on German flanks. Both were subsequently given much higher command assignments.

The critical day of the battle was 9 September 1914. The newly formed French Sixth Army pressed the German right flank near the town of Meaux while the British attacked in support. In the centre of the line, Foch's Ninth Army (also newly formed) pressured a critical hinge point in the German line near a swamp known as the St Gond Marshes. The attacks forced one German army to withdraw, opening a dangerous gap that could be closed only by the entire German line retreating. Paris was saved, and generals began to think in terms of a longer war.

Opposite The Battle of the Marne was then the largest battle ever fought, both in terms of the numbers of men and the amount of space it covered, from Paris to Verdun.

Below This colour dramatization of the Battle of the Marne, by Ferdinand Desnier, shows French troops in their impractical 19th-century-style blue-and-red uniforms.

Bottom German ammunition abandoned at the Battle of the Marne. None of the combatants was prepared for how quickly their stocks of shells would be exhausted.

	ALLIES	GERMANY
COMMANDERS	Joseph Joffre (French) Sir John French (British)	Helmuth von Moltke
STRENGTH	c. 1,100,000	c. 1,480,000
CASUALTIES	c. 263,000	c. 230,000

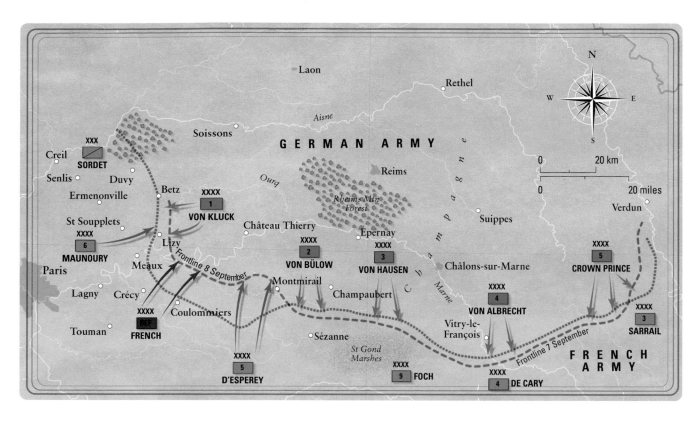

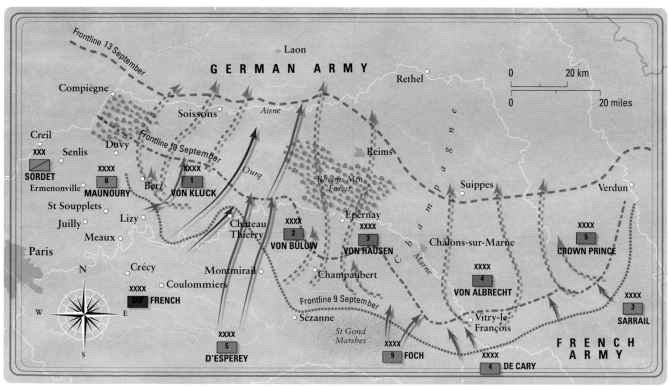

process continued until the two sides had reached the English Channel in the north and the Swiss border in the south. Then began the second process: the digging of parallel trench lines to protect men from the elements and the murderous machine guns of the other side (see box, p. 44). Most officers expected the trenches to be a temporary condition that would buy time until spring while the armies found more men to put in uniform, more guns to put in their hands and new war plans for them to execute.

THE EASTERN FRONT

The stasis in the west was a significant problem for the Germans. The Russians had devised a surprisingly flexible plan that allowed them to mobilize units as they became available. The system allowed the huge, but largely unskilled, Russian army to put large numbers of men in the field quickly. Because the German war plan sent so many men west, and because Germany's Austro-Hungarian allies mainly headed south to crush the Serbs they held responsible for the crisis that had begun the war, there was no large force to stop the Russian steamroller. Consequently, the German commander of the lone army in the east, an ageing court favourite named Max von Prittwitz, opted for a massive withdrawal behind the Vistula river. Although the move made a good deal of operational sense, the German high command reacted with horror at ceding so much initiative and land to the Slavs they held in contempt. Prittwitz's proposed withdrawal would yield much of East Prussia, the traditional home of the Prussian aristocracy known as the Junkers, to the Russians. It was thus unthinkable politically.

The Germans therefore made a change of command, removing Prittwitz and sending two officers, the veteran Paul von Hindenburg and the fast-rising Erich Ludendorff, east to handle the Russians. Hindenburg, who had spent much of his

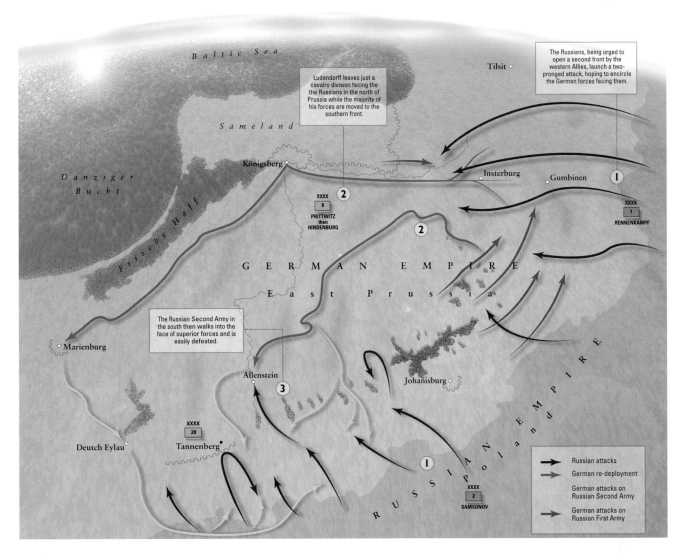

Ludendorff leaves just a cavalry division facing the the Russians in the north of Prussia while the majority of his forces are moved to the southern front.

The Russians, being urged to open a second front by the western Allies, launch a two-pronged attack, hoping to encircle the German forces facing them.

The Russian Second Army in the south then walks into the face of superior forces and is easily defeated.

Baltic Sea

Tilsit

Sameland

Königsberg

Danziger Bucht

Insterburg

Gumbinen

XXXX **2** 8 PRITTWITZ then HINDENBURG

XXXX **1** RENNENKAMPF

Frische Haff

G E R M A N   E M P I R E

E a s t   P r u s s i a

Marienburg

Allenstein

3

Johanisburg

R U S S I A N   E M P I R E

Deutch Eylau

Tannenberg

XXXX 20

1

R u s s i a n   P o l a n d

XXXX **2** SAMSONOV

→	Russian attacks
→	German re-deployment
→	German attacks on Russian Second Army
→	German attacks on Russian First Army

Above During the Battle of Tannenberg, 26–31 August 1914, German forces cut off the Russian Second Army and annihilated it almost completely.

Opposite The command team of Erich Ludendorff (right) and Paul von Hindenburg (left) briefing Kaiser Wilhelm (centre). The Kaiser became increasingly irrelevant to German war operations.

retirement designing defensive schemes against the Russians in his native East Prussia, had taken the precaution of heading to the train station at Hanover in order to be able to assume command as quickly as possible. When the telegram informing him of his command arrived as he expected, he replied with a simple 'Ready'. Meeting him at Hanover was Ludendorff, a hard-driving and efficient officer who had recently made a name for himself in the Belgian fortress town of Liège by pounding on the door of the citadel with the hilt of his sword to demand its surrender.

As its train sped east from Hanover, the new command team of the German Eighth Army planned its next moves. Rather than retreat further, Hindenburg and Ludendorff devised a plan to attack two Russian field armies when their lines of march took them to opposite sides of the large Masurian Lakes chain, which would keep them too far apart to offer mutual support. The skilfully redeployed German Eighth Army pounced on the unsuspecting Russian First Army on 27 August near the town of Tannenberg, surrounding it and forcing tens of thousands of trapped and panicked Russians to surrender. Before news of the disaster could reach the Russian Second Army, the Germans had repeated the trick, surrounding the Russians

and cutting them off from their avenues of retreat. Tannenberg alone cost the Russians 30,000 dead and more than 125,000 prisoners of war; the second battle, called the Battle of the Masurian Lakes, cost them another 100,000 casualties. The great twin success of Hindenburg and Ludendorff partly redeemed the failure of the German armies in the west, but the massive size of the Russian army meant that the two battles, incredibly lopsided victories though they were, would not by themselves force Russia out of the war.

> '*I can only now think with disgust of the battle pictures which one sees in books. They show a repulsive levity.*'
>
> German soldier Paul Rohweder on 29 October 1914, after seeing his first battle

The failure of the Germans to achieve a victory on either front posed a serious problem to a generation of German generals taught to fear the long-term consequences of a two-front war. The abysmal performance of the armies of the Austro-Hungarian Empire in battles along the foothills of the Carpathian Mountains further underscored the German dilemma. Having started the war with 1 million men under arms, the Austro-Hungarians lost 300,000 men (100,000 of whom were POWs, which indicates the low morale of many units) and 300 artillery pieces in its first months. The Germans therefore knew they were, in the words of one senior German official, 'shackled to a corpse' that could be of little value in the time ahead.

GLOBALIZATION AND STALEMATE, 1915

Two major themes dominated the second year of the war. The first was the war's increased globalization. Italy entered on the side of the Triple Entente (France, Russia and Britain), putting pressure on an already overextended Austro-Hungarian army that was also engaged in fighting the Russians in the Carpathian Mountains. Italy's entry into the war also ensured Britain and France had virtually free use of the

Opposite Allied battleships lined up across the entrance to the Dardanelles in an attempt to remove the Ottoman Empire from the war, but they could not operate safely in narrow waters.

Above and above right After the failure of the naval attacks on the Dardanelles, the British landed troops on the Gallipoli peninsula on 25 April 1915. This decision proved to be a strategic and operational disaster.

Mediterranean shipping lanes. More importantly, however, the British Empire had made a critical decision to pursue a global strategy aimed at knocking out the Ottoman Empire, which was seen as the weakest member of the Central Powers (the others being Germany, Austria-Hungary and Bulgaria). The new leaders of the Ottomans, the so-called Young Turks, had allied themselves with Germany in large part for some protection against an expected Russian power play for Constantinople and the warm waters of the Dardanelles. Ottoman possessions in the Middle East and the sultan's decision to declare jihad threatened British interests from Suez to India that the British thought worth defending, even at the risk of removing men and weapons from the Western Front. The British choice to fight a sustained war in multiple theatres against the Ottomans, along with decisions to pursue a campaign in Africa and to support a Japanese naval campaign against Germany's Pacific colonies, helped to convert the European war into a true world war.

BRITAIN AND THE OTTOMANS

The most famous manifestation of the new British strategy involved a grand scheme to force the Ottomans out of the war by relying on naval power. The scheme, largely the brainchild of the First Lord of the Admiralty, Winston Churchill, aimed to push powerful British battleships through the Dardanelles Straits and to threaten the Ottoman capital. The British had presumed that Ottoman determination to fight the war was weak and that Ottoman leaders would respond to a show of British force by suing for peace. The British might then be able to pursue a landward strategy against the faltering Austro-Hungarian Empire, perhaps in conjunction with armies from several of the Balkan states. British advocates of this strategy, however, badly underestimated Turkish resolve. A combination of mobile shore artillery batteries (manufactured in Germany and manned by German specialists) and mines blocked the battleships' progress in February and March of 1915. Britain's most powerful

The Machine Gun

All armies began the war with machine guns capable of firing at least 500 rounds per minute and accurate up to 550 m (600 yards). Most of these weapons were heavy – the French Hotchkiss weighed 40 kg (88 lb) without its mount, and the British Vickers weighed 33 kg (73 lb) – but they quickly proved their effectiveness on the battlefield. Easy to conceal and difficult to destroy, a single machine gun could replace the firepower of a battalion of men. During the course of the war, all armies endeavoured to reduce the weight of machine guns and thereby improve their mobility. The German MG 08 'Spandau' machine gun used a smaller water jacket and a lighter mount to reduce the weight to 18 kg (39 lb). An air-cooled version weighed even less.

Smaller, lighter machine guns could be used in aeroplanes or by infantry on the advance. Light machine guns, such as the British Lewis gun, the German MG 08/18 and the American .30 Browning, helped to restore mobility to the battlefield in the last months of the war. At the conflict's very end, the Americans introduced the extremely light (10-lb) Thompson submachine gun that had a theoretical cyclical fire rate of 700 rounds per minute. Although it was nicknamed 'the trench sweeper' in honour of its expected battlefield role, it arrived too late, and instead became connected with gangsters and its later use in World War II.

Above Like all such weapons, the British Vickers machine gun proved to be a powerful defensive tool and was especially devastating against advancing infantry.

Below A German heavy machine gun based on a design by the famous American weapons maker Hiram Maxim. It fired 7.92-mm (.3-inch) ammunition at a rate of 400 rounds per minute.

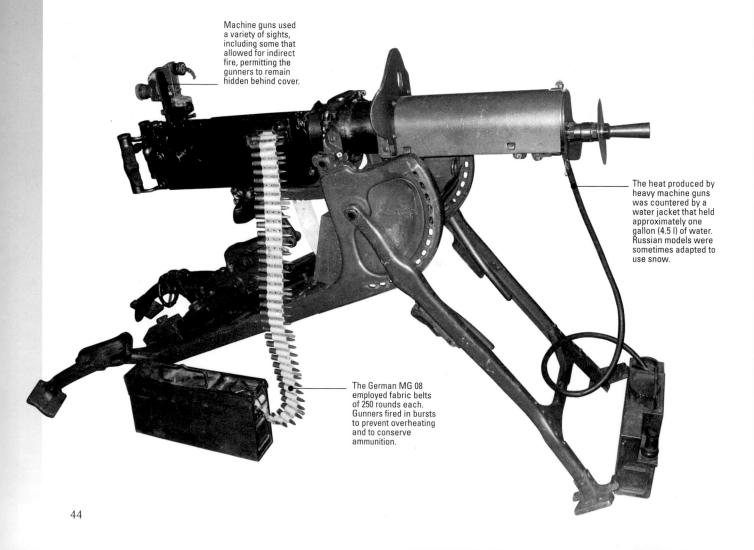

Machine guns used a variety of sights, including some that allowed for indirect fire, permitting the gunners to remain hidden behind cover.

The heat produced by heavy machine guns was countered by a water jacket that held approximately one gallon (4.5 l) of water. Russian models were sometimes adapted to use snow.

The German MG 08 employed fabric belts of 250 rounds each. Gunners fired in bursts to prevent overheating and to conserve ammunition.

weapons had been stopped by relatively cheap German and Turkish defences.

To clear the way for minesweepers and to make a second push by the battleships possible, Churchill convinced a reluctant army to land an amphibious force on the Gallipoli peninsula. This army would clear the peninsula of the mobile artillery batteries and small fortifications that had blocked the first British attempt. On 25 April, French troops made a diversionary landing on the Asian side while British and Anzac (Australian and New Zealander) troops landed on five separate beaches at Gallipoli. Almost nothing went as the British had hoped: units landed in the wrong places; Turkish units fought with great tenacity; and supplying the British force with basics such as fresh drinking water proved to be a great challenge. The Gallipoli campaign, intended to be a quick and cheap solution, instead became bogged down in the very trench warfare that it was supposed to have helped end.

> ‘I do not order you to attack. I order you to die.’
> Mustafa Kemal at Gallipoli

Gallipoli was but one of several campaigns that pitted the British and Ottoman empires against one another for control of the Middle East. Several Ottoman attempts to cross the Suez Canal and inflame an anti-British rebellion inside Egypt failed, although they did lead the British to devote significantly greater resources to the Suez region, which eventually resulted in a major campaign to take Palestine in 1917. This campaign, involving an alliance with Arab warriors loyal to the independence-minded Emir Faisal, set up a difficult and tense post-war period for the region. In Mesopotamia, too, the British pressed the Ottomans. Using mostly Indian soldiers, British forces invaded Mesopotamia in spring 1915. They advanced up the Tigris–Euphrates valley before they were stopped near Kut al-Amara in December. There the Ottomans encircled and trapped the British 6th Division. Concerned about British prestige and unable to rescue the men through military means, Churchill proposed paying the Ottomans a £2 million ransom in gold, but the Ottomans refused. The weakening British force at Kut, 9,000 men in all, surrendered in April 1916 after a gruelling siege. It was then the largest capitulation in the history of the British army and a great blow to British prestige in Muslim Asia.

Indian soldiers using a machine gun in an anti-aircraft role, Mesopotamia, early 1916. Light machine guns such as the Lewis shown here could also be used on board aeroplanes.

FIREPOWER ON THE WESTERN FRONT

The British pursued such far-flung strategies in large part because they suited British strengths, namely their great naval dominance and the manpower of the empire. Many British officials, moreover, grew disenchanted at the prospects of victory on an increasingly stalemated Western Front. Throughout 1915 both sides pursued victory in France and Belgium, but found that the new trench systems were too strong to be broken. The general Allied approach to breaking the stalemate involved a massive preparation of the battlefield with an increasing weight of shellfire. In theory the shelling would destroy the enemy's field defences (especially barbed wire) and kill enemy soldiers in the trenches. Infantry units could then advance in reasonable safety to kill remaining enemy soldiers and exploit gaps in the line. Then cavalry could charge through the secured passages, targeting enemy communications and cutting off avenues of retreat, thus turning a victory into a rout.

All such plans on the Western Front failed in 1915, but not for lack of trying. Part

German artillery pieces captured by the French in September 1915. Artillery was the largest single killer on the Western Front and came to be used in a wide variety of roles and missions.

Scènes Vécues à TROYES pendant la Grande Guerre Européenne - TROPHÉES de Guerre pris aux Allemands à la Bataille de Champagne (25 sept. 1915) exposés à TROYES du 29 septembre au 8 octobre 1915
Vue d'ensemble des 20 canons de 77

of the problem involved the nature of artillery at this still early stage of the war. The guns were still mostly light field pieces of 75 mm (3 inches; French) or 18 pounds (8 kg; British). Both types of gun were designed to support attacking infantry. They were not well suited for destroying solid trench systems, nor were they especially effective at destroying barbed wire. Much of the ammunition, moreover, was shrapnel, which sent down showers of deadly lead pellets. Once underground in their trenches, German soldiers could find reasonable protection from shrapnel, which was too light to penetrate. Finally, the great haste with which much of the ammunition was manufactured caused many duds and misfires.

As a result, artillery rarely cleared the way for the infantry, to say nothing of the cavalry. In their defence, the generals who designed these plans, often derided as 'butchers and bunglers', hoped that the artillery would win the battle, thus sparing the lives of the infantry. A favoured French maxim of the time preached that 'Artillery conquers. Infantry occupies.' Still, when the artillery failed to do its job, infantrymen were helpless in the face of enemy machine guns, artillery pieces and rifles. The most tragic offensive of this type occurred in Champagne, where the French fired an astonishing 800,000 artillery shells in support of a massive offensive in September 1915. The French had a superiority of numbers in the region and were confident of success. Nevertheless, the German defences survived a four-day artillery barrage by moving many of their machine guns and artillery pieces further to the rear, and therefore out of effective French artillery range. The French offensive failed completely, gaining just 40 square km (15 square miles) at a cost of 144,000 Frenchmen dead, wounded or taken prisoner.

Even when the artillery did its job, infantry could rarely exploit the success. Artillery barrages might destroy some German field defences, but they also chewed

'This is not war. It is the ending of the world.'
Hindu soldier on the Western Front, 1915

up the ground and made any rapid advances extremely difficult. Commanding and controlling a large infantry advance was difficult in an era when battlefields were too big to be observed by the commanders, and field communications were often unreliable. As a result, local successes quickly evaporated as the Germans often brought reserves into threatened areas faster than the French and British could. Infantry advances, moreover, had to be supported with more men and supplies, a logistical task that proved too great for most armies. At the simplest level, armies could occasionally create break-ins, but they could not sustain breakthroughs.

The campaigns of 1915 demonstrated the need for much more effective artillery. All sides began to manufacture much larger guns with more destructive power and greater ranges. Gunners demanded high-explosive ammunition powerful enough to hit targets below ground. Command and control of the guns became more sophisticated as well. Gunners became innovative in the complex ways they designed barrages, and they learned to work with spotters to hit targets they could not see, a process known as 'indirect fire'. Chief among these spotters were aviators, who could fly over enemy lines and both locate likely targets and assess the effectiveness of their gunners' fire. Aviation thus became an increasingly

'Seeing a modern battle demolishes all one's preconceived ideas.'

Eric Fisher Wood, 1915

British pilot at Gallipoli, 1915. Aviation grew exponentially during the course of the war as generals recognized its military potential, intially for reconnaissance of large battlefields and for the correction of indirect artillery fire.

Above Many casualties of gas attacks recovered, although others were left permanently blinded or were killed. The novelty and impersonality of the weapon added to its ferocity.

Below A German gas mask – part of an elaborate cat-and-mouse game in which scientists struggled to produce both more deadly types of gas and better ways to protect soldiers.

important element of warfare, as pilots tried both to observe 'the other side of the hill' and to deny the enemy the ability to do the same, through the creation of dedicated hunter or pursuit squadrons that targeted enemy observation aircraft. The dogfights between aces may have captured public attention, but these dramas were merely ancillary to the much more important task of controlling the skies so that one side could simultaneously see the battlefield from above and prevent the enemy from doing so.

Armies also became increasingly interested in poison gas, which was first used on the Western Front by the Germans in April 1915. Although the weapon was banned by international treaty, all armies had experimented with gas and had amassed stocks of it. Unlike artillery, poison gas (which was heavier than air) could seep down into the trenches and reach the very deepest recesses of a trench network. Gas was a terrifying weapon, both because of its novelty and because of the grotesque effects it could have on men unequipped to deal with it. Nevertheless, it was an imperfect weapon, dependent on weather and primitive delivery systems, and vulnerable to the fear that one's own soldiers often had of it. Armies soon began to train men to fight with it, and they also enlisted their scientists to develop new gases and effective countermeasures such as gas masks.

THE ITALIAN AND EASTERN FRONTS

The entry of Italy into the war on the Allied side was supposed to make possible a 'walk to Vienna', as promised by the Italian commander Luigi Cadorna. Austro-Hungarian forces had, however, taken dominating positions on the high ground of the Julian Alps in the Isonzo river valley. Commanded by a talented Croatian general, Svetozar Boroevi, Austro-Hungarian forces used terrain to their advantage and stopped a series of Italian attacks. The Austrians found it easy to motivate their men against the Italians, who had reneged on treaty obligations in 1914, then joined the Triple Alliance the following year in exchange for promises of large tracts of Austro-Hungarian land. The Isonzo campaign involved nine separate and uncreative attempts by Cadorna to break Austro-Hungarian lines. Freezing cold weather, high altitudes and the barren but stubborn strategy of Italian generals made this front miserable for all sides.

The stalemate on the Western and Italian fronts in 1915 stood in stark contrast to a massive war of movement in the east, where much greater distances meant that armies could not create dense lines of defence. Instead, they had to make decisions about where to place precious resources along broad fronts. As a result, there were inevitably weak spots. In May 1915 the Germans found one such spot between the Galician towns of Gorlice and Tarnow in the Carpathian foothills, and blasted it with 700,000 artillery shells in four hours. Russian defences, being much weaker than the German defences in France, crumbled. More than 30,000 Russians surrendered in less than a week. An entire Russian army collapsed, giving the Germans open flanks and chances at pursuit. Soon the entire German army in the east was involved in a massive campaign of conquest that took Poland from the Russians in the most successful campaign of the war in terms of the amount of land taken. Still, the Russian army, though battered, had reserves on which it could depend. The war in the east would continue.

Russian prisoners of war on the Eastern Front. None of the combatant powers was prepared for the tens of thousands of prisoners that were captured.

OLD STRATEGIES AND NEW STRATEGIES, 1916

Allied generals on the Western Front concluded that their operational approach to war in 1915 had been essentially sound. They blamed the lack of appropriate artillery for their failures and believed that they had learned the right lessons from the bloody reverses of that year. More and better artillery, commanded by more experienced officers and used by more experienced soldiers, would provide the desired results in 1916. The necessary elements, they concluded, would be available by summer, when the French, British, Italians and Russians would conduct a series of roughly coordinated offensives that would pressure the Germans and Austro-Hungarians from all sides. A major conference held at the headquarters of the French General Joseph Joffre at Chantilly in December 1915 led to a rough agreement to that effect by all the major Allied powers.

The German high command, still stuck in its two-front quandary, was not sure it could afford a 1916 that looked like 1915. The Germans had no interest in chasing the Russians further east and risking the same fate as Napoleon's *Grande Armée*. Neither did the German high command want to repeat the mistake the French made in Champagne and lose tens of thousands of men in a futile attempt to force a breakthrough. Even if they had wanted to do so, it was unclear that German industry could sustain such a massive programme of artillery building. The British blockade was also beginning to bite into the German home front, and the angry American response to the sinking of the *Lusitania* in May 1915 had forced the Germans to become more circumspect in their use of submarine warfare as a deterrent to the British. Germany's submarine warfare campaign had shown some signs of effectiveness, but in 1915 the German government was unwilling to antagonize the United States, the world's most powerful neutral state.

ATTRITION AT VERDUN

Faced with these difficulties, General Erich von Falkenhayn, the hard-nosed German commander, developed a plan to force the French out of the war by fighting a titanic battle at the strategic fortified city of Verdun on the Meuse river. Verdun's historic significance, dating back to the days of Charlemagne, may have played on Falkenhayn's mind, but much more important to him was the nature of the large salient around Verdun that allowed the Germans to dominate the rail and road lines into the region. Consequently they could supply themselves much more reliably than the French could. Falkenhayn may also have been aware that the French had removed most of the heavy guns from Verdun's mighty fortresses in order to use them elsewhere on the Western Front. There remains much debate about exactly what the mercurial Falkenhayn hoped to accomplish at Verdun. The so-called 'Christmas memorandum' he wrote to the Kaiser has never been found, but Falkenhayn later claimed that it laid out a plan to win the war at Verdun. Exactly what that plan involved remains a mystery. Some historians think he was trying to capture the city and its ring of imposing forts as a prelude to an advance on Paris, but most think he was using it as bait, hoping to draw French reserves into the area in order to use his superior artillery and logistics to grind them up. This approach is consistent with how Falkenhayn says he presented the battle to the Kaiser. Oddly, his ultimate target was not France but Britain, a nation that most members of the

A propaganda poster produced after the German sinking of the *Lusitania* on 7 May 1915. Such imagery was used in the US to encourage enlistment and to stir up public opinion in favour of intervention in the war.

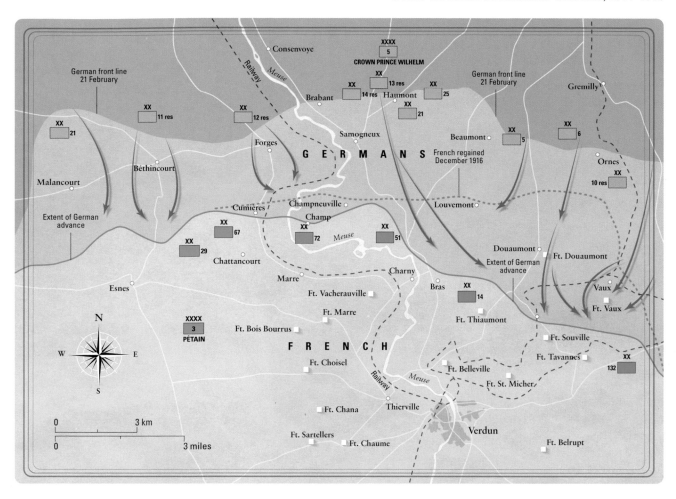

The Battle of Verdun (1916), a terrible struggle in which the Germans aimed to inflict unbearable casualties on the French. The terrain surrounding the fortress city was dominated by the Meuse river, a series of fortified hills and thick woods.

German elite held in deep contempt. Only by knocking 'England's best sword' (France) from its hand, he assumed, could Germany force the British to sign a maritime and colonial treaty on German terms.

The British may have been Falkenhayn's long-term target, but it was the French who suffered under the tremendous bombardment the Germans unleashed on 21 February 1916. Using almost 2,000 well-supplied guns, the Germans blasted exposed French positions. French forces were utterly unprepared for the attack, despite warnings in the weeks beforehand from an important front-line commander. Lieutenant Colonel Emile Driant, stationed in a forest just opposite the Germans, had warned Joffre's staff of the German build-up around Verdun, but French headquarters had ignored him. As a member of the French Chamber of Deputies, Driant had used his parliamentary connections to urge that Verdun should be better defended, but Joffre responded by threatening to court-martial Driant for insubordination. As a result of Joffre's stubbornness, the French army did little to reinforce Verdun; France had just 244 heavy guns and 2 under-strength French divisions to face 7 powerful German divisions in the sector. Driant himself was among the first casualties, killed by a sniper's bullet in the forest he was defending. The situation grew so dire so quickly in the battle's early days that the local French commander at Verdun advocated demolishing the forts and abandoning the city.

Although there was much to recommend that course of action, Joffre instead ordered a senior general to go to Verdun and reassess the situation there. General Edouard Noël de Castelnau ordered all of Verdun's forts to be defended and told French soldiers to die where they were rather than retreat. The French then sent General Philippe Pétain to assume command at Verdun with orders to hold both banks of the river. Pétain soon became a household name in France, using his expertise in defensive warfare and artillery tactics to slow the German attacks. He also oversaw a massive programme of troop rotation and a new logistical infrastructure that allowed the French to hold on at Verdun, despite the morale-crushing loss of the city's two most powerful forts. Both sides saw little choice but to commit more and more men and materiel to the battle, which dragged on into the summer and autumn. The lines barely moved as soldiers focused their efforts on small local objectives. The conditions of the battle were appalling: men could see and smell the 'slaughterhouse' of Verdun from miles away.

Verdun became a laboratory for testing new methods and weapons. The Germans introduced flame-throwers to the battlefield and developed the first dedicated aerial fighter squadrons and systematic air-warfare tactics. The French innovated as well, developing leapfrog infantry tactics that allowed one squad or platoon to cover the advance of another. The French also devolved command authority to lower and lower levels, encouraging their men to act with initiative and giving them the chance to exploit local successes. By far the most important innovations, however, came in artillery. French gunners developed a rolling or creeping barrage that preceded the carefully measured advance of the infantry. The goal was less to kill enemy infantry (which the experience of 1915 had shown to be unrealistic in any case) than to force them to take cover, thereby suppressing their fire long enough to allow the infantry to advance. These methods made it possible for the French to retake their two lost forts and in November to return the battle lines to where they had been in February. Verdun had been a bloody, gruelling test that left 700,000 men dead, wounded or taken prisoner.

THE ALLIED SUMMER OFFENSIVE

Nor had either side been able to seek a decision on the seas. The British fleet was strong enough to keep the German fleet bottled up in its home ports, but not strong enough to challenge the Germans behind their defences. Unbeknownst to the Germans, the British had a copy of the German codes, which made the British position even stronger. As a result, there was only one large engagement on the high seas. In the Battle of Jutland, on 31 May and 1 June 1916, the German fleet was able to damage its British counterpart, but not enough to change the essential balance of power in the North Sea. Victory would have to be found on land.

Verdun meant that the French could not participate in the great Allied summer offensive to the extent that they had anticipated. Instead, the French army assumed a supporting role for the British army, which took over planning for the offensive to target German positions on high ground near the Somme river: the river was the dividing line between the British and French sectors of the Western Front, and the Allies had held out high hopes that the two sides might be able to help one another during the offensive. French generals urged the British to begin the attack as soon

British officers on the Somme. None of them had ever commanded an operation of this size before, and their inexperience contributed to the disaster of 1 July 1916.

Watercolour painted during the Battle of Jutland (31 May – 1 June 1916). World War I's only large naval battle ended in a stalemate, but it discouraged the German surface fleet from leaving its ports again.

as possible in the hopes of drawing German troops away from Verdun, but the British commander Douglas Haig wanted to wait until he thought he had the resources he needed to succeed. Despite some reservations from several of his senior advisers, Haig planned to use tactics broadly similar to those used in 1915. A massive artillery barrage would clear the way for the inexperienced infantry. The ultimate goal was to break through German lines, which would enable the British to pursue the Germans and defeat them in open warfare.

Final preparations began in late June. The British fired almost 1 million shells at German positions over a one-week period. The British reasonably assumed that the gunners had cleared away any possible German resistance, but they were wrong. The Germans had either buried their machine guns deep under the chalky soil of the Somme region (the British still used far too much shrapnel ammunition to kill men buried deep underground) or pulled the machine guns back to rear positions out of range of the British guns. Tragically, British soldiers, most of them seeing their first battle, went over the top expecting little resistance. A rolling barrage broadly similar to what the French had used at Verdun had preceded them, giving young British soldiers even more confidence, but (unbeknownst to them) it had been too poorly coordinated to offer meaningful protection to soldiers on most parts of the Somme front.

German machine guns opened fire as soon as the poorly choreographed barrage had passed them, shooting with impunity at slow-moving British soldiers. In far too many cases, British soldiers were laden down with heavy packs and in some divisions ordered to go forward at a

'They were singing some music-hall tune, with a lilt in it, as they marched towards the lights of all the shells up there in the places of death . . . something of their spirit seemed to come out of the dark mass of their moving bodies and thrill the air.'
Correspondent Philip Gibbs
on the Somme, 1 July 1916

British troops going over the top on the Somme, August 1916. They faced an enemy defensive line that had survived British artillery bombardment and that inflicted a terrible toll on men such as these.

walking pace in a straight line in order to maintain the integrity of the advance. British soldiers were mown down in no man's land or, in many cases, on the front steps of their own trenches. German machine gunners fired as furiously and quickly as they could, pausing only to reload and to cool red-hot barrels. British generals, unable to get a clear picture of the massive battlefield, sent second and third waves into the battle. Their fate was little better. On 1 July 1916, the first day of the Battle of the Somme, 19,240 British soldiers died and 38,230 more were wounded or taken prisoner. It remains the single bloodiest day in the long history of the British army.

Far from the expected fast-moving battle of pursuit, the Battle of the Somme slowed down to a muddy and inconclusive slogging match. The Germans, faced with fighting on the Somme and at Verdun simultaneously, suffered greatly as the British changed tactics. This involved a daring night attack on 14 July, brave assaults over open fields and into forests (many conducted by imperial troops from Australia, New Zealand, South Africa and Canada), and the introduction of tanks (see box on pp. 66–67) to the battlefield in September. None of these efforts brought the British the victory that Haig was looking for, but they did make the Somme a bloody battle that bled both sides terribly. The Somme campaign lasted 142 days and cost 419,000 British and 194,000 French casualties, for the gain of approximately 185 square km (70 square miles) of strategically

'Victory was to be bought so dear as to be almost indistinguishable from defeat.'
Winston Churchill, 1917

insignificant (and now devastated) terrain. German losses were never officially calculated, but historians estimate them to be near 600,000.

Once again, the stasis on the Western Front stood in contrast to the movement on the Eastern Front. Surprisingly, though, that movement came as a result of a successful Russian, not German, attack. Russia's best general, Aleksei Brusilov, found an isolated weak spot in the Austro-Hungarian line and attacked it on 4 June. His success temporarily shocked the Central Powers, which responded quickly, thereby preventing the Russians from gaining anything more than a stunning local success. The Germans blamed Austro-Hungarian ineptitude for the setback and took steps to assume control over Austro-Hungarian operations, effectively ending their ally's military independence. For their part, the Russians had scored an unexpected success, but the campaign had used up much of their country's remaining military assets, leaving it in poor shape as domestic hardship inside Russia led to increasingly strident calls for political and social change.

By February 1917 those calls had become too strong for the Russians to ignore. German advances in the Baltic region and in Romania negated any strategic advantage the Brusilov Offensive had given to Russia. A poor harvest in 1916 and the obvious bankruptcy of the Russian approach to war had led to demands for change. Strikes in the cities, draft evasion in the countryside and desertions within the army created a dangerous situation that led to the tsar's abdication. At almost the same time, the Germans announced their intention to resume unrestricted submarine warfare. World War I was about to enter a new phase.

DIE
GROSSE
SCHLACHT
IN
FRANKREICH
NEUESTER FILM

3

World War I: The Decisive Conflict, 1917–1918

JOHN BOURNE

Opposite An imposing image of Field Marshal Paul von Hindenburg in a film poster for *Die grosse Schlacht in Frankreich* ('The Great Battle in France'), 1918.

World War I has been described as 'the seminal catastrophe of the twentieth century'. During the second half of the war the shape of the catastrophe began to emerge. The war in 1917–18 would be about the demand for 'more' – more soldiers, more workers, more food, more weapons, more resources, more money, more skills – and about the effort to balance those competing demands while maintaining political solidarity and social cohesion at home. Victory would be the product of the home front as well as of the fighting front. Only those states that fully mobilized their resources and maintained their political legitimacy would prevail.

HOME FRONT

The year 1917 was one of strain. There were 95 strikes in France in 1915, 659 in 1917. Food shortages became serious, and 300,000 troops had to be withdrawn from the front to bolster the war economy. In Britain there was a wave of strikes between March and May, especially in the engineering districts, involving some 860,000 workers. The British prime minister, David Lloyd George, launched an investigation into the causes and was comforted by a report that showed an absence of revolutionary aims. Even so, Lloyd George made some important concessions to the strikers while imprisoning their more radical leaders. This method was followed by the new French prime minister, Georges Clemenceau, when he was confronted by similar problems in 1918. British morale, especially in London and the south-east of England, was further tested by a bombing campaign launched on 25 May 1917 by German fixed-wing aircraft. Public outrage and desire to retaliate in kind led eventually to the establishment of the world's first independent air force, the Royal Air Force, on 1 April 1918. The last eighteen months of the war were also a bitter trial to Germany. Food shortages became severe, exacerbated not only by the increasingly effective Allied naval blockade, but also by Germany's decision to privilege meat production over that of grain, and by its failure to impose an effective and fair system of rationing, which did much to undermine national solidarity. But it was in Russia that the strain was greatest. Tsarist autocracy collapsed in March 1917 in the face of a wave of war-weariness and industrial and political unrest. The liberal Provisional Government decided to remain in the war, but itself succumbed to military defeatism and revolutionary violence in November.

STARING INTO THE ABYSS

War is a political act, with political purposes and political consequences. By the end of 1916 the political consequences feared from the outset by many – not least in

President Woodrow Wilson addressing the US Congress on 2 April 1917, four days before the US declaration of war on Germany.

Germany – became apparent. The prospect of the dissolution of the old order in Europe gave statesmen of both sides pause for thought. But in the event, the European great powers walked to the edge of the precipice, stared into the abyss and jumped.

The appointment of David Lloyd George as British prime minister in early December 1916 provided little encouragement to those at home and abroad who favoured a negotiated settlement. Lloyd George came to power as a result of the British political elite's dissatisfaction with the apparently somnolent leadership of H. H. Asquith. Ironically, his political aims were actually more grandiose than those of his senior military advisers and commanders, notably the chief of the Imperial General Staff, General Sir William Robertson, and the commander-in-chief of the British Expeditionary Force, General Sir Douglas Haig. Robertson and Haig believed in what would now be called 'deterrence'. Lloyd George's aims were much more far-reaching, embracing not only the dismantling of 'Prussian militarism' but also the destruction of the Ottoman Empire, something that Robertson looked on with alarm. Lloyd George baulked at the human costs of offensive attrition, however, and constantly sought alternatives to costly frontal assaults on the Western Front. This was to bring him into friction with his military advisers and commanders and, to some extent, with his allies.

Politically, the war both widened and narrowed in 1917. In the United States President Woodrow Wilson had been narrowly re-elected in November 1916 on the promise that he would keep his country out of the war, but it became increasingly apparent to him that, if the United States was to have a role in the post-war settlement – something he wished and believed vital – then it must take part in the fighting. The United States declared war on Germany on 6 April 1917. US belligerency was made easier by the foolishness of German policy, especially the promise to help Mexico in an invasion of the United States, and the unrestricted submarine warfare campaign that began in February 1917, and by the fall of the tsar in March 1917. The United States would no longer have to take its place on the same side as one of the world's greatest autocracies.

The unprecedented human and economic costs of the war had made it increasingly difficult to justify the conflict in the abstract language of diplomacy. Death and destruction on such a scale needed the justification of higher ideals; the United States provided them. Wilson was careful to distance himself from the European imperialist powers: the United States would enter the war as an 'Associated Power'. This reflected the US government's noble purposes, which were to end war as an instrument of international relations and to 'make the world safe for democracy'. In the wake of the American declaration of war, the world began to take sides. Bolivia, Brazil, China, Costa Rica, Cuba, Ecuador, Guatemala, Haiti, Honduras, Liberia, Nicaragua, Panama, Peru and Uruguay declared war against the Central Powers in the months after April 1917. Although only Brazil participated militarily, politically the writing was on the wall. No state joined the Central Powers after Bulgaria's entry into the war in October 1915.

The decision of the German military to allow Lenin to travel back to Russia across Germany in a sealed train from his exile in Switzerland must rank among its more disastrous. The hope was that Lenin would foster unrest, undermine the Provisional Government and take Russia out of the war, allowing Germany to concentrate its

'We can now deploy our entire strength in the West. To be sure that is our last card.'

Colonel Albrecht von Thaer,
assessing the opportunities created
by the collapse of Russia, 1918

forces in the west. This typically put short-term military advantage before longer-term political and strategic considerations. Lenin certainly wished to take Russia von of the war, advocating a policy of 'revolutionary defeatism'. This was in contrast to other Bolshevik leaders who wanted to stay in the war as a means of fomenting revolution in Germany. Although the Bolsheviks accepted an armistice in December 1917, no peace treaty was signed until March 1918, and then only after a German renewal of hostilities. The Treaty of Brest-Litovsk (3 March 1918) was punitive: Russia was compelled to cede Poland, the Baltic Provinces, Ukraine, Finland and the Caucasus to Germany. The delay in signing meant that the German army was forced to retain almost 1 million mainly second-rate troops in the occupied territories. The thought of having to sign such a treaty themselves also sustained the resolve and solidarity of the Allied leaders in the crises that followed Germany's spring offensive, which was launched eighteen days after Russia left the war.

Lenin gives a speech from the back of a vehicle, November 1917. Lenin's concept of 'revolutionary defeatism' played a key part in taking Russia out of the war.

THE SEARCH FOR VICTORY

The German army was the 'motor' of World War I. In 1917 the motor changed gear and direction. Falkenhayn's failure at Verdun, coupled with the unprecedented British offensive on the Somme, saw him replaced at the end of August 1916 by the successful duo from the Eastern Front, Field Marshal Paul von Hindenburg and General Erich Ludendorff. Both had been contemptuous of Falkenhayn's strategy of being strong enough everywhere to avoid defeat, but not strong enough anywhere to achieve victory. They believed they had been starved of men and munitions in the campaign against Russia. German strategy in 1917 would be to stand on the defensive in the west and to seek a decision with Russia. To this end, German operational doctrine was rewritten and based on the concept of 'elastic defence in depth'. In February and March the so-called retreat to the Hindenburg Line shortened the German line in France and Belgium, provided a reserve and frustrated the forthcoming French offensive on the Aisne.

The Germans also sought a decision with the British at sea. Britain was greatly dependent on imported food supplies, and the North and South Atlantic shipping lanes were the country's lifeline. German desire to sever this cord was militarily sound (at least in theory – whether the German navy had the resources for the job is another matter) but politically inept. The policy explicitly risked American belligerency. The contempt for the United States as a military power, and the economic, financial and industrial strength that underpinned it, is one of the most extraordinary misjudgments made by two generations of German leaders. The United States was assuredly not a great military power in 1917, but it was a great naval power. The German declaration of unrestricted submarine warfare not only made US entry into the war more likely, but also made German success in cutting off Britain from its food supplies less likely. The military and political leadership of the US Navy showed a statesmanlike understanding of the realities of the naval war, preferring to build escort vessels over prestige battleships and making possible a much more effective convoy system that eventually began to negate the U-boat menace.

In Britain, Lloyd George's rise to the premiership meant that there would be a reassessment of the 'Western' strategy. Lloyd George had always favoured fighting Germany where it was weak and not where it was strong. In 1915 and 1916 he had advocated an 'Eastern' strategy, variously in the Dardanelles, in the Levant, in Palestine and in Salonica. He was encouraged in this reassessment by the first clear British victory of the war, General Sir Stanley Maude's capture of Baghdad in March 1917. This helped purge the stain of one of the British Empire's most embarrassing defeats, the surrender of General Townshend's army to the Ottomans at Kut al-Amara in April 1916. Maude took a battered and demoralized army, rested it, retrained it and re-equipped it, helped by a much more effective mobilization of the resources of the Raj in India, marshalled by General Sir Charles Monro. Lloyd George saw an opportunity to strike further blows against the Ottoman Empire in Palestine. After the unsuccessful British offensives known as the First and Second Battles of Gaza (March–April 1917), he replaced the British commander-in-chief, General Sir Archibald Murray, with a veteran commander from the Western Front, General Sir Edmund Allenby. Allenby reinvigorated the British forces in Palestine and – displaying a subtlety not always obvious in his Western Front battles – employed his superior

Opposite A German U-boat sinking a ship. Allied shipping losses to U-boats peaked at 860,000 tons in April 1917, the month the US entered the war.

Below This photograph of a German U-boat engine room captures the claustrophobic nature of submarine warfare.

British troops entering Jerusalem in December 1917 – an event described by Lloyd George as 'a Christmas present for the British people'.

numbers, artillery and aircraft to damaging effect against the Ottoman armies at the end of a long and uncertain supply chain increasingly harassed by Arab irregulars. Allenby's armies entered Jerusalem on 9 December 1917. In 1918 he was able to complete the destruction of the Ottoman armies in Palestine, despite losing nearly all his British infantry to the fighting in France and Belgium.

By the end of 1916 war-weariness was everywhere apparent in France. Voices were raised in support of a negotiated settlement, but as with Germany in 1914 (and again in 1918) France sought to disperse political pessimism with strategic and operational optimism. General Joffre, whose great victory on the Marne in September 1914 now seemed a long way off, was replaced by General Robert Nivelle, who had made his reputation in the French counteroffensives at Verdun. Nivelle believed he had found the operational key to success in trench warfare, but in truth this was little more than an exaggerated faith in the power of artillery to rupture the enemy's line, allowing infantry to pour through the resulting gap. His salesmanship was sufficiently slick to convince some, but not all, of the French political leadership. The British prime minister was also a believer. At a conference in Calais towards the end of February 1917, ostensibly called to resolve logistical problems, Lloyd George attempted by devious means to subordinate the BEF to French command – to the outrage of Haig and Robertson. Lloyd George was compelled to labour under what has been called 'the yoke of Calais' until the end of 1917, when reverses suffered by the BEF at Cambrai gave him sufficient leverage to attempt a major restructuring of the British high command.

The Nivelle Offensive (April–May 1917) was a disaster for France. Prospects of its success were seriously undermined by the German retreat to a strong defensive position (the Hindenburg Line) that had taken place in February–March. French security was virtually non-existent, and the Germans were well aware of Nivelle's intentions. His boast that he could break the German lines in 48 hours proved illusory, and so did his belief that if the plan failed the battle could and would be brought to a halt. The fighting assumed the characteristics of previous battles. After some initial success, progress stalled, territorial gains were few, and losses rose precipitously. The offensive spirit of the French army, already blunted at Verdun, was broken here on the Aisne. Widespread mutinies occurred, affecting some 16 corps. Nivelle was dismissed and replaced on 15 May by the cautious and pessimistic General Pétain. For the rest of 1917 the French army was capable of only limited operations.

The near collapse of the French army threw the main burden of Allied offensive operations in the west onto the BEF, whose commander, now Field Marshal Sir Douglas Haig, took up the struggle with relish. Haig had always favoured an offensive in Flanders, where he believed that the German army would have to commit troops to a killing ground or yield vital positions that would compromise its entire position in the west. The British War Cabinet was dubious about Haig's claims but allowed

'The general situation at present requires a great deal of watching. The strain everywhere is becoming great and we need to consider every move in all theatres very carefully.'

General Sir William Robertson to Field Marshal Sir Douglas Haig, 4 June 1917

him to go ahead. The consequences of the Nivelle Offensive's failure meant that it was June before Haig could start the Flanders campaign. Since 1915 the British Second Army, under General Sir Herbert Plumer, had been digging mine galleries under the Messines Ridge, a key German-held position south-east of Ypres in Belgium. On 7 June 1917, at 3.10 a.m., 19 of the surviving 21 mines, totalling 447,200 kg (986,000 lb) of ammonal high explosive, were detonated. The effect on the German defenders was devastating, and the British infantry swept forward to capture the ridge.

Haig then made a decision that came to haunt him. He gave command of the main Flanders attack to his protégé General Sir Hubert Gough, by some years the youngest of the BEF's five army commanders. The transfer of command wasted another six weeks of precious summer weather. Gough launched his assault on 31 July, and almost immediately ran into the heavy rain that would dog the offensive in the wettest autumn in Flanders for seventy-five years. Although the attack once more enjoyed initial success, it failed to take the vital Gheluvelt Ridge, from whose reverse slopes the massed German artillery was able to enfilade the British advance. Haig became dissatisfied with the pace of the battle and handed the main southern part of the attack back to Plumer. This necessitated yet more delays. Plumer's methods were more methodical and conservative than those of Gough: he preferred set-piece attacks, utilizing enormously powerful rolling artillery barrages on narrow

German dead on the Messines Ridge in the aftermath of the huge British mine explosions, June 1917.

fronts. The most successful of these attacks, at the Menin Road Ridge, Polygon Wood and Broodseinde, did great damage to the German army and lessened its faith in 'defence in depth'. But the return of very wet weather in October made accurate artillery-spotting difficult, and it became virtually impossible to move guns forward. Plumer, for all his successes, was unable to develop the kind of operational tempo that could achieve strategic results. Haig's decision to continue the campaign through worsening weather, deepening mud and stiffening German resistance after the failure at Poelcapelle (9 October) was one of the most controversial of a controversial career, lending the Third Battle of Ypres ('Passchendaele') its characteristic image of futile infantry assaults across a battlefield that had become a quagmire.

'Only a few have survived the battle. Dog tired we report in to the company assembly point. Three men of the hundred who were forward answer their names at roll call.'

Fusilier Karl Böhme, 5 October 1917

It is not difficult to portray the Flanders campaign as a clear British defeat. This was certainly the view taken by Crown Prince Rupprecht of Bavaria, whose group of armies defended the Flanders position. None of Haig's grandiose strategic aims was achieved. The U-boat bases on the Belgian Channel coast were not captured. Neither was the important German communications centre of Roulers. After three months of bitter fighting the BEF had finally managed to stagger on to the Passchendaele Ridge, which had been an objective of the initial attack in July. The British army's numbers had been much reduced and its morale undoubtedly damaged. The Flanders campaign had not prevented the defeat of Russia, nor had it prevented a German-reinforced Austro-Hungarian attack at Caporetto, which began on 24 October, from

almost knocking Italy out of the war. Since Italy had entered the war in May 1915, the Italian army had valiantly, but ineffectually, tried to drive the Austro-Hungarian army off the high ground in the north-east of the peninsula, in eleven 'battles of the Isonzo', suffering heavy casualties for little gain. The twelfth battle, however, was an Austro-Hungarian–German offensive, marked by the appearance of German-led artillery and infantry tactics emphasizing surprise, shock and infiltration. The Italian Second Army virtually collapsed, and the Third and Fourth armies were pushed back beyond the Piave river.

Despite Germany's military successes in 1917, however, Ludendorff viewed the future pessimistically. The state of the German home front was a cause for concern. More serious still was the condition of Germany's most faithful ally, Austria-Hungary, whose preservation as a major power was a principal German war aim. The Russian Brusilov Offensive of 1916 had done grave damage to the Dual Monarchy. When the new young emperor, Karl, came to the throne in November 1916, he immediately put out peace feelers to France. By the end of 1917, with the prospect of the Americans joining the fighting in France, he was even more desperate for an end to the war. Ludendorff was rightly sceptical of the German navy's boasts that they could prevent the US Army from deploying to Europe. (During 1918 American troops were landing in France at the rate of 150,000 a month.) And then there was the problem of the British. They showed no sign of flagging in their resolve to attack the German army in the west. Ludendorff's military instincts were aggressive. He could see no outcome to the war satisfactory to German interests that passively acquiesced in another 'Passchendaele'. If Germany was to win the war, the German army needed to resume the offensive.

The attack had to be soon. But no offensive was possible until Russia was taken out of the war. The Germans attacked along the whole of the Russian front on 18 February 1918. The Bolshevik surrender on 3 March freed between 30 and 40 divisions for deployment elsewhere. Even with these troops, however, Ludendorff had worryingly limited manpower. Germany had sufficient troops only for a single-front attack on a grand scale. For the attack to be decisive it had to be on the decisive front. This meant an attack on the Western Front in France and Belgium. Once these issues were resolved, Ludendorff was able to give his most earnest consideration to the fundamental question: how was the attack to be made decisive?

Ludendorff could not rely on weight of numbers. Nor could he rely on tanks, which – unlike the British and French – the Germans had failed to develop (see box overleaf). He recognized that what was strategically desirable in this war was often not tactically possible. He therefore reversed the formula. German success was to follow from what was tactically possible. He emphasized this in a meeting with his army commanders in late January 1918. When Rupprecht asked what the strategy was, Ludendorff dismissively replied, 'We just chop a hole and the rest will follow of its own accord.' This turned out to be a disastrous misjudgment.

Ludendorff was depending on sophisticated artillery tactics developed and organized by the German army's artillery expert, Colonel Georg Bruckmüller, allied to the aggression of elite infantry formations of specially trained storm troops. The artillery would deliver a short preliminary bombardment of violent intensity, opening without warning. Its principal aim would not be to kill the enemy's soldiers, but to

Opposite British soldiers bearing a wounded comrade at Passchendaele – a powerful image that encapsulates the difficulties of casualty evacuation.

Left An A7V tank, nicknamed 'the Monster' – the only German tank to see action, and the first to take part in tank-to-tank combat, at Villers-Bretonneux in April 1918.

Below A British Mark IV Female tank, sent to Australia in June 1918 as a propaganda tool to raise money for war loans – a common use for tanks during the war.

The Tank in World War I

The tank was one of the most important technological innovations to emerge from World War I. The onset of trench warfare focused the minds of inventors and tactical theorists on a weapon capable of crushing barbed wire, overrunning machine-gun positions and crossing trenches. The British deployed tanks in the field as early as 15 September 1916, and French tanks made their debut on 16 April 1917. After initial shock, the German infantry and artillery developed tactics to deal with the new machines, and their influence on the battlefield remained disappointing until the British used them en masse at Cambrai in November 1917. During the second half of 1918 the British and French integrated tanks into an effective tactical framework, together with infantry, artillery and ground-attack aircraft. But tanks remained extremely vulnerable, slow and prone to mechanical breakdown, and they were never able to act as an instrument of breakthrough and pursuit.

Mark IV Female tanks were armed with six light machine guns, four of which were located in sponsons on each side of the tank.

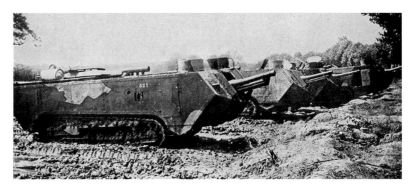

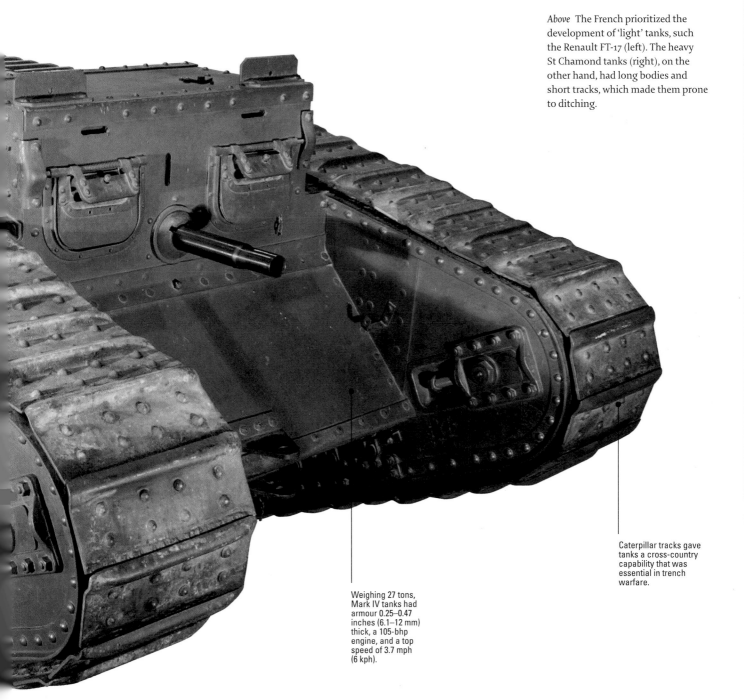

Above The French prioritized the development of 'light' tanks, such the Renault FT-17 (left). The heavy St Chamond tanks (right), on the other hand, had long bodies and short tracks, which made them prone to ditching.

Weighing 27 tons, Mark IV tanks had armour 0.25–0.47 inches (6.1–12 mm) thick, a 105-bhp engine, and a top speed of 3.7 mph (6 kph).

Caterpillar tracks gave tanks a cross-country capability that was essential in trench warfare.

paralyse his command and control system by targeting telephone exchanges, command posts, crossroads, forming-up areas, billets and bivouacs. A deep, creeping barrage would precede and protect the infantry assault. Storm troopers would infiltrate enemy positions, ignoring centres of resistance, which would be dealt with by follow-up troops. In this way it was hoped to unlock the stalemate of trench warfare and to roll up the enemy's line in a war of movement.

THE ENDGAME

The 'Kaiser's Battle' (Operation Michael) began at 4.40 a.m. on 21 March 1918. Part of the huge blow fell on the weak and elongated front of General Gough's British Fifth Army on the Somme. Field Marshal Haig had come under intense pressure to agree to a 45-km (28-mile) extension south of the British line. This was at a time when the BEF was also forced into a major restructuring, owing to manpower shortages, that resulted in the reduction of the number of battalions in an infantry division from twelve to nine (though this reorganization did not apply to the excellent Dominion divisions). The British were certain that they would be attacked in 1918 and had decided themselves to adopt a German-style system of 'defence in depth', but this was poorly understood by subordinate formations, and the necessary defence works barely existed in places. Gough found himself holding a 68-km (42-mile) front with only eleven divisions in line, much of whose infantry he still deployed in the front trench system, where they felt the full violence of the German bombardment. The Fifth Army was forced into a dramatic retreat. In less than a week the British found themselves behind the positions from which they had launched their Somme campaign in July 1916. The army lost 160,000 men and 1,000 guns.

This degree of success was far beyond anything achieved by the British and French in 1915, 1916 and 1917. It has dazzled many commentators ever since. Unfortunately for the Germans, it also dazzled Ludendorff. The logic of 'tactics first' began to unravel. The German Eighteenth Army's advance led nowhere except across the shattered battlefields of the Somme. The troops came within 20 km (12 miles) of Amiens, a vital rail hub, but no one in the German high command, certainly not Ludendorff, seems to have had the slightest idea of the advantages to be gained from taking, or even interdicting, the town. Its significance was not lost on Haig, however, and appropriate measures, taken in conjunction with the French, were made to protect it. By the end of April all chance of taking Amiens had gone.

Despite the scale of the German advance on the Somme, it fell short of a breakthrough. Ludendorff began to look elsewhere, swinging punch after punch like a drunk in a brawl, desperately trying to find someone he could knock out. Succeeding offensives at Ypres (Operation Georgette), on the Aisne (Operation Blücker-Yorck) and on the Marne (Operation Gneisenau) produced moments of crisis for the Allies, increasingly strengthened by American divisions, but by the summer it was clear that they had survived.

The spring offensives were a disaster for Germany. One of their main aims was to shatter the Anglo-French alliance. They not only failed in this, but in fact actually strengthened the union. The French and British political leaderships became closer. Neither Lloyd George nor Clemenceau was prepared to contemplate defeat. Political solidarity was also replicated at the military level. The appointment of General

Opposite above British heavy artillery on the Aisne, 1918. The awesome power and accuracy eventually achieved by British (and Allied) artillery was a major factor in the victories of 1918.

Opposite below A French soldier in a barbed-wire-protected trench near Champagne, indicative of the improvised nature of the Marne fighting in 1918.

Allied and German positions on the Western Front in 1918. The German spring offensives had failed to bring a decisive victory, and from August a series of vigorous Allied counter-attacks resulted in German retreat and ultimate surrender.

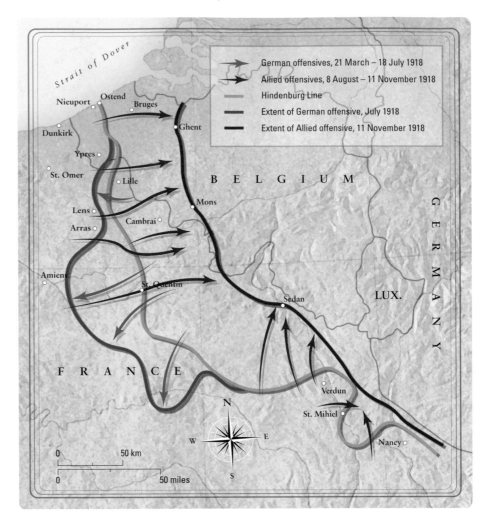

Ferdinand Foch, a man with a seemingly inexhaustible supply of courage and optimism, as Allied supreme commander on 26 March 1918 ensured more effective coordination of the Allied defence and (soon) the Allied counter-attack. The German army's casualties, especially in the irreplaceable assault divisions, were calamitous. Almost 1 million men had been lost in six months, and the Germany army was forced to call up the 'class of 1919'. Desertion from the army was running at record levels, and economic privations began to undermine civilian solidarity. Ludendorff also deteriorated mentally and physically as he began to see that the war was lost.

> '*I will fight before Paris, I will fight in Paris, I will fight behind Paris.*'
>
> Georges Clemenceau,
> French prime minister, 1918

During the final three months of the fighting the full military lessons of the conflict were at last absorbed and implemented by the Allies in the field. From mid-1916 onwards World War I had been characterized by the accumulating weight of firepower, especially the firepower of artillery. At the beginning of 1917 the fundamental problems of artillery – target acquisition, accuracy, survivability, destructiveness, effective cooperation with other arms – remained to be solved. But in the last two years of the war solutions to these problems emerged, thanks to the effective mobilization of the resources of modern industrial states and of their scientific and technological infrastructures. Techniques of sound ranging and flash spotting made the identification of enemy guns more certain. Improved maps, which were printed in huge numbers, and accurate surveying permitted artillery to be fired effectively without a tell-tale preliminary bombardment, a technique pioneered by the British at Cambrai in November 1917, and returned surprise to the operational agenda. Better-quality ammunition – mostly high-explosive rather than shrapnel, fitted with instant percussion fuses – became more effective against barbed wire, and did less damage to the ground over which attacking forces would have to advance. The deployment of gas and smoke shells made battlefield deception another option. Creeping barrages of incredible density required not only mass production on a previously unheard-of scale, but also efficient and flexible logistical arrangements and slick staff work.

But this was not all. No matter how powerful the artillery, it could not kill all the enemy's soldiers. The infantry still had to be able to fight their way forward. In order for them to do this they were provided with much greater firepower, a process that began in 1916 but did not reach tactical maturity until later. Rifle grenades, hand grenades, automatic rifles and trench mortars, allied to flexible tactics based on the platoon, allowed the infantry once more to 'fire and manoeuvre' on the battlefield. Command and control arrangements also changed. In the battles of 1915 and 1916

Workers painting shells in a British munitions factory. Millions were fired, causing more deaths than any other weapon.

too often the man who had the power of decision did not have the information to act, while the man who had the information to act did not have the power to do so. In 1918 authority was increasingly devolved to the level at which decisions could effectively be taken, however low it may be. This put increasing responsibility on junior officers and NCOs, and changed traditional perceptions of military leadership, discipline and morale.

The combined effect of the integration of more powerful and accurate artillery, constantly replenished, with more powerful and flexible infantry, supported by ground-attack aircraft and – when available – tanks, was to increase operational tempo. The 'flash to bang' time of operational planning was dramatically reduced. Despite these huge and impressive changes, however, it was never possible to achieve 'breakthrough'. Tactics win fire-fights; operational art wins battles; strategy wins wars. The abandonment of 'breakthrough' was, perhaps, overdue, but the decision no longer to reinforce failure became fundamental to Allied success in the last hundred days of the war. Attacks were now switched from front to front once enemy resistance stiffened.

The Allied counter-stroke, spearheaded by the US 1st and 2nd divisions and supported by 225 mostly new French light tanks, began on 18 July 1918 on the Marne, a river of ill omen for German military ambition. By 6 August the Germans had lost 793 guns and about 170,000 men, including (worryingly) 29,000 prisoners. This debacle was almost immediately followed by an even more serious reverse. On 8 August ('the black day of the German army') at Amiens, Australian, British and Canadian formations inflicted a major defeat on the Germans, capturing 400 guns and 27,000 men (15,000 of whom were prisoners). Amiens demonstrated the evolution of British operational art, based on 'all-arms cooperation', surprise, flexible infantry tactics and the numbing power of artillery. By the end of September the German army had been forced back to the decayed (but still formidable) defences of the Hindenburg Line, from which they had launched their fateful offensive on 21 March. The emerging power of the US Army was demonstrated on 12 September in the attack against the St Mihiel Salient, followed by the impressive transfer of the US army northwestwards to the Meuse–Argonne front two weeks later, a logistical triumph that first brought to prominence the name of George C. Marshall, a future US chief of staff and secretary of state. The British took up the baton on 29 September, when the veteran 46th (North Midland) Division spearheaded the Fourth Army's breaking of the Hindenburg Line at Bellenglise. Foch described this as the 'blow from which there could be no [German] recovery'. Nor was there.

In the (almost) hundred days after the attack at Amiens the German army in the west finally broke under the strain of repeated Allied blows. German military power was insufficient to sustain its allies, who also began to crumble. Bulgaria accepted an armistice at the end of September, the Ottoman Empire at the end of October. A

> '*Tonight, I issued a Note to Army Commanders . . . "It is no longer necessary to advance step by step in regular lines . . . All units must go straight for their objectives, while reserves should be pushed in where we are gaining ground."*'
> War diary of Field Marshal Sir Douglas Haig, 22 August 1918

New Yorkers celebrating peace, November 1918. News of the Armistice was greeted with an outpouring of relief and joy among the victors that was not always expressed as decorously as in this photograph.

'The last shot is fired: The slaughter is over: The enemy people are in revolution: What will come of it?'

Diary of Florence Lockwood, British feminist, 12 November 1918

British–Italian army routed the Austrians at Vittorio Veneto (24 October to 3 November). Hungary defected from the union with Austria on 31 October. The German fleet mutinied at Wilhelmshaven on 30 October. Germany descended into revolution. And, on 11 November, Germany itself accepted a humiliating armistice.

The integration of strategy, operational art and tactics into the 'all-arms deep battle' during the autumn of 1918 arguably marked a 'revolution in military affairs'. As so often in the history of war, it was the losers rather than the winners who drew greatest inspiration from the changes. In the years ahead, it was the Soviet Union and Germany that would lead the way in the art of war.

73

4 An Unstable Peace, 1919–1930

John Ferris

KEY DATES

11 November 1918 Armistice signed; hostilities cease

28 June 1919 The Treaty of Versailles officially ends the state of war and sets out concessions to be made by Germany

June–October 1920 Iraqi Arabs rebel against the British Mandate

12–25 August 1920 Battle of Warsaw sees Polish victory over the Red Army

14 November 1920 The last major White Army evacuates Russia

17–23 July 1921 Spain suffers defeat at the Battle of Annual; revolt in Morocco lasts for several years

23 August – 13 September 1921 Turkish troops block the Greek advance on Ankara at the Battle of Sakarya River

25 August – 14 September 1922 Destruction of the Greek army in Anatolia

15 September – 3 November 1924 Second Zhili–Fengtian War

July 1925 – July 1927 Great Syrian Revolt against French control

July 1926 – March 1927 The Northern Expedition sets out to suppress the warlords and unify China

Opposite French colonial soldiers preparing against Arab insurgents, Damascus, 1925. In fact little street fighting occurred, but the city suffered heavy damage from bombardment.

The 1920s often are seen as a decade of peace. In fact they were one of war. World War I did not really end on 11 November 1918. Several belligerents were beaten, or broken, but what would happen to their territories, or who would control them, was unclear. Some defeated states had the strength to attempt a comeback. The victorious ones were limited in power. They maintained their empires and order in Western Europe, through their own forces and the Treaty of Versailles, which limited German military strength; but, tired and divided, the Allies could not impose their will everywhere. In 1918 millions of French, American and Commonwealth soldiers defeated Germany; by 1919 just a few thousand of them could be deployed against Bolsheviks and Turkish Nationalists. Political chaos emerged from the collapse of the great powers that had dominated Eastern Europe and the Middle East (Russia, Austria-Hungary and the Ottoman Empire), from the attempts of new regimes to seize power in those territories, and from the Allies' efforts to create states based on the principles of national self-determination.

Wars of succession to the defeated empires, and struggles by the victor powers to maintain or extend their positions abroad, raged from the Danube to the Pacific between 1919 and 1921, and until 1926 in the Middle East and North Africa. China remained at war between 1917 and 1948. Some of these conflicts could have reshaped the world – if the Soviets had defeated Poland during 1920 and then tried to spread revolution through Europe, for example, or had Britain and Turkey gone to war during 1922. Even so, these struggles determined power and politics in eastern Europe, East Asia and the Middle East. In terms of defining which state would control what territory, conflicts between 1919 and 1923 affected the world almost as much as did World War I itself.

POWER AND FORCE

The 1920s marked the apogee of Western control over the world, and also the moment when it began to fade. New weapons bolstered imperial states. Spain used poison gas to subdue guerrillas in Morocco, as did the Red Army against one major rising in Tambov province, south-east of Moscow, and Britain applied tear gas in Iraq. Aircraft were used routinely against opposition, whether to attack warriors, villages or flocks. These weapons, and the willingness of Western states to use them, combined with political disorganization among their subjects, enabled counter-insurgents to achieve unusual success in guerrilla wars. Yet Britain, which controlled the largest European empire, was inhibited about using such weapons. British authorities never used poison gas in imperial wars and applied air policing far less than they could have done, because they believed it might start more hostility than it stopped, while their public opinion would not tolerate indiscriminate attacks on civilians. Meanwhile, the spread of means of mass political mobilization boosted the military power of non-Western states. Afghanistan, China, Persia and Turkey pushed European power from their territories, revolts rocked French and British colonies in the Middle East, and Britain voluntarily began to transfer power in India.

During these conflicts forces used the weapons of World War I, but in small numbers. Armies often had few guns and machine guns. Aircraft or mechanized forces were rare, except in colonial wars. These struggles usually involved just a few thousand or, less often, tens of thousands of soldiers. Armies reached the hundreds of thousands only in the Russian and Chinese civil wars. In the largest campaign of the period, the Russo-Polish War (see p. 84), each side fielded 800,000 men, barely a fifth of the size of the tsarist, German and Austro-Hungarian forces that had contested the same territory just a few years before, with perhaps a tenth of the guns and machine guns. Absolute strength and force-to-space ratios were low, while prepared defences were rare. Weakness in finances and economics, reserve and training systems, morale and political cohesion prevented belligerents from raising mass armies. None could inflict or absorb the punishment taken even by inefficient powers, such as Italy, in 1914–18. Political divisions splintered the power of the Bolsheviks' enemies during the Russian Civil War. The Bolsheviks briefly fielded 5,500,000 men in 1920 – half the size of the tsarist army at its peak strength – but immediately had to demobilize 80 per cent of them as the strain cracked the state. The fragmentation of alliances and the treachery of subordinates marked the civil war in China more than did the manoeuvres of divisions.

These conflicts involved the types of forces seen in World War I, but not their style of operations, nor the phenomenon of total war. They were more like the wars of the 1860s and

1870s in Europe. The power of the defence declined, while breakthrough and exploitation were common. Major and cheap successes were easy to achieve and, once achieved, to keep; small forces and battles had major consequences. The dominant arm in 1914–18 was artillery; from 1919 to 1930, for the last time, it was cavalry, serving especially as mounted infantry but also as lancers, valuable for breakthrough and essential for manoeuvre and exploitation. Particularly when married to the power of railway logistics, radio communication and successes in intelligence and deception, these forces could conduct fast, mobile and decisive campaigns in the classic manner. Many of these wars were fought between not just two sides, but several of them; hence political skill and the ability to become the single strongest player in a multilateral situation were central to military power.

GUERRILLA WARFARE AND COUNTER-INSURGENCY

During the 1920s, guerrilla warfare and counter-insurgency were widespread in Asia and to a lesser degree in Africa. Most irregular forces were small, numbering hundreds of men, opposed by thousands in colonial forces, but some insurgencies were great in scale. Perhaps 100,000 armed men participated in the Iraq Revolt of 1920 against Britain, as did much of the population of Syria during the rising of 1925–27 against France. Thousands of Islamic guerrillas struggled against Soviet rule in Central Asia throughout the decade, beaten only by the deployment of tens of thousands of Red cavalrymen. Britain deliberately did not try to control hundreds of thousands of armed Pushtuns within the north-west frontier of India. Some struggles between guerrillas and counter-insurgents were among the largest of the decade. During 1920–21, for example, Spain attempted to control the centre of Spanish Morocco by scattering 20,000 men across the territory. In 1921, through assault, ambush and infiltration, 4,000 guerrillas led by a local chief, Abd el-Krim, annihilated the overstretched Spanish army, killing 8,000 men, forcing the remainder to flee, and acquiring modern weapons for the first time – 20,000 rifles and hundreds of guns and machine guns.

From 1921 to 1926 the Rif Republic, with 10,000 fighters and an effective government, controlled much of Spanish and some of French Morocco. It was finally defeated in 1925–26 only by a great amphibious assault, supported by naval gunfire, aircraft and tanks, on the heartland of the Rif. Afterwards, 250,000 French and Spanish soldiers used overwhelming numbers in a classic cordon system. They systematically cleared guerrillas from one area, killing insurgents and intimidating the population, then moved on to the next, backed by air strikes (see box overleaf) and gas attacks on recalcitrant villages. In order to suppress a mass revolt in Syria during 1925–27, France launched full-scale conventional attacks on hostile forces, involving aerial attack and artillery bombardment of villages and, on two occasions, of Damascus, which killed 10,000 civilians. In 1920–21, 100,000 Red Army soldiers, using a cordon system and ruthless attacks on

Above Abd el-Krim after surrender to French forces in 1926. He lived abroad in exile until 1963 and saw the end of French rule in North Africa.

Opposite Goumiers – irregular Moroccan auxiliaries to the French – advance through rough terrain during the Rif War. They proved invaluable adjuncts against guerrillas.

'The Arab and Kurd . . . now know that within 45 minutes a full-sized village can be practically wiped out and a third of its inhabitants killed or injured by four or five machines which offer them no real target, no opportunity for glory as warriors, no effective means of escape.'

Squadron Leader Arthur Harris, 1924

Air Policing

Colonial states learned to control guerrillas through more modern and less bloody means, particularly by air policing. Between 1904 and 1918, for example, the British lost control of central Somalia to Mohammed bin Abdullah Hassan, the so-called 'Mad Mullah of Somaliland', who maintained an effective administration and defeated several British expeditions. In 1919–20, however, Britain struck at him with 800 paramilitary soldiers and thousands of tribal auxiliaries, spearheaded by air power. An air strike against the Mullah's encampment wounded him, killed some of his lieutenants and scattered his flocks – the economic basis for his power. Hostile tribesmen then seized 60,000 of his animals. He fled into exile, and died. Air power was only one element of Hassan's defeat, no more important than tribal politics, but still it was significant. Similarly, between 1921 and 1925 Britain contained a substantial Kurdish rebellion in Iraq by targeting guerrillas with air strikes mounted from garrisoned airfields, which were supplied by mechanized forces escorted on roads by armoured cars. In 1927–28 British armoured cars and aircraft ended assaults on Iraqi tribes by Ikhwan ('Brethren') raiders in Saudi Arabia. However, the limits to such forces were notable. In 1929 air policing collapsed in Palestine during riots between Arabs and Jews, as it would again during the Arab Revolt in 1936–39. Air policing in itself could not prevent major revolts, but when they occurred aircraft became auxiliaries to ground forces, most useful in bombing cities.

A light bomber, standard policing aircraft of the 1920s, over Baghdad in 1925. This image embodies contemporary ideas of Western power over colonized peoples.

civilians, were needed to suppress guerrillas in the Russian province of Tambov. In 1925–26 Turkey suppressed tens of thousands of Kurdish rebels only by flooding the countryside with soldiers, killing or driving out all rebels, and by the use of mass executions and deportations.

TURKEY DEFEATS THE ALLIES, 1919–1923

In the Middle East, World War I did not end until 1923. Although Turkey surrendered in 1918, that really was just an armistice. Thousands of men retained personal arms, and the army hid more. In 1919, convinced, correctly, that the Entente allies intended to crush Turkey, a leading general, Mustafa Kemal, and other officers formed a movement to drive out foreigners and create a Turkish nation state. Initially their position seemed dire. The Allies occupied Istanbul and European Turkey, and aimed to form an Armenian state in north-eastern Turkey. Greece controlled the Aegean coasts of Anatolia, with its large Greek population. Muslim and Christian partisans conducted ethnic cleansing against each other's people. However, the Turkish Nationalists had several strengths. They included the best Turkish officers of the war – excellent men – thousands of veterans, and motivated soldiers. They controlled the administration and armouries of Anatolia, and worked effectively to gain the political support of

'We will not defend a line, but we will defend an area. That area is the whole nation.'
Mustafa Kemal, August 1921

Turkish troops at the turning point. Mustafa Kemal inspects Turkish soldiers at Eskisehir in late 1921, after defeating the Greek attack on Ankara and breaking Entente solidarity through a separate peace with France.

both the Turkish elite and the general population.

Being surrounded by enemies had advantages as well as perils. The Nationalists concentrated their strength against their weakest enemies, one at a time, while dividing the rest by diplomacy. First, they occupied the territory assigned to Armenians and populated by Greeks on the Black Sea coast, deporting the people and seizing their resources. They beat French forces in Syria, forcing them into a local armistice and seizing some frontier regions. Together with the Soviets they divided the Caucasus, regaining territory Turkey had lost generations before. The Soviets were eager to weaken the West, and supplied hundreds of guns and machine guns, thousands of rifles and millions of rounds of ammunition. By 1921 Kemal controlled most of Anatolia, a strong base of resources, though his armies were barely a tenth the size of those fielded by Turkey in 1915. The Allies, demobilized and divided, could do no more than garrison Istanbul. Turkey's main enemy, Greece, held coastal areas with long borders, which would be difficult to defend in the best case, and the country was financially and politically unable to maintain enough soldiers in Anatolia to hold these territories for long. Ironically, the Turkish Nationalists might have fractured politically had the Greeks been just slightly more successful.

In 1921 the Greeks tried to escape this difficult position by sending 100,000 men against 80,000 Turkish regulars. These small armies had little in reserve – victory would go to whoever blinked first. The Greeks, too small to occupy Anatolia, could win only by destroying something vital to Turkey – its army. They struck Turkish forces at the main rail junctions of Eskisehir, just beyond their lines. These forces, defeated but not destroyed, fell back behind a cavalry screen. Then the Greeks moved on the Nationalist capital of Ankara, 320 km (200 miles) from Eskisehir, to make the Turks stand or else lose their administrative base. The Turks avoided combat until 80 km (50 miles) from Ankara, just past the Sakarya River, in rough terrain. The Greeks, unable to use their numerical advantages in soldiers and firepower easily either to outflank or smash through this position, were forced into a series of assaults, often disconnected. Deaths in this ferocious but localized struggle for hilltops were equal, around 15,000 men each. Both sides were tired, sick, hungry and low on ammunition. The Greeks fought well, alarming Kemal, but they could neither win nor stay. So they withdrew. Greece lacked the money and morale to advance again and had an impossible position to defend, with 80,000 men scattered over an 800-km (500-mile) front. Often just 1,000 men and 8 guns held a 16-km (10-mile) line, in rough terrain.

In August 1922 Kemal secretly moved 100 guns and 6,000 cavalrymen south of Eskisehir. After a short but intense bombardment, which neutralized defensive firepower, infantry broke the crust of Greek defences and cavalry drove through, rupturing Greek command and morale and encircling its forces. Greek forces were captured or else withdrew to the coast for evacuation. For the next year Turkish and Allied forces engaged in a tense stand-off around Istanbul, as their masters negotiated a peace that met most of Kemal's demands. The Turkish army declined in strength, and the Allies believed they could hold Istanbul and European Turkey if they wanted to do so, but no longer cared to try. By force of arms, in remarkably small numbers, Turkey overturned much of the outcome of World War I in the Middle East, even if Britain and France held many of their Arab provinces of 1914.

Opposite above Armenian defenders of Aintab in south-eastern Turkey, December 1920. The Turks soon drove these irregular soldiers, their families, and small French garrisons out of the region.

Opposite below Greek soldiers entrained in Anatolia, September 1922. Trains – often overloaded, as here – were a key means of military transport in the struggles of the 1920s.

THE RUSSIAN CIVIL WAR

In Russia World War I turned into a civil war, in which military power stemmed from politics. The Soviets, who now controlled the cities, industries and armouries, and most of the railway system in a contiguous bloc, could raise forces and resources easily and move them. Their minister of war, Leon Trotsky, was a talented administrator, and he and the Bolshevik chief, Vladimir Lenin, were able strategists. The Bolsheviks, the strongest force in a multilateral struggle, controlled 60 million people. The largest population under White domination, in Ukraine, numbered just 9 million (swollen, for a few months, to 30 million). The Bolsheviks also had greater political support than any other faction, though still only from a minority. All sides relied heavily on murder to defeat their enemies, and terror to intimidate the population. The Bolsheviks' rivals included ethnic nationalists, other socialist parties and the Whites, a political movement of army officers, disliked by most of the population and ignorant of how to create support, even from groups opposed to Lenin. The Whites were divided into three separate theatres – Ukraine, Petrograd and Siberia – and were dependent for weapons on aid from other powers. Because of their administrative incompetence, many of these weapons never reached the front. The Whites initially possessed more veteran officers than the Bolsheviks and were better led. Their best forces were good, but many of their units, conscripted from peasants

A Russian White cavalry advance in skirmish order in Siberia, 1919. Note the mixture of lances and rifles carried by individual soldiers, and the open terrain in which they operate.

'While in the ponderous positional warfare of the imperialist conflict, cavalry . . . was a subsidiary type of weapon, in our "light" war (light as regards the rapidity of advances and retreats, though not in the casualties involved), our war of field manoeuvres, cavalry plays an immense, in some cases decisive, role.'

Leon Trotsky, Soviet minister of war, 1919

or captured Red Army soldiers, were poor. The Reds built a larger army that improved steadily in competence, aided by former tsarist officers who dominated command but were controlled by commissars – loyal Bolsheviks with veto power over military decisions.

The Bolsheviks concentrated their strength against one enemy at a time, annihilating it while absorbing limited blows from the others. In 1918–19 they spread their influence and power down the railway lines, relying on armoured trains carrying artillery and shock detachments to seize towns and smash enemy forces. Such units could move fast and deep in the key centres of population and industry. The Bolsheviks moved first for victory in Siberia, where they outnumbered the Whites by 200 per cent, and then around Petrograd. Finally they focused on a prolonged campaign in Ukraine, which turned on the manoeuvres of divisions in open country. By December 1919, 200,000 White soldiers had moved north towards Moscow on a 1,600-km (1,000-mile) front. However, they had little control over the

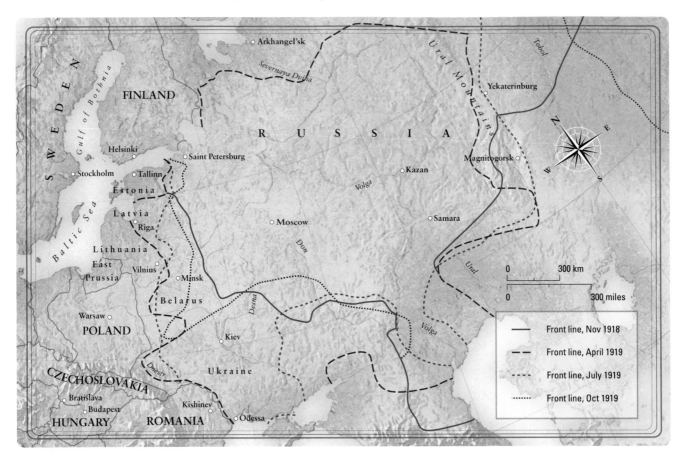

The progress of the Russian Civil War between November 1918 and December 1919.

territories and resources they seized, and were stalled by equal numbers well short of Moscow. Their position collapsed when the peasant anarchist forces of Nestor Makhno, based on horse-drawn sledges that combined machine guns with mobility, surged across Ukraine, cutting the supply lines of the Whites and ravaging their administration. Simultaneously, Red cavalry smashed the front and soon drove the White armies into the Black Sea, and Makhno into exile.

THE RUSSO-POLISH WAR

As the civil war ended, the Bolsheviks entered a great struggle with Poland, which began as a conflict over Ukraine and came to involve national survival and the spread of revolution across Europe. In this national war the Bolsheviks were joined by 14,000 tsarist officers, which boosted their professionalism. In mid-1920 the Bolsheviks pushed the Poles 650 km (400 miles) from Kiev to Warsaw, often driving 30 km (20 miles) per day. The Poles, trying to hold long lines with weak forces – 120,000 men on a 320-km (200-mile) front – were chivvied by the Soviets, who concentrated infantry and guns to break their defences, with cavalry armies penetrating to the rear, slashing Polish logistics and command. As the Poles fell back, however, their forces grew in size, the front became narrower, and the Bolsheviks became overconfident and factionalized.

> '*To the West! Over the corpse of White Poland lies the road to worldwide conflagration.*'
> General Mikhail Tukhachevsky, order of the day to the Soviet western front, 2 July 1920

Right Members of the Legion of Polish Women, an element of the Polish forces during 1919–21. Its 2,500 members – volunteers determined to prove that women could serve their country – provided support and combat, suffering many deaths in operations.

Below Bolshevik propaganda poster of Red cavalry, 1919, produced in an expressive graphic style.

By August 1920, Bolshevik forces, refusing to cooperate with each other, divided to attack different objectives far to the north and south of Warsaw, leaving a great gap in the middle. Polish radio intelligence discovered Soviet deployments, and their commanders exploited the position, concentrating their forces against the weak centre while leaving minimal strength to hold the main Soviet armies. The Poles shattered the Soviet front, dividing it into two disconnected groups, and then turned to encircle the tired and overstretched forces of the Soviet western front to the north. Many of those formations collapsed, and the rest were routed. The Poles then drove all the Red divisions back in confusion, which culminated in victories at the last great cavalry battles in history – at Komarów and Hrubieszów – in August–September 1920, involving hundreds of thousands of men and horses. The two sides reached a peace of exhaustion, leaving the Bolsheviks controlling most of the pre-war tsarist empire, but with an independent Polish state occupying western Ukraine.

THE CHINESE CIVIL WAR

The civil war in China was even more bewilderingly multilateral than that in Russia. So many adversaries were involved that battles were dangerous even to the winner, because victory weakened one for some time against third parties that might attack before one had recovered. This situation made politics in its various forms – mobilization, subversion, treachery, assassination and diplomacy – the safest and strongest tool for war. Only when politics had prepared the ground could an effective and economical use of force be made and combat lead to gain. When the central government collapsed in 1916, the struggle initially was conducted by warlords, commanders of the forces in one or more provinces, often aligned in loose coalitions. Warlords needed to control provinces in order to secure the economic resources required to maintain their armies, hold their territory and take more. Usually warlord armies were small and badly armed, and their regimes weak, without much political support. The greatest of these campaigns, however – that waged by and against the

Chinese soldiers fighting communists around Shanghai in 1927. Note the Western-style uniforms and 3-inch (75-mm) field gun. Most regular Chinese forces of the day, however, were far less well equipped.

Fengtian alliance in 1924 and 1925–26 – involved armies of a million men, using a few light tanks and aircraft.

Meanwhile, new political and military actors entered the fray: the Kuomintang (KMT), a nationalist movement seeking to rule the entire country, closely affiliated with the Chinese Communist Party (CCP). They were aided by thousands of Bolshevik political and military advisers, trained and armed by the Soviets, and able to create networks of political support across the country through unions, newspapers, student groups and secret societies. By 1924 the KMT and CCP had grasped control of the wealthy region around Canton and built the most powerful army in China, 100,000 strong, politically loyal, militarily competent and well equipped. Exploiting the weakness of all other forces after the Fengtian wars, in 1926–27 they launched the Northern Expedition, seizing control over much of central China. In the process, KMT field artillery bombarded British gunboats on the Yangtze river, while mass riots and boycotts rocked European concessions in Chinese towns, beginning the end of the great age of Western power there. In 1927, however, the KMT and the CCP split, turning to a ruthless war against each other. Ironically, in the short term a KMT army trained and equipped by the Soviet Union defeated the

Chinese communists. The KMT emerged as the strongest faction in China, with an army of 250,000 men, but failed to conquer most of the warlords or to destroy the CCP. China, in a state of political stalemate and civil war, remained a standing invitation for Japanese intervention and communist revolution.

TOWARDS WORLD WAR II

The sorts of military force that fought conventional wars between 1919 and 1930 were not those that mattered most in 1939. These wars were mobile and decisive because belligerents were too weak to raise mass armies, while the armies themselves possessed little firepower. During this period, however, major states developed advanced weapons such as aircraft, mechanized forces and radio, and tried to incorporate them into their forces. They did not do so with complete success, because the correct lessons were hard to learn and the technology was primitive. Thus until 1936, the power of aircraft and airborne ordnance was so small that aircraft carriers were ancillary to battleships, and were also routinely destroyed during naval exercises at night. Nonetheless, between 1919 and 1930 several states did undertake military modernization. All major navies trained not merely to fight in line of battleships, but also for actions by individual ships at night, and worked to integrate aircraft carriers into their fleets, an area in which the US Navy developed an important lead. All leading armies experimented with mechanized forces, although decisions during the 1930s gave Germany the greatest gains from these events. Meanwhile, Britain refined a remarkable system for strategic air defence that would pay dividends in 1940, at a time when France was suffering from earlier decisions about the development of mechanized and air forces.

'As I said the last time, when the war of giants is over, the wars of the pygmies will begin.'
Winston Churchill, 1944

These wars had great costs: 7 million people died in the Russian Civil War, and 4 million in the Chinese. Perhaps 1 million perished during the Greco-Turkish War, and 2 million were deported in the population exchanges that accompanied it. These wars determined which regimes would control what territory, and the very existence of nation states. Although ideas of national self-determination guided peacemaking in 1919, this really benefited only states that had armies of their own. Large populations that could have formed nation states but possessed inadequate armies, such as Armenians, Kurds and Ukrainians, were occupied by their neighbours. Above all, these conflicts shaped the international system that emerged after World War I, and also the roots of its collapse. Where the Versailles system survived in Europe, ensuring that Germany did not immediately recover from defeat, Turkey achieved that end. The Soviet Union controlled most of the pre-war tsarist empire; Eastern Europe was divided between several weak and squabbling successor states; and China remained fractured. These circumstances shaped the military rise of Germany and Japan during the 1930s, the dilemma of the 'status quo' powers, and the outbreak of another war of the giants in 1939.

5 Gathering Clouds: The 1930s

WILLIAMSON MURRAY

Opposite Viennese women greet their German blood brothers with unalloyed enthusiasm at the start of what Austrians would later refer to as the rape of their country, March 1938.

The 1930s began with the grim spectre of depression haunting the global landscape and ended with the even darker prospect of the outbreak of a second great world war in a quarter century. Certainly the period was not without its wars (for the Sino-Japanese conflict, see Chapter 7). Yet in many ways the technical and doctrinal developments, as well as the surge of rearming powers in the last years of the decade, were far more important than the conflicts that were sprinkled throughout it.

In September 1931 Japanese troops guarding the Manchurian railway manufactured an incident and simply seized the whole province; their government in Tokyo did not respond. The world took no action beyond numerous speeches in Geneva and innumerable telegrams between foreign offices. In retrospect the lack of action is not surprising, given the memories of the previous world war and the fact that the global economy was sliding into an abyss. Yet, if the world's attention was focused on desperate internal matters, trends and currents were abroad that would lead to disaster by the decade's end.

The Depression brought Adolf Hitler to power on 30 January 1933, an event that accelerated the strategic and military processes towards making a second great world war a reality. As the new chancellor explained to the army's senior military leaders during his first week in power, he had no intention of simply regaining the minuscule territories the Reich had lost by the Treaty of Versailles. Instead, he intended to remake the global map in pursuit of his biological world revolution. And, he added, if Germany's potential opponents possessed any toughness, they would seek war with the Reich now, rather than later.

> '*When today so many preach that we are entering the age of peace, I can only say: my dear fellows, you have badly misinterpreted the horoscope of the age, for it points not to peace, but to war as never before.*'
>
> Adolf Hitler,
> November 1930

The generals may not have taken his prognostication of world conquest seriously, but they were to worry throughout the 1930s about the Reich's enemies acting against Hitler's moves. Nevertheless, they were delighted to hear that their new leader would provide them with a blank cheque to begin rearmament. None of the generals should have been surprised by Hitler's declaration that he was aiming at war: he had made

Die Kriegsbeschädigten grüßen den Führer
auf dem Appell der Amtswalter, zu dem auf der Nürnberger Zeppelinwiese 160 000 Träger
der Politischen Organisation antraten

announcements to this effect on a number of occasions during his political campaigns and could hardly achieve his aims without it.

The Germans escaped their considerable economic difficulties and established the military power for the strategic base from which they could fight a great world war and destroy much of Europe in the process. While German rearmament caused some concern among the European powers, none was willing to take action to halt the Third Reich's growing strength. Winston Churchill, however, warned of what events in Germany portended.

THREE POINTS IN THE PREPARATION FOR WAR

Before turning to the conflicts that provided signposts to the coming world war, we might examine three crucial military developments that occurred in the early to mid-1930s. The first concerned the solidification of the German combined-arms doctrine (involving the use of infantry, artillery, engineers and armour together as a team) in 1933 with the publication of *Die Truppenführung*, largely written by generals Ludwig Beck and Freiherr Werner von Fritsch. *The Leadership of Troops* summarized the careful lessons learned from the study of World War I that General Hans von Seeckt had initiated in 1920. Not only did Beck's opening statement encapsulate the fundamental nature of war, but it provided the basis for the combined-arms, decentralized (with leadership and

'I marvel at the complacency of Ministers in the face of the frightful experiences through which we have all so newly passed. I look with wonder upon our thoughtless crowds disporting themselves in the summer sunshine, and upon this unheeding House of Commons, which seems to have no higher function than to cheer a Minister; [and all the while, across the North Sea,] a terrible process is astir. Germany is arming.'

Winston Churchill, summer 1934

initiative pushed down to the lowest tactical level) exploitation approach that provided the Germans with an enormous advantage in the early years of the coming world war.

The second major development was related to the intellectual ferment occurring in the Red Army during the early years of this period. A group of forward-thinking generals led by M. N. Tukhachevsky and V. K. Triandafillov conceptually thought through how technology was already changing the face of battle. Well before the Germans, the Red Army created its first armoured division in 1931 (the first German panzer division came in 1935). Moreover, the Red Army's manoeuvres in 1935 would see the first large-scale drop of paratroopers. In this atmosphere of innovative thinking, Tukhachevsky and Triandafillov had developed the concept of 'deep attack', which aimed at far-ranging operational exploitation of breakthroughs in the enemy's front lines. In this respect, the Red Army was far in advance of its German counterpart, the Wehrmacht. Admittedly, the Red Army confronted severe problems, particularly in the training of masses of illiterate peasants from the collective farms.

Yet in the short run all these advances came to naught. In May 1937 Stalin began a ferocious purge of the army. For the next three years his secret police savaged the Red Army's officer corps, targeting the leading military reformers. The result reduced much of the officer corps to a dull-witted, unimaginative group, incapable of initiative. The purges led directly to the catastrophes of 1941 and 1942. However, there is a dim echo of Tukhachevsky's and Triandafillov's concept of 'deep battle' in the Red Army's great victories of 1944 and 1945.

The third major development came in Britain under the leadership of a single individual, Hugh Dowding. Early in the decade he was head of the Royal Air Force's research and development command. In that position he set the specifications for what would eventually be the Hurricane and Spitfire fighters. Even more important was his support for scientists such as Robert Watson Watt in the development of radar. Then in the mid-1930s, having failed to become the chief of the air staff, Dowding was appointed head of Fighter Command, newly established to meet the growing threat of the German air force, the Luftwaffe. He was thus ideally placed to integrate the new technologies coming on stream, since he had played a crucial role in their development. Building on the RAF's experiences in defending London during World War I, Dowding integrated radar into a systemic approach to air defence which maximized the forces available, something the Germans would fail to do until 1943.

THE ITALIAN WARS IN ETHIOPIA AND THE SPANISH CIVIL WAR

On 3 October 1935, after a period of sustained build-up, the Italian dictator Benito Mussolini unleashed his legions without a declaration of war on a hapless Ethiopia (Abyssinia). The Duce believed that the Western powers, fearful of Germany's increasing military might, would not interfere. Eight months before the start, he made clear the kind of war the Italians would wage against the Ethiopians: he ordered his commanders to employ mustard gas liberally, should they run into any substantial resistance. They did, and from the opening days of the campaign they used gas against Ethiopia's ill-prepared tribal levies. Nevertheless, the initial Italian advance was hardly impressive, soon coming to a halt in a welter of ineptitude.

From December 1935 to March 1936, Marshal Pietro Badoglio reorganized Italian

Opposite Hitler passes war veterans at the 1933 Nuremberg rally, already determined to launch a bigger and more ferocious war.

Below The Duce, Hitler's partner in crime. He had similar megalomaniacal views, but lacked the tools to attempt global conquest.

forces, while Mussolini, unwilling to accept the humiliation of a negotiated settlement, deployed massive reinforcements through the Suez Canal. In April the Italians resumed their offensive. Helped by liberal doses of mustard gas and the fact that the Ethiopians attempted to fight a conventional war, the Italians captured the capital of Addis Ababa in May. Emperor Haile Selassie fled. Sporadic guerrilla warfare, marked by murderous Italian reprisals, flickered until British troops liberated the country in 1941.

While the Italians were slaughtering the Ethiopians, the League of Nations stood by and did nothing. Its sanctions failed to harm the Italians. The British public demanded a strong stand behind the League, but those most vociferous in support of Ethiopia enthusiastically supported disarmament. With a democratic public

Right The Italian vision realized: their murderous triumph with modern weapons over the tribal levies of Ethiopia. Magazine cover, 1936.

Opposite A Spanish poster produced by the Republicans, *c.* 1937, displaying the ferocious attitudes of their communist backers.

ILLUSTRAZIONE DEL POPOLO

26 gennaio - 1° febbraio 1936 (XIV)   Supplemento della "GAZZETTA DEL POPOLO,,   Anno XVI - Numero 5

RAS DESTA SBARAGLIATO DALLE TRUPPE DEL GENERALE GRAZIANI. — Durante la grande offensiva sul fronte somalo gli armati abissini hanno tentato un'accanita resistenza nella zona tra Torbi e Ringhi. L'intervento di reparti nazionali, sostenuti da autoblindate e dall'aviazione, ha infranto la difesa dei nemici che furono travolti in rotta disordinata.
(Vedere nelle pagine centrali l'articolo «Nella morsa di Graziani» con fotografie dal fronte somalo).
(Disegno di E. Mainetti).

completely out of touch with reality, Stanley Baldwin's government dithered, while the French looked on appalled that anyone would take the League seriously or court a confrontation with Italy as the Germans rapidly rearmed. The British chiefs of staff painted a dismal picture of Britain's prospects in a war with Italy, but largely because they hoped to use the crisis to speed the government's lackadaisical rearmament policies. The German remilitarization of the Rhineland in March 1936 ended the possibility of a serious stand over Ethiopia, while it also altered the strategic landscape. The upshot was that the Italians gained a bloody victory over Ethiopia, and Mussolini, whose inclinations were already turning towards the Germans, now moved firmly into Hitler's camp.

On 18 July 1936 the Spanish military revolted against the liberal Republican government. The coup achieved only partial success, the rebels seizing control of Seville and Cadiz, while Madrid, Barcelona, south-east Spain and much of the Basque country remained in the Republic's hands. The result was a bloody and prolonged civil war that killed nearly a million Spaniards and devastated the country. Almost immediately, Europe's ideologically committed flocked to one side or the other. Britain and France attempted to impose an embargo on the shipment of arms to Spain, which only they honoured, while the Soviet Union, Fascist Italy and Nazi Germany rushed 'advisers' and equipment to the contending parties. The Germans provided crucial support early on by using their fleet of Ju 52 aircraft to fly General Francisco Franco's Moroccan mercenaries from North Africa to southern Spain. There was considerable irony in the fact that Moroccan Muslims were now defending 'Christian' Spain. The Nationalists soon launched a major offensive against Madrid, which reached the capital by early November 1936. Four months of fierce fighting followed, but the forces of the Republic, aided by large numbers of foreign volunteers, held.

By autumn 1936 the Italians and Germans were pouring aid into Franco's Nationalists, while the Soviets were doing the same for the Republicans. The Italians also sent a number of combat formations, most of dubious combat value. In March 1937 two Fascist divisions launched an attack at Guadalajara that collapsed into a shambles – a defeat Lloyd George described as the 'Italian skedaddle'. As usual the rout had little to do with the bravery of the troops, but rather reflected poor planning, appalling leadership and general incompetence by commanders. That incompetence reflected the gross weaknesses of the army's officer corps, whose shortcomings had been responsible for the slaughter of 600,000 Italian soldiers in the murderous campaigns of World War I. Italian supplies of weapons and ammunition, however, were of considerable help to the Nationalists, but substantially delayed Italy's own rearmament programmes, something that would prove a major factor in the Italian defeats early in the next world war.

Like the Italians, but on the other side, the Soviets supplied substantial amounts of equipment and 'volunteers' to the Republic. But accompanying that aid was the dark shadow of the NKVD (predecessor to the KGB); Stalin's hounds were soon pursuing the 'enemies of the Republic' – not surprisingly their own enemies – with a vengeance. These purges in the Soviet Union soon spilled over to include the enemies of the people among the Republic's ranks. Those advisers who survived Spain did not long survive Stalin's camps and firing squads on their return to the Socialist 'Motherland'.

The Spanish Civil War (1936–39).

	Nationalist territory July 1936
	Nationalist territory October 1937
	Nationalist territory February 1939

Right The Spanish Civil War (1936–39).

Below 11 May 1939: Franco's tanks parade through the streets of Valencia to celebrate the Nationalist victory.

Hitler, unlike Mussolini, had no interest in ending the war quickly; as he told his advisers in November 1937, Spain was providing a wonderful smokescreen for the steadily growing power of Nazi Germany. The Germans made little effort and learned much, although the real lessons they absorbed were quite other than those historians have suggested. The primitive tactics employed by the Nationalists confirmed to the German advisers that they were on the right track at home. The war in the air reinforced what the Germans had learned from their analysis of air power in World War I: strategic bombing would be difficult; close air support could be useful in the breakthrough battle, but would be costly; even in clear weather bombing accuracy was questionable; and air superiority was a crucial enabler.

The war in Spain involved a series of slow and costly – to both sides – advances of Nationalist forces into the Republic's strongholds. There is some evidence Franco deliberately prolonged the war so that he could maximize his purge of Spain's leftist elements. In a series of offensives the rebels conquered the Basque provinces; and by summer 1938 they had managed to split Republican-held areas in two, but Barcelona and Madrid continued to hold. At the end of the year Franco's forces launched a major offensive against Barcelona, and the Republican defences crumbled. On 26 January 1939 the Nationalists captured Barcelona; Madrid and Valencia followed two months later, and the Republic was dead. But Spain was in desperate shape, and in no condition to participate in World War II, despite Franco's enthusiastic attempts to join Hitler's war in July 1940.

THE EUROPEAN CRISIS: WAR IN 1938 OR 1939?

In November 1937 Hitler held a highly secret meeting with his leading military and diplomatic advisers. He made clear that Germany would have to move in the near future because of its serious economic situation, and identified the first stops on the journey: Vienna and Prague. During the conference three individuals – the war minister, Field Marshal Werner von Blomberg; the army's commander, Werner von Fritsch; and the foreign minister, Baron von Neurath – expressed considerable doubts as to whether Germany was ready for war.

There would be no further such meetings to discuss Germany's strategy, and the three nay-sayers would soon be gone. In early January 1938 Blomberg married a woman with a 'dubious' past; when, within the month, evidence of this past emerged, senior generals demanded his removal from office. Hitler immediately moved: along with other prominent figures, he dismissed Blomberg, Neurath and Fritsch, the last on the basis of fictitious charges manufactured by Heinrich Himmler's SS. And therein lay the start of the only significant civil–military crisis in the history of the Third Reich. Himmler's case immediately unravelled, and a number of senior generals demanded Fritsch's reinstatement.

Confronted with serious internal problems, Hitler, ever the gambler, created a political and diplomatic crisis with Austria. The upshot was the collapse of the Austrian regime, and unprepared German troops occupied the country to the enthusiastic cheers of most Austrians. The occupation itself was not an unalloyed success. There were no plans for such an operation, tanks broke down all over the Austrian roads, and traffic discipline proved to be a nightmare. But the Germans gained major advantages from the annexation of Austria, the Anschluss. They

Right Neville Chamberlain returns from the Munich Conference in September 1938 to the acclaim of the oblivious in Britain. His government would not begin serious rearmament until the following March.

Opposite A woman is overcome with emotion as Nazi forces march into Eger in the Sudetenland, October 1938.

'Personally, I just sit and pray for one thing, namely that Lord Runciman [Britain's 'mediator', whose task was to settle the differences between the Czechs and the Sudeten Germans] will live up to the role of an impartial British liberal statesman. I cannot believe that he will allow himself to be influenced by ancient history or even arguments about strategic frontiers and economics in preference to high moral principles.'

Sir Nevile Henderson, British ambassador
in Berlin, summer 1938

seized substantial reserves of hard currency (a major aid to furthering rearmament), now surrounded Czechoslovakia on three sides, possessed a common border with Italy and could reach deep into the Balkans.

Czechoslovakia was obviously next on Hitler's list, and here the French had a real problem, since they were allied with the Czechoslovakians. By early June the Führer had decided that his forces would destroy the Czechoslovakian state in early October. He immediately applied himself to that task by manufacturing a crisis in the Sudetenland – on the basis that Germans inhabited Czechoslovakia's border districts, which were essential to Czechoslovakian defence and independence – while mobilizing and deploying German forces around the Czechoslovakian Republic. In effect, the Germans were able to throw 'the right of self-determination', on which the Treaty of Versailles had been based, in the face of the Western powers.

The French hoped that the British prime minister, Neville Chamberlain, could appease the Germans sufficiently to save France from having to honour its treaty obligations to defend Czechoslovakia. At the height of the crisis, in September 1938, Chamberlain flew three times to Germany in a desperate attempt to persuade Hitler to agree to a negotiated settlement. The fact that Hitler rejected the terms that Chamberlain brought to Godesberg on his second journey to the Reich underlines the Führer's deep desire to smash the Czechoslovakians, and his unwillingness to acknowledge that he was courting a general European war. On the other

'All is over. Silent, mournful, abandoned, broken Czechoslovakia recedes into the darkness. She has suffered in every respect by her association with France, under whose guidance and policy she has been actuated for so long ... Every position has been successively undermined and abandoned on specious and plausible excuses.'

Winston Churchill, October 1938

hand, Chamberlain remained obdurately unconvinced about the evil nature of the Nazi regime. At the last moment, Hitler backed down and agreed to a peaceful settlement, one that dismembered Czechoslovakia. The meeting at Munich, which completed the sorry story of appeasement in the summer of 1938, has quite rightly gone down in history as a strategic and political disaster, in contrast to the wild cheering that greeted Chamberlain's return to London.

Had war broken out in October 1938, there is little doubt that the Germans would have conquered Czechoslovakia, although probably at a far higher cost than was to be the case with Poland in 1939. But what then? The Luftwaffe was making the transition to a newer generation of aircraft in summer 1938, with under 50 per cent of its aircraft in commission; the army was still unprepared and possessed only three panzer divisions; the economy was a shambles; the navy did not possess a single heavy unit and had only a few submarines; and Germany had no access to petroleum in 1938. Moreover, there was every possibility that the Poles would have taken advantage of any difficulties the Germans encountered. Whatever the outcome of the initial fighting in Eastern Europe, the German military quite simply did not possess the ability to win the stunning victories in spring 1939 that it was to win in 1940.

Germany won an enormous strategic victory at Munich. When it completed its peaceful conquest of Czechoslovakia in March 1939, it gained control of the substantial reserves of hard currency the Czechoslovakians possessed, their vast arms industry and the up-to-date equipment of their army, some of which Germany used to equip the formations of the Waffen SS, and some of which was bartered to the Eastern European countries in exchange for raw materials. Munich completely undermined France's system of alliances in Eastern Europe. Ironically, the only power capable of replacing the Czechoslovakian divisions lost to the French was Britain, which had steadfastly refused to prepare its army for service on the continent.

Despite the immense strategic, economic and military gains the Germans had made, Hitler always regarded Munich as one of the greatest mistakes of his career. German rearmament continued at its frantic pace, now fuelled by the additional resources of Czechoslovakia as well as of Austria. But in Britain, despite the fact that the government had used the supposed unpreparedness of the British military for war as an excuse, Chamberlain refused to undertake any serious measures to speed up rearmament. The government did announce an increase of 50 per cent in the number of fighters on order, but in fact it only extended the two-year contract for a third year, which meant that no more fighters would be delivered for the next two years. In February 1939 Chamberlain grudgingly committed a small ground force to the defence of the continent, but only because the French

'History, which we are told is mainly the record of the crimes, follies, and miseries of mankind, may be scoured and ransacked to find a parallel to this sudden and complete reversal of five or six years' policy of easy-going placatory appeasement and its transformation almost overnight into a readiness to accept an obviously imminent war on far worse conditions and on the greatest scale.'

Winston Churchill, reflecting on the approach of war

suggested they would not be in a position to support the Low Countries should they be invaded by the Germans unless the British provided ground troops.

Hitler met with little resistance in Czechoslovakia. There were exceptions: one fighter pilot, Jozef František, machine-gunned a column of German troops on the way out. He would fly with the Poles, escape to France, fly with the French, and escape to Britain to become the leading ace in the Battle of Britain, only to be killed in a flying accident on 8 October 1940. Czechoslovakian industry, and workers with no means of escaping, would continue to produce arms and ammunition for the Nazi war machine until late April 1945.

The mask was off, but Chamberlain dithered about continuing the policy of appeasement until it was clear that the country, including many appeasers, demanded that the government take a strong hand. He then offered up guarantees to Poland and virtually all the other small countries of Eastern Europe.

Hitler's response was immediate. He ordered the Wehrmacht to plan for an invasion of Poland to begin in early September. Frantic diplomatic scrambling took place over the summer, but this time Hitler was not to be sweet-talked out of war. In August he cobbled together a non-aggression pact with Stalin. The efforts of the Western powers to enlist the Soviet Union in an anti-German coalition had never really got off the ground. But the crucial point was that the pact allowed Stalin to sit on the sidelines, watching the capitalists tear each other to pieces, with a view to mopping up large amounts of territorial booty in Eastern Europe. And so Hitler launched his forces, partly in the belief that the Western powers would not react. To a certain extent he was right: for their part they undertook no significant military actions, even while the Poles died in their tens of thousands.

The Polish cavalry rides out to meet the armies of the Third Reich at Konskie, 1939.

POINTING TO THE FUTURE: POLAND, NOMONHAN AND FINLAND

Hitler's war began on 1 September 1939 as the Wehrmacht smashed into what most Germans referred to as a 'season state' (a state that would last no longer than a season). The Poles fought tenaciously, but they had not completed their mobilization when the Germans struck. Moreover, they had spread their forces out across their frontiers in the hope of defending everything. In the end they defended nothing. The Wehrmacht broke through Polish defences in a number of places and then the mobile forces, still organized in only corps-sized units, penetrated deep into Polish rear areas. The Poles were able to make no response. Within a week they were in a hopeless position, and by the end of the month the fighting was over. A long, dark nightmare had begun for Poland.

Yet the German campaign was anything but an unalloyed success. The army found most units, including those of the active duty force, to be under-trained, unskilled in the execution of basic doctrine and generally lacking the aggressive

The Dive Bomber

Although between the wars the US and Britain both emphasized strategic bombing above almost any other potential mission, the US Navy, unlike the Royal Navy, was able to keep control of its aircraft development programme. The naval aviation community had quickly appreciated the need for accuracy at sea, and by the early 1930s the US Navy had devised aircraft capable of launching themselves in deep angles of attack and then recovering successfully, meaning they could steer their bomb loads quite accurately against targets at sea or on land.

While visiting the US in 1931, the future Luftwaffe field marshal Ernst Udet had seen one of the US Navy's early dive bombers, the Curtiss F8C Helldiver, in action, and subsequently urged Göring to authorize the purchase of two examples. These formed the basis for what eventually became the Stuka dive bomber. Despite the myth that the Luftwaffe of the 1930s was merely 'the handmaiden of the army', and thus interested only in close air support, this was in fact the least of its priorities. The Germans too had come to realize that bombing accuracy represented a major problem. As a result, the Stuka was developed specifically for air interdiction against targets that required the utmost accuracy, and efforts were made to provide bombers such as the Ju 88 with dive bombing capabilities.

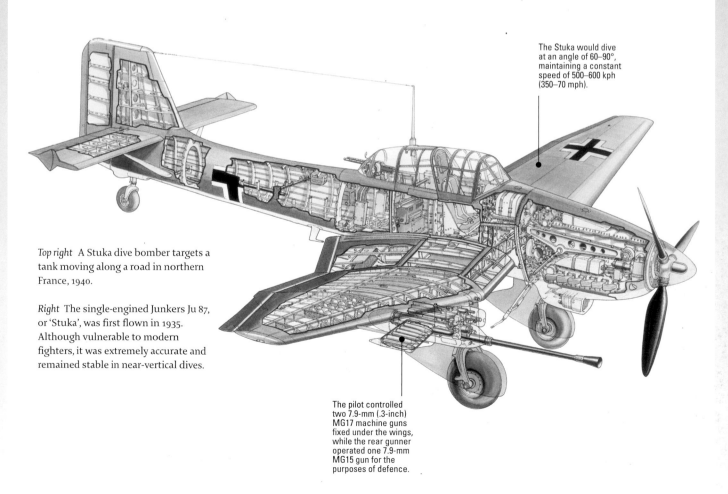

The Stuka would dive at an angle of 60–90°, maintaining a constant speed of 500–600 kph (350–70 mph).

Top right A Stuka dive bomber targets a tank moving along a road in northern France, 1940.

Right The single-engined Junkers Ju 87, or 'Stuka', was first flown in 1935. Although vulnerable to modern fighters, it was extremely accurate and remained stable in near-vertical dives.

The pilot controlled two 7.9-mm (.3-inch) MG17 machine guns fixed under the wings, while the rear gunner operated one 7.9-mm MG15 gun for the purposes of defence.

'Hence, the Reich appears to have suffered relatively little wear and tear during the first six months of the war, and that mainly as the result of the Allied blockade. Meanwhile, it has profited from the interval to perfect the degree of equipment of its land and air forces, to increase the officer strength and complete the training of its troops, and to add further divisions to those already in the field.'

Allied Military Committee, April 1940

spirit of exploitation that it expected. Moreover, the Stuka dive bomber (see box on p. 99) team that Dr Goebbels's propaganda pictured simply did not exist. The Luftwaffe was capable of providing close air support in static battles only. It had no ability in 1939 to support mechanized forces in a mobile battle of manoeuvre. In fact, the Luftwaffe regularly bombed the army's mobile units, most of which accepted that fact in their after-action reports suggesting that the air force had dropped more bombs on the Poles in close air-support missions than on German units. One panzer regiment, however, which had one of its lead units harried for several hours by Luftwaffe attacks despite desperate attempts to warn German aircraft off, suggested that large numbers of courts martial for the pilots were in order.

The overall picture was not that of an army ready to conquer the world. The German high command therefore instituted a massive programme to retrain its forces to meet the tactical standards it expected, and over the coming six months the army trained for twelve hours a day, six days a week. That autumn a serious argument exploded between Hitler and the army high command. Most historians have depicted that disagreement as being one over operational plans: it was not. On one hand the generals believed that the army required a massive training overhaul. On the other hand Hitler, looking at Germany's serious strategic and economic situation, believed that German forces needed to move immediately against the West; if they did not they would be incapable of moving in the spring. Hitler would have won the argument if it had come to the final decision to attack. But it did not, because one of the worst winters in European memory prevented the Germans from launching an offensive in the late autumn of 1939, an offensive that would have had little chance of success.

Triumphant German troops march through Warsaw, September 1939. In their wake they brought the SS and a regime that would slaughter Poles, both Jews and non-Jews, by the million.

On the other side, the Allies did nothing. The French sat behind their fortifications, principally the Maginot Line, and watched the Germans. The British sent Bomber Command in night missions over the Reich dropping leaflets rather than bombs, thus – as suggested by Arthur Harris, the ferocious future head of Bomber Command – supplying Germany with its toilet-paper needs; the French turned down British proposals to mine the Rhine river; and the British chiefs of staff talked the government out of mining the Norwegian Leads until it was too late, which would otherwise have cut off that winter's crucial supplies of Swedish ore coming out of Narvik and probably made a German invasion of Norway impossible. Most important was the failure of the British to force the Italians into the war. Here for once Chamberlain was correct in divining that it would be to the advantage of the Allies to crush the Italians as soon as possible. But the British chiefs of staff took a pusillanimous and inept position that allowed Mussolini to determine when Fascist Italy would enter the war. The result was that the Germans were ready and waiting in spring 1940 to launch their devastating attack.

Soviet officers examine the wreckage of a Japanese Imperial command post after the Battle of Khalkhin-Gol, August 1939. The battle should have been a warning to the Japanese military of how ill prepared they were. It was not.

While these events were unfolding, two military confrontations occurred in the second half of 1939 in theatres peripheral to most of the fighting in World War II. The first occurred in August 1939 in the far-western reaches of Manchuria, as part of the continuing dispute between Japan and the Soviet Union over areas of China and Mongolia. In July a small Japanese force occupied a piece of territory claimed by the Soviets – known as Nomonhan to the Japanese and Khalkhin-Gol to the Soviets. Skirmishing ensued and both sides rapidly built up their forces. By late August the Japanese had concentrated a reinforced division along the disputed area and had seemingly gained the upper hand. But the Soviets were merely biding their time. Stalin sent the future marshal of the Soviet Union Georgy Zhukov along with three armoured divisions and five tank brigades. In late August, Zhukov struck. Within two days the attackers had destroyed almost to a man the entire Japanese division against fanatical resistance. The message to the Japanese was clear: do not mess with the Soviets. When in late 1940 and early 1941 the Japanese were deciding whether to move south against the European colonial empires or north against Siberia, Nomonhan provided a clear answer and warning. In November 1939, Finland rebuffed Stalin's demands that they surrender large swathes of territory – a clear prelude to losing their independence. Stalin ordered the Red Army to invade. In this case the Soviets threw together hastily mobilized, ill-equipped, ill-trained and unprepared reservists under a slapdash command, and ordered them to attack in the middle of winter. The result was an unmitigated, humiliating disaster that underlined how badly prepared portions of the Red Army were.

Of these two singular confrontations, the Germans probably never heard of the former, while the latter would convince the Führer and his military that the Soviet Union would prove to be a pushover. The resulting invasion of the Soviet Union encompassed great German tactical victories, but eventually spelt the doom of the Third Reich and contributed mightily to Allied victory in World War II.

6 World War II in Europe

DENNIS SHOWALTER

KEY DATES

1 September 1939 Germany invades Poland

3 September 1939 France and Britain declare war on Germany

10 May 1940 Germany invades France and the Low Countries; Churchill becomes British prime minister

22 June 1941 Germany invades the Soviet Union

28 June 1942 German offensive towards the Caucasus and the Volga

1–9 July 1942 German and Italian forces defeated at El Alamein by the British Eighth Army and Allied contingents

31 January – 2 February 1943 Germans surrender at Stalingrad

18 May 1943 German forces in North Africa surrender unconditionally

24 May 1943 German U-boats withdraw from the North Atlantic

22–26 November 1943 Churchill, Stalin and Roosevelt meet in Tehran to begin post-war planning

6 June 1944 The Allies land in Normandy

22 June 1944 The Red Army launches Operation Bagration, the first of the offensives that will bring it to Berlin

16 December 1944 Germany begins its final major offensive, the Battle of the Bulge

30 April 1945 Hitler commits suicide

8 May 1945 Germany surrenders formally and unconditionally

Opposite 'For the Motherland, for Honour, for Freedom': Soviet propaganda poster depicting the Red Army and Air Force on the attack, 1941.

World War II had its origins in a toxic blend of unfinished business and new traumas. The decades between the two world wars saw the decline of the Weimar Republic, the resurgence of Germany under National Socialism, the rise of Fascism in Mussolini's Italy, the emergence after a bloody civil war of the communist Soviet Union under Stalin, and a civil war in Spain that involved fighters of many nationalities, culminating in the dictatorship of Franco.

THE APPROACH TO WAR

Hitler was determined to provoke war in his bid for global hegemony. The military occupation of the Rhineland in 1936 was followed that same year by overt intervention in the Spanish Civil War. In the spring of 1938 a jubilant Austria was brought 'home to the Reich'. Three months later Hitler demanded cession of the Czechoslovakian borderlands inhabited by a 'Sudeten German' minority, and in March 1939 he occupied Prague. As the 1930s came to an end appeasement was seen to have failed, and to all but the most optimistic war had become inevitable. France and Britain guaranteed the territorial integrity of Poland and increased their rearmament programmes. The conclusion in August 1939 of the German–Soviet Non-Aggression Pact was a golden opportunity for Hitler. On 1 September 1939 the German army rolled into Poland in the first stage of the new war.

The Polish campaign of 1939 has been widely described as the first test of *Blitzkrieg*: the 'lightning war' that dominated military operations in Europe in 1942. Blitzkrieg was not a comprehensive principle for mobilizing Germany's resources for a total war waged incrementally. Nor was it a structure of concepts, expressed in manuals, taught in schools and practised in manoeuvres. It is best understood in the context of the war of movement that was historically at the heart of the German army's operational planning, and a central feature of its doctrine and training. 'War of movement' involved forcing an enemy off balance mentally and physically. Between the world wars tanks, trucks and aircraft were understood in Germany not as elements of a military revolution but as facilitators of traditional German operational objectives: outflanking an enemy, threatening his lines of communication, and forcing him to fight on unfavourable terms and as quickly as possible. As long as armies moved essentially at the same pace, war of movement remained a theoretical concept. The combination of radio communication (see box overleaf) and internal combustion engines now made it possible in practice for an army to run rings around an enemy – if, and it was a big if, its moral and intellectual qualities were on a par with its materiel.

103

What the Germans were good at was exploiting opportunities. In that context they initially benefited significantly from 'obliging enemies' who made of their own volition decisions that suited German purposes. It was not, for example, German doctrine that led Poland to deploy its army in a cordon along its frontiers, nor France to send some of its best mobile divisions lunging irrelevantly into the Netherlands in May 1940. Blitzkrieg was to a great degree old-fashioned professionalism.

Determined resistance could not stop the German armoured spearheads that took full advantage of an unexpectedly dry summer in a country with few paved roads. As the Polish army began recovering from the initial shock, Soviet troops crossed its eastern border and shook hands with the panzer crews. The extermination squads of their respective governments went to work on 'subversive elements': anyone, Gentile or Jew, who might pose an objective threat to the new orders.

As Poland died, France and Britain marked time. They had rearmed slowly and reluctantly. Their governments had as yet no coherent war aims beyond avoiding the bloodbaths of 1914–18. Their forces had neither the doctrine nor the spirit for offensive operations, even against the weak screen of second-line troops that was all Hitler could spare for the Western Front. Instead, the Allies went to ground behind the Maginot Line, designed to break the spine of any direct attack. The German army digested its experiences and corrected its mistakes, while Hitler fumed over his generals' lack of offensive spirit. The USSR, seeking to secure its northern flank, provoked a war with Finland that highlighted the drastic shortcomings of the Red Army, whose command echelons had been bled white by repeated purges.

WAR ON THE LOW COUNTRIES

The phony war, the so-called *Sitzkrieg*, came to a brutal end in the spring of 1940. In February Hitler, influenced by his admirals' demands for a coastline long enough to provide some operational flexibility, launched an invasion of Denmark and Norway. Allied response was limited and ineffective. Outnumbered, at the far end of a long supply line, the Wehrmacht nevertheless bested the British at their own historic game of power projection – albeit at the cost of most of the ships originally expected to take advantage of the Norwegian bases. Scandinavia, however, became a strategic backwater when, on 10 May, Nazi Germany launched an all-out offensive through the Netherlands, Belgium and northern France.

The Allied high command, expecting a repeat of the Schlieffen plan of 1914, rushed every available man, gun and tank into Belgium (see box on p. 118). The weight of the German attack, however, was further south, through an Ardennes forest considered impassable by large motorized forces. Brushing aside weak screens of cavalry and cyclists, the Germans fought their way across the Meuse against second-line French troops whose tactics and commanders, rather than their courage, failed them at crucial points. As German tanks swung west and thrust deeply into the Allied rear, the French commander Maurice Gamelin, asked where his strategic reserves were, replied laconically 'aucune' ('there are none'). British and French troops already facing strong German forces to their front did the best they could to cut off the German spearheads. It was not enough. By 21 May the British Expeditionary Force and most of a French army group were cut off without hope of relief, withdrawing towards the English Channel and wishing for a miracle.

Parachute troops jump from a German transport plane, May 1940. It was attacks of this type that helped overrun southern Norway and the Netherlands.

Radio and Radar

World War II was an electronic war. Radio and radar played decisive roles across the globe and in all elements. On land, radios made possible close communication and flexible cooperation of all arms. Radios reduced the battlefield isolation of the infantry, and enabled unprecedented control of artillery barrages. Admirals Karl Dönitz and Chester Nimitz used radio transmissions to command entire fleets from shore bases in major operations. Radio was the key to controlling carrier aircraft and coordinating convoy escorts. Air–ground radio communications were decisive in the Battle of Britain and in the long air battle over Germany. They enabled artillery and armour to give close support to infantry. And from ULTRA's Bletchley Park to individual field agents, radio was a key facilitator of intelligence operations.

Radar, an independent development, first proved its worth in the Battle of Britain and then again in the Battle of Germany, both in an early-warning role and in tracking air attacks. In the Battle of the Atlantic radar was crucial for picking up U-boat signatures. In the Pacific, radar direction was a force multiplier for US carrier fighters, and eventually came to replace the proverbial 'Mark I eyeball' in surface operations as well.

The BC-611 allowed for two-way communication over a distance of up to 5 km (3 miles). The unit was switched on by raising the aerial.

The first true hand-held radio, the US-made BC-611 was widely used in the second half of World War II.

Above A radar set of the kind deployed as part of the air defence system during the Battle of Britain.

Above left The hand-held, battery-powered field radio was increasingly used by all armies during World War II. Convenience and ease of operation made up for low power and short range.

Left A signaller operates a British radio set, designed primarily for communications in forward areas, Libya, 1943.

The miracle – often overlooked – was that the alliance held. Winston Churchill, who succeeded a thoroughly discredited Neville Chamberlain on 10 May, sent most of Britain's remaining effective ground troops to France to help restore the line. The Royal Air Force fought the Luftwaffe to a stalemate in the skies over beaches where jetties – improvised from now-useless vehicles – carried British and French soldiers to the waiting ships of the Royal Navy, undeterred by brutal losses. None of this was enough for an increasingly despairing French government. It sufficed, however, for the French in the Dunkirk pocket, who held to the end to give the last of the BEF a chance to get home and fight again.

Did Hitler hold the panzer divisions back from Dunkirk as a goodwill gesture to a Britain he hoped to conciliate? Or did Hitler's generals see an unnecessary risk in sending armour across broken ground against fixed defences? There is no doubt that the tank-men were far more comfortable when they turned against France on 5 June. Within days a new government, headed by Great War hero Marshal Philippe Pétain, was suing for peace while it still had some negotiating room.

Britain's refusal to follow suit arguably owed as much to Churchill's belief in imminent US intervention as to any military or moral factors. In any case Britain's defiance confronted the Wehrmacht with a situation in which naval weakness made air supremacy a prerequisite for a successful invasion. During the summer and early autumn of 1940 an outnumbered RAF stood off a Luftwaffe handicapped by short-range aircraft and by a leadership unable to pursue a consistent strategy. Radar, centralized operations rooms and single-engine monoplane fighters were the technical triad of British air defence. But victory ultimately rested with RAF Fighter Command, its dour commander, Air Chief Marshal Sir Hugh Dowding, and the 'Brylcreem boys' who flew the Spitfires and Hurricanes and scored two for one against the Luftwaffe's best – 1,000 British aircraft lost compared with 2,000 German. At the end it was the German invasion force that stood down, leaving to the U-boats the task of bringing Britain to reason.

STEPS TO GLOBAL DOMINATION

Hitler, in the meantime, had increasingly focused his attention on the Soviet Union as his next objective. In a strategic context, the destruction of Russia would deprive Britain of its 'continental sword'. Ideologically, the USSR was both the home of Bolshevism and the source of the 'living space' needed to make the dream of Greater Germany a reality. Operationally, the Wehrmacht was convinced it had developed a way of war that negated traditional Russian advantages of numbers, space and resources.

The Mediterranean campaign

Planning the invasion of Russia, however, absorbed only part of Hitler's attention. His long-range goal of global domination could be achieved only by war with the United States. In the autumn of 1940 he began working to secure bases in North Africa to sustain future operations in the Atlantic. He promptly ran foul of the ambitions and interests of his Mediterranean clients – Vichy France, Falangist Spain and its wily caudillo Francisco Franco, and Mussolini's Italy. The last-named state had pursued its Mediterranean objectives independently, by a quickly stalemated

Above Free French pilots of the Royal Air Force run to their Spitfire fighter planes for immediate take-off, England, *c.* 1940.

Opposite Erwin Rommel, the master of mobile warfare in North Africa, *c.* 1941.

invasion of Greece and an attack towards the Suez Canal that met with a series of disasters at the hands of a far smaller, far more effective British opponent. Even after France's surrender, an Italian navy built at tremendous cost and effort proved no match for the Royal Navy's Mediterranean Fleet and its pugnacious commander, Admiral Sir Arthur Cunningham. The pilots of the Italian air force were as skilled and courageous as any, but their obsolescent aircraft could achieve no more than temporary local successes.

By the spring of 1941 it was clear to Hitler that saving Mussolini from the consequences of his mistaken attacks was a necessary prelude to securing the southern strategic flank of the campaign that would end the European phase of the war. Armour-tipped German armies overran Greece and Yugoslavia. An airborne assault captured the island of Crete, inflicting near-crippling losses on the Royal Navy, once again standing in to take off the survivors of a land disaster. And General Erwin Rommel, with an Africa Corps improvised from the Reich's military leftovers, began giving the British in North Africa an eighteen-month lesson in mobile warfare.

Invasion of the Soviet Union

Given the imbalance between resources and successes in the first months of Germany's Mediterranean campaign, it has frequently been asked whether Nazi Germany missed an opportunity by not increasing its commitment to that theatre. Even a small proportion of the tanks lost in Russia, it is argued, could have opened Rommel's way to the Caucasus, to Persia and its oilfields, perhaps to India itself.

Critics respond that the US, by this time a belligerent in all but name, would have sustained Britain in the war no matter what losses a declining empire might suffer. The issue was rendered moot by Hitler's determination to pursue the Russian option as quickly as possible. On 22 June 1941 the Wehrmacht, supported by a mixed bag of to some degree reluctant client states, crossed the borders of the Soviet Union.

The USSR was still digesting the geographic fruits of its earlier agreement with Hitler. Stalin had adamantly refused to credit comprehensive intelligence reports predicting an imminent invasion. For two months, as panzer spearheads sliced deep into Russia and foot-marching infantry ground up suddenly isolated Russian units, the Germans won a string of tactical/operational victories unprecedented in military history. Thousands of tanks, guns and aircraft; hundreds of thousands of prisoners; civilian populations welcoming the Wehrmacht as liberators from Soviet tyranny – it was the raw material for an epic. But the Red Army and the USSR refused to crack.

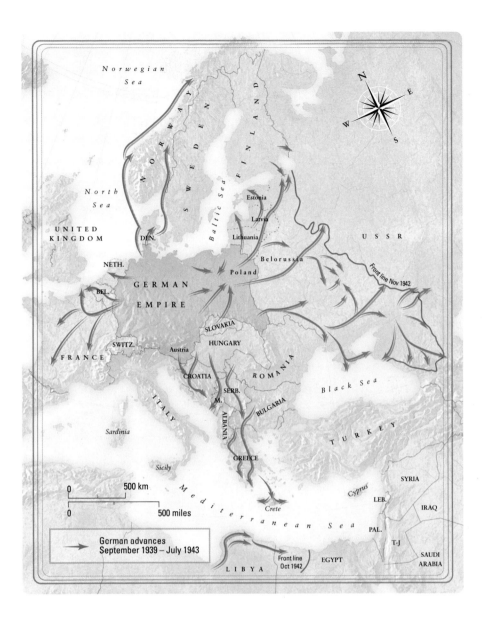

Opposite German Mark IV tank and supporting infantry in action on the Russian Front, summer 1941.

Right German advances in Europe from September 1939 to July 1943.

As the Germans drove deeper into Russia, their losses mounted. Hitler and his generals could agree on neither objectives nor time frames. At the front and behind the lines, Nazi ideology generated atrocities and massacres, with Wehrmacht participation more the rule than the exception. Nor was the Reich able even to exploit its conquests effectively. The materiel cornucopias so confidently expected before the war began turned out to be mere trickles of resources and manufactured goods. Slave labour, on the other hand, was a flourishing commodity – one whose use further alienated the civilians on whom production depended.

The road to Auschwitz

Well before the invasion of Russia the Nazis had begun implementing the 'Final Solution' of the 'Jewish question' that was at the centre of their racially based ideology. What has been called a 'twisted road to Auschwitz' becomes a little straighter once it is understood that the Nazis believed that Jews were literal parasites. Isolating them from their 'host communities' of more or less unsuspecting Gentiles was itself a final solution. Left to their own resources and devices, the Jews could reasonably be expected to die off with only minor assistance.

Isolation, impractical in Germany even during the war, could be implemented more openly and comprehensively in Poland, which was viewed in any case as a test bed for Nazi racial principles. Ghettoization began in the autumn of 1939, steadily increasing the concentration of Jews in particular areas of large cities. Deportation was added in 1940, as the first of hundreds of trainloads of Jews from Germany, Austria and the conquered states of Western Europe began arriving in Poland. The Nazi cover story, to the victims and their neighbours alike, was that the Jews were being deported for forced labour. Jews were indeed put in work gangs and used as factory slaves. But despite steadily reduced rations, steadily worsened environments and steadily increased oppression, the Jews stubbornly refused to die en masse.

It was that stubbornness that led Heinrich Himmler and the SS to employ more direct methods in Russia. *Einsatzgruppen* ('action squads') of killers followed the armies into the Soviet Union. With help from the Wehrmacht and local Gentiles, they accounted for the deaths of over a million and a half Jews, Gypsies and Slavs, most between June and December of 1941. The psychological strain of direct mass murder, however, led to a movement in favour of establishing an organized structure of genocide. Some time in the autumn of 1941 Himmler, with Hitler's approval, began establishing facilities for mass killing by poison gas. On 20 January 1942 the Wannsee Conference accepted the proposal for the 'complete solution of Europe's Jewish question' – ultimately involving the projected murder of around 11 million people.

Deportations from the ghettoes to the killing centres began in early 1942. By year's end many of the Jews in Eastern Europe were dead. The years 1943 and 1944 witnessed the round-up and extermination of those overlooked and those deported from Western and Southern Europe. The exact number of Jews and other 'enemies

of the Reich' killed in the camp system and its offshoots has never been determined. Perhaps the most noteworthy feature of the operation is the relatively limited direct impact it had on the Nazi war effort. The Holocaust was accomplished with the spare change of a total war.

GERMANY FALTERS

As the Germans struggled to cope with success, the Soviet Union, which had moved much of its industrial plant beyond the Ural Mountains, caught its second wind. Autumn mud slowed German tanks; winter snow immobilized them. By December 1941 the Wehrmacht had reached the outskirts of Moscow. It would get no farther, as Russian counter-attacks stabilized the front and forced Hitler and his generals to wait till next year.

The United States joins the war

The Japanese attack on Pearl Harbor on 7 December 1941 brought the United States into a war that President Franklin D. Roosevelt had increasingly regarded as inevitable. Critics and admirers alike have described Roosevelt's policies as 'two steps forward, one back' – a judgment excessively Machiavellian. Certainly since September 1939 Germany had not behaved in any way Washington might interpret as conciliatory. Instead, the Battle of the Atlantic had brought the war to America's Atlantic coast, as British and Allied merchantmen fought their way past the U-boats to sustain Britain's lifeline. By the summer of 1941 the US Navy was engaged in what amounted to an undeclared war with its German counterpart, the Kriegsmarine, which was increasingly insistent that Hitler should allow retaliation. The Führer for his part enthusiastically declared war against America on 11 December. He was confident that Japan would distract a decadent country ruled by a paralytic long enough for the 'real' war in Eurasia to be ended, after which the United States alone, facing two warrior cultures, was likely to seek negotiations.

Opposite left Jews being shot near Ivangorod in 1941 by one of the special killing teams innocuously named 'action squads' (*Einsatzgruppen*).

Opposite right Jews undergoing 'selection' on the station platform at Birkenau. Those considered unfit for work were immediately gassed.

Right Soviet propaganda poster, 1941. The legend states: 'Napoleon was wiped out. Hitler will be wiped out.'

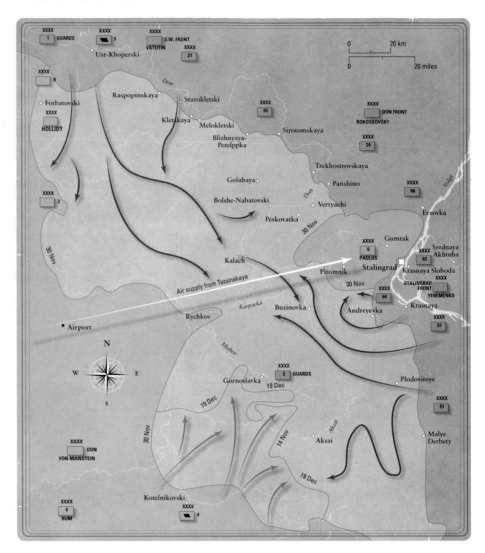

Above German prisoners taken at Stalingrad, February 1943. Over 90,000 were captured.

Right The Soviet counter-offensive against the German Sixth Army at Stalingrad, 19 November – 18 December 1942.

> 'History knows no greater display of courage than that shown by the people of the Soviet Union.'
>
> Henry L. Stimson, US secretary of war, 1941

Hitler takes command

On 19 December 1941 Hitler also assumed supreme command of the Wehrmacht. Many key commanders were relieved or reassigned. In their places stood new men, hard men convinced that will power and fighting power would end the war in the next campaign – particularly after Soviet offensives in the early spring were repelled with relative ease. The Führer Directive of 3 April 1942 provided for the concentration of all available resources in southern Russia. Their mission was to destroy the enemy in that sector, and secure the oilfields of the Caucasus and the mountain passes to the Middle East. On 28 June the great offensive began. This time, however, the Russians fell back rather than staying in place to be overrun. Then Hitler changed the plan, making the city of Stalingrad, on the left of the German axis of advance, the principal objective. Forces already stretched dangerously thin were further divided, then committed to the kind of close urban combat that nullified German skills in manoeuvre war. As Hitler's obsession with its capture increased, Stalingrad became at once magnet and mousetrap, drawing in forces from other sectors, leaving them vulnerable to the hammer blow Stalin and his generals were preparing. On 19 November the Russians struck – not Stalingrad itself, but the open steppe on the city's flanks. Defences largely manned by poorly equipped German client forces crumbled. Within a week the Germans in Stalingrad were surrounded. Not a single general had the moral courage to defy Hitler's order to hold the city at all costs. On 2 February 1943, 200,000 survivors surrendered to a Red Army that had learned its lessons and was preparing to become the teacher.

El Alamein

During 1942 another learning curve had been demonstrated in the Mediterranean. On land, British forces had been able to do no more than keep the field against Rommel, in a series of wide-open see-saw battles that highlighted British shortcomings in mobile warfare. At sea and in the air the story was the opposite, as Britain reversed Axis control of the Mediterranean. In the process Italy's remaining material and moral resources were steadily eroded. The tide definitively turned in August, when a physically exhausted Rommel launched his final attack against the British Eighth Army, which was finally balancing its material superiority with operational skill. Checked and stalemated by Claude Auchinleck, the German Africa Corps was hammered into defeat at El Alamein by a new commander, one who understood the capacities and the limitations of his forces better than any of his predecessors. Bernard Law Montgomery would be heard from again.

TOWARDS TOTAL WAR

US participation made what had begun as an essentially European conflict into unquestionably a global war. It also highlighted an increasing movement towards total war in all the major belligerents. The Soviet Union's adjustments were more operational than social; the country had been on what amounted to a war footing since the introduction of the first five-year plan in 1928. Of the liberal democracies, Britain was most efficient in mobilizing its limited resources, while Germany was slower to achieve full mobilization – in good part because Hitler believed that in World War I the home front had collapsed from privation while the army was still fighting on. Even after Stalingrad, the Reich's civilians continued to live well on the plunder of Europe. As for the United States, its large population and efficient economic system enabled a national mobilization that was effective even with permitted loopholes: for example, major-league baseball was able to continue fielding teams throughout the war (see box overleaf).

Even before the entry of the United States into the war, Britain had been striking back at Germany the only way possible – by air. Pre-war expectations of the effect of strategic bombardment, however, proved wildly optimistic. The RAF, unable to survive by day, was also unable to find, much less strike, specific targets by night. The result was a shift of emphasis to area bombardment, a shift initially hardly noticed because of the small numbers and the short range of the aircraft available.

British General Bernard Law Montgomery watches his tanks move up during the Battle of El Alamein, November 1942.

'Before Alamein we never had a victory. After Alamein we never had a defeat.'

Winston Churchill

JOIN US in a VICTORY JOB

APPLY AT YOUR NEAREST NATIONAL SERVICE OFFICE

Left Australian war propaganda poster, 1943. The wide range of occupations shown here – including the armed forces, nursing and factory work – implies that there was a job for every woman.

Below A woman working on a dive bomber in Tennessee, 1943. African-American women were recruited for war work and military service.

Bottom The US armed forces remained officially segregated throughout the war.

Gender, Race and War

Of all the social changes brought about by the necessity of direct conflict, those involving women and racial minorities were among the most significant. Nations approached the problems posed by home labour and conscription in different ways, according to their individual needs and cultural prejudices. Britain was obliged to make the most of what meagre resources it had, to the point of conscripting women for war work and eventually integrating them into home-defence anti-aircraft batteries. In Germany, on the other hand, it was not until after Stalingrad that the country began to tighten its belt and to add women in

significant numbers to its labour force. The United States had a large population at its disposal, which, combined with the benefit of a healthy economy, meant that it could even indulge its racist elements by virtually ignoring the military potential of 10 per cent of its citizens. Whether draftees or volunteers, most African Americans spent the war as uniformed labourers. Despite the large numbers engaged in direct support of the war effort, in factories and in uniform, American women's contributions as well were largely gender-conventional, involving keeping home fires burning and home cooking on the table.

MILITARY POLICE
COLORED

*'The dominant feeling
of the battlefield is
loneliness.'*

General William Slim,
June 1942

The Americans were more robust in their approach, calling for a land invasion of continental Europe in 1943 – or perhaps as early as 1942, should Soviet collapse become imminent. Churchill and his military chiefs considered both ideas folly. Apart from the shortage of the landing craft that the US Navy insisted were needed in the Pacific, Britain had been consistently and embarrassingly defeated wherever it had fought the Germans in Europe on a scale larger than pinprick commando raids. The Dieppe fiasco of August, an unsuccessful probing attack on the Channel port, was only the most recent example. Time and experience would be needed to tackle the Reich on its home ground. In the end Roosevelt agreed that Allied ground resources would be better employed initially in an invasion of North Africa.

The North African campaign and the Mediterranean strategy

Mounted in November 1942, Operation Torch highlighted the tactical and operational weaknesses of the US and British armies while proving a significant success on strategic and policy levels. The North African campaign forced the Axis off the continent with a loss of over 150,000 prisoners, and put an end to Italy's commitment to the war. It also established the framework for successful cooperation among senior British and US commanders, who had no previous experience of working together. The latter achievement owed a great deal to General Dwight Eisenhower, whose developing mastery of coalition war would make him one of the 20th century's great captains.

Victories in North Africa, however, were irrelevant – at least for negotiating purposes – to Stalin, who demanded a 'second front now' in north-west Europe to relieve pressure on the Soviet Union, which was strained to the limit against a still-formidable Wehrmacht. Anglo-American pursuit of 'unconditional surrender', announced in January 1943, did not placate the Soviet dictator. Neither did the Western Allies' decision that African success was best followed up directly by invading Sicily then mainland Italy. This 'Mediterranean strategy' particularly disturbed a US army still committed to a cross-channel invasion in 1943 and a navy arguing for the deployment of American resources to the Pacific. It made sense, however, to a president committed to maintaining an equal partnership with the steadily weakening Britain, and to the British army chief of staff, General Alan Brooke, who persuasively argued that a full-scale Italian campaign would tie down enough German divisions to make it difficult for the Wehrmacht to reinforce its army in France against a cross-channel invasion.

General Dwight D. Eisenhower, Supreme Commander of the Allied Forces in Europe, 1944–45.

'We Polish soldiers, for our freedom and yours, have given our souls to God, our bodies to the soil of Italy, and our hearts to Poland.'

Inscription, Polish cemetery,
Monte Cassino, Italy

Operational implementation of the 'Mediterranean variant' has ever since been grist for critics' mills. Sicily was overrun easily enough. But the plans for invading Italy took little account of the terrain, and paid even less attention to the Germans. Italy's surrender in September 1943, exploited only half-heartedly by the Allies, enabled the Germans to convert Italy to a glacis and a killing ground. An increasingly multicultural Allied force fought its way up the peninsula mile by mile against a defence whose conduct remains a tribute to Wehrmacht skill at arms. The single effort to open up the campaign, the amphibious landing at Anzio in January 1944, was quickly contained, becoming just another static front in a theatre where advances were achieved at a single price: soldiers' lives.

Retreat after Stalingrad

Allied successes in the Mediterranean nevertheless influenced Hitler and the Wehrmacht. In the aftermath of Stalingrad, the Germans had succeeded in re-establishing their lines in south Russia, even throwing the Russians out of the key city of Kharkov in February 1943. That counterpunch generated plans for a larger attack against the salient around the city of Kursk. Far from being just a large-scale local counter-attack, Operation Citadel was regarded as a response to Allied gains in the west, and as a means of regaining the operational superiority lost at Stalingrad. The Red Army for its part viewed Kursk as an integral part of its own offensive plans, an opportunity to wear down German mobile forces on Russian terms. The result was history's biggest tank battle (see box overleaf). At its end the panzers had been stopped, then forced into a retreat that ended only in the streets of Berlin. The Russians followed their victory by unleashing their own offensive – a series of operationally sophisticated, well-coordinated attacks that by late autumn had recaptured Smolensk and Kiev, forced the Germans back across the Dnieper and set the stage for the denouement of the Russo-German War after the turn of the year.

The Battle of the Atlantic

Meanwhile, Britain and the United States had won a decisive victory in one sector and were expanding operations in another. The Battle of the Atlantic had gone into high gear in the aftermath of Pearl Harbor. U-boats took advantage of American inexperience to launch a devastating offensive along the Atlantic coast and in the Caribbean. The Royal Navy, stretched to breaking point, and the Royal Canadian Navy, so new that its ships were named after inland towns such as Moose Jaw and Kamloops, made heavy weather of transatlantic escort missions.

For a year it seemed that the Kriegsmarine might indeed sink merchantmen faster than the Allies – or, rather, the Americans – could build them. The U-boats counted success in terms of tonnage sunk. Totals reached 600,000 tons a month. As late as March 1943 the wolf packs accounted for almost half a million tons of shipping, and in Britain there was concern about the country's ability to continue the war. By the end of 1942, however, US yards were launching ships on a daily basis. All three

Opposite A US Liberty ship under construction. American shipyards built over 2,700 of these cargo vessels between 1941 and 1945. One particular example was constructed in a record four-and-a-half days.

Right A woman of the Women's Royal Naval Service operating Colossus, the world's first electronic programmable computer, at Bletchley Park in Buckinghamshire, the British forces' intelligence centre during the war.

Below The radio room of a U-boat: an operator decodes a message on the four-rotor Enigma machine.

Allied navies were learning the techniques of anti-submarine warfare. Improved escorts, including small aircraft carriers, were increasingly coming into service. Air forces obsessed with bombing Germany were persuaded to release enough long-range bombers to cover the air gap between Britain and the United States. And ever in the background was an intelligence war decisively won by the Allies.

'ULTRA' was the cover name for the information obtained by decrypting messages intercepted largely from the German Enigma machine developed between the wars. Its code was regarded by the Germans as unbreakable, to the point that communicators often failed to take normal security precautions in its use. The first steps in cracking it were undertaken by Polish intelligence. The British continued to make advances, joined after Pearl Harbor by the Americans. Significant in assisting fighter control during the Battle of Britain, ULTRA came into its own during the Battle of the Atlantic in enabling convoys to avoid U-boat wolf packs and, as Allied resources grew, in directing hunter-killer teams against the U-boats themselves. The battle for control of the North Atlantic culminated in May 1943, with Allied escorts and aircraft inflicting losses so high that Admiral Karl Dönitz 'temporarily' withdrew his boats to safer sectors. They would never return in force.

Tanks in World War II

From their introduction in 1916, tanks were considered by advocates such as the strategist J. F. C. Fuller as having the potential to change the nature of war. But technical limitations restricted their actual performance until the 1930s. Even then, French planners considered tanks in the context of infantry support, while the British saw them as assuming traditional cavalry roles.

The Germans and Russians went further, seeing armour as the key to restoring tactical mobility to battlefields gridlocked by firepower. That conception shaped ground combat in Europe between 1939 and 1942. The standard tank developed along the lines of the US Sherman and the Soviet T-34, built to a medium-weight design with a medium-calibre gun, moderate armour protection and extended range. During the second half of World War II, tactics and technology caught up. Anti-tank weapons became more effective, and anti-tank defences became more sophisticated. In response, tanks' protection and gun power were increased at the expense of mobility, along the lines of the German Tiger.

Kursk, history's largest tank battle, marked the operational turning point of

The Panzer Mk-IV was designed for a support and anti-infantry role. By 1942, it weighed 23.6 tons and could achieve a top speed of 38 kph (24 mph).

Right The M4 Sherman was the principal tank used by the US in World War II. Designed in 1940, it was still in service with the IDF during the 1973 Yom Kippur War. The version shown here is the M4A3, with a 75-mm (3-inch) gun.

Below right A Soviet T-34 tank at the Battle of Kursk. The medium-weight T-34 was in production from 1940 until 1958.

Below left The Panzer Mk-IV was a mainstay of the German armoured force throughout the war. The Mk-IV G version shown here, introduced in 1942, was mounted with a 75-mm (3-inch) gun.

After the Germans had encountered the Soviet T-34, the Mk-IV's armament was upgraded to the high-velocity 75-mm (3-inch) KwK 40 L/43 anti-tank gun. The tank's hull carried 80 shells.

The Panzer Mk-IV G had wider tracks for use in the snow and mud of the Eastern Front.

the German–Soviet war and was a defining event of armoured conflict. The German army, far from beaten even after Stalingrad, proposed to cripple its adversary by committing the best of its panzers against a salient around the city of Kursk. For their part, the Russians intended to draw the Germans onto a killing ground and break their fighting power once and for all. On 5 July 1943 the Germans struck; the climax came on 11–12 July, around the country railway station of Prokhorovka. A thousand tanks fought it out at point-blank range in a tangle of ravines

and ridges. When the fighting was over the panzers held the ground, but their losses were so heavy they could not exploit their advantage.

As the Germans regrouped, the Red Army launched an all-out counter-offensive. More important than the ground it gained was the army's success at subjecting the Wehrmacht to two months of comprehensive bloodletting from which it could not recover. After Kursk, the Germans were able to mount no more than local operations on any front – ripostes that postponed, but could not avert, final defeat.

War in the air

As the war at sea intensified, so too did the battle over Germany. The RAF, whose strength and effectiveness were steadily increasing, was joined in 1942 by growing numbers of US heavy bombers, committed by doctrine and design to daylight precision bombing, even in a theatre where cloud cover was often as high as 90 per cent. Daylight raids proved costly in the face of a Luftwaffe that, indifferent to defensive operations before the war, had made brisk progress. They were no less costly than British night operations. Both Allied air forces took pride in never having abandoned a raid, despite losses as high as 60 out of 230 US bombers sent against Schweinfurt on 14 October 1943, and 95 of the 800 RAF aircraft that attacked Nuremberg on the night of 30–31 March 1944.

The scale and scope of the raids steadily increased. As early as 1942 the British were able to send a thousand planes against a single target in a single night – but only in western Germany. That same year the first fire raids began, incinerating cities the size of Hamburg. In 1943 the 'Combined Bomber Offensive' took on Berlin, the Americans by day and the British by night. But the Reich survived, its morale and its production capacities proving unexpectedly resistant to the worst that two of the world's greatest industrial powers could throw at them.

THE TIDE TURNS

The year 1944 brought the turning of the tide in the European war. In the air, the P-51 Mustang, the war's best piston-engine fighter, enabled daylight raids to penetrate anywhere in the Reich – and destroyed its Luftwaffe opponents. Electronics increased British successes after dark. As D-Day approached (see box on pp. 124–25), both air forces were diverted from bombing cities and factories to strike oil-production facilities and railway networks. By September Luftwaffe fuel supplies were so low that fighter pilots were being sent to squadrons with no more than a few hours' cockpit time – cold meat for their Allied opponents, who were undeterred by the small-scale introduction of jet fighters exponentially superior to any piston-engine craft. The bombers ranged virtually unchallenged across the shrinking Reich. By the end of the year, the Combined Bomber Offensive had for practical purposes run out of targets – military targets, at least.

Red Army offensives

On land, the Red Army began the year with a coordinated sequence of offensives. One broke the siege of Leningrad, the Baltic city that had held out for 900 days at the cost of as many as 800,000 lives. Other spearheads isolated the Crimean Peninsula, and drove across the Bug and Dniester rivers into Romanian territory. Hitler responded by replacing most of the generals – about all that could be done, given the steep and worsening decline in German resources relative to a USSR that had risen like a phoenix from the disasters of 1941–42. As he had done consistently since 1941, he ordered a policy – it cannot be called a strategy – of no retreat. Implemented along a front of 2,250 km (1,400 miles), it was a recipe for catastrophe.

On 22 June no fewer than four Soviet army groups opened Operation Bagration against an overstretched German defensive system in central Russia. Army Group Centre disappeared in a typhoon of fire and steel; it took a quarter century to

Opposite top The B-17 Flying Fortress was the backbone of the daylight bomber offensive against Nazi Germany. These aircraft are from the 398th Bombardment Group, 8 April 1945.

Opposite below The bombing of Dresden in February 1945 by the USAAF and the RAF was the last major operation of the Combined Bomber Offensive. It remains one of the war's most controversial episodes.

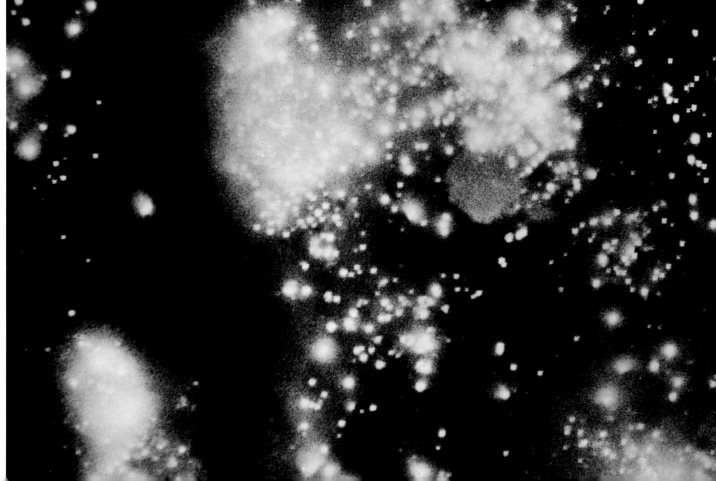

reconstruct the fate of individual divisions from survivors and returned POWs. To the north, Russian forces pushed the Germans back into the Baltic states, then swung left to trap an entire army group in the Courland Pocket on the Baltic Sea. On 7 August elements of the 1st Ukrainian Front reached the Vistula. The underground Polish Home Army reacted by staging a rising in Warsaw. Its savage suppression by German forces was uninterrupted by Soviet commanders, who claimed their advance units were too overstretched to make a further effort.

The Red Army had enough vital energy remaining to mount a drive into Romania, beginning on 20 August, that drove Romania to capitulate and left two German armies isolated in the land of their erstwhile ally. Some of the men made it back to their own lines. Most were lost, along with their irreplaceable equipment, as the Russians slashed into Hungary and occupied Belgrade – the latter operation with some help from a Yugoslav partisan movement that had fought internal rivals almost as much as the Germans over the previous few years.

The Soviet Union's achievement in the second half of 1944 is arguably the greatest operational victory of World War II. The Red Army had retained the virtues of mass that gave it consistent and significant numerical superiority. It had developed a fighting spirit fuelled by German atrocities and enhanced when necessary by the secret police. It had introduced sophisticated combined-arms tactics, and developed commanders who had learned their trade at the front against an unforgiving, highly

The changing tide of war, 1942–45.

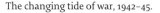

Russian soldiers load a rocket inscribed 'To the Reichstag' during the final battle for Berlin, April 1945. The truck-mounted rocket launchers known as Katyushas were among the Red Army's most devastating weapons.

skilled enemy. The T-34 and JS II main battle tanks, the Katyusha multiple rocket launcher and the heavily armoured Shturmovik ground-attack aircraft all contributed firepower and mobility. Soviet intelligence left the Germans deceived or blinded. Soviet partisans provided a rear-area threat to Germans already facing all they could handle to their front. Rear-echelon services, with the aid of thousands of lend-lease US trucks and jeeps, kept forward units supplied and mobile. Engaged on its own terms, the German army had been outfought as well as overwhelmed.

The Normandy landings

D-Day was an operation that could be undertaken only once. Britain's moral and material capital was nearly exhausted, its fighting manpower so limited that the army sent to north-western Europe had to cannibalize itself: entire divisions were broken up to keep the rest operational. Failure, to say nothing of disaster, would have had incalculably negative consequences for the war effort of the island kingdom. The United States was powerful enough to bear and recover from the material consequences of defeat on Europe's beaches. The psychological impact there would have been a different story entirely. June 1944 in Britain invites comparison in US military history with July 1863 in Pennsylvania. Both occasions generated a sense of participation in something Hegel might have called a world-historical event. Seen in this light, the cross-Channel invasion was more than a military operation – too much more to risk its launching in anything but the most favourable circumstances possible.

'We sure liberated the hell out of this place.'

US soldier in a Normandy village, 1944

From 1942 Britain experienced such an influx of American men and equipment that it was jokingly said only the ubiquitous barrage balloons kept the island from

D-Day

D-Day began just after midnight on 6 June 1944, when over 20,000 British, Americans and Canadians were landed by parachute and glider on the flanks of the landing beaches. On the right the US 82nd and 101st Airborne divisions dropped between the villages of Ste-Mère-Eglise and Carentan. The British 6th Airborne went in on the left, east of the Orne river. The main attack came from the sea at 6.30 a.m. On the far right the 4th US Infantry Division landed on Utah Beach. Next to them the 1st and 29th hit Omaha. Gold Beach was assigned to the British 3rd Infantry, Juno to the 3rd Canadian, and Sword to Britain's 'Fifty Div'. Soldiers, sailors and airmen from a dozen countries participated. Over 130,000 men and 20,000 vehicles were brought ashore during the day by 4,000 landing craft. Over a thousand warships provided fire support. Allied aircraft flew over 14,500 sorties; the Germans managed only 2. And yet Operation Overlord was by no means a walkover. Plans for an immediate breakout were thwarted by a determined, sophisticated German defence. The Allies suffered around 10,000 casualties – 5,000 of them on Omaha Beach alone, where the loss ratio approached one in five. 'The longest day' nevertheless made inevitable the Third Reich's defeat, and remains the most significant event of the war's second half.

The D-Day landings in Normandy, June 1944 – the start of the Allied campaign to free continental Europe from the occupying German forces.

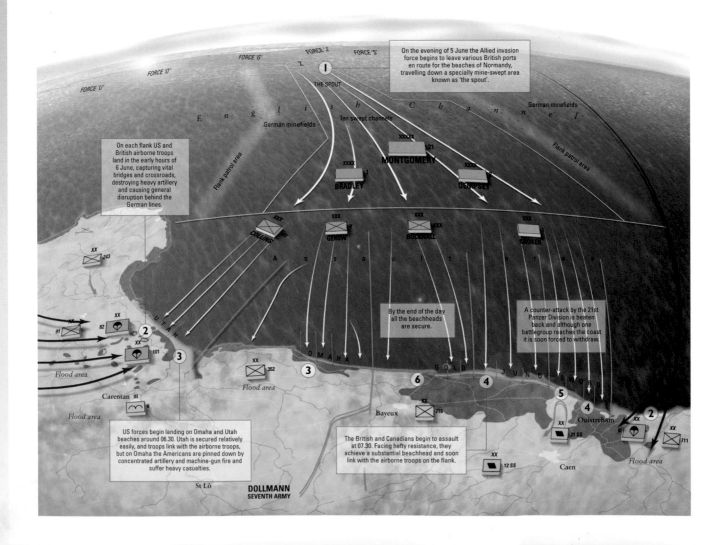

	ALLIES	GERMANS
COMMANDERS	Dwight D. Eisenhower Bernard Montgomery Omar Bradley	Gerd von Rundstedt Erwin Rommel Friedrich Dollmann
STRENGTH	c. 175,000	c. 380,000
CASUALTIES	c. 10,000	4,000–9,000

Top US troops landing under fire on Omaha Beach, 6 June 1944. The fighting here was particularly intense, and the beach was not under Allied control until early evening.

Above Allied troops build up on the Normandy beaches, preparing to move inland.

sinking. Extreme measures were taken to maintain security. Elaborate deceptions were contrived to throw the Germans off track regarding the timing, location and strength of the landings. Planning epitomized an Anglo-American war effort that sought to maximize materiel at the expense of human resources.

The half-dozen divisions that crossed the beaches and the two airborne divisions that landed behind them constituted the largest amphibious assault force in history up to that time. They were supported and sustained by the factories and laboratories of two of the world's greatest industrial nations. Unprecedented air and naval bombardment, armoured vehicles specially modified for beach assault, artificial harbours ('Mulberries') to support the invasion until a port could be captured, and underwater pipelines to provide fuel were all deployed. Yet after months of preparation, the landing was delayed for a day by bad weather. Despite the high-tech support, in the end it was fighting power that secured and expanded the beachheads. Not for five bloody weeks were the Allies able to develop their positions enough to coordinate a breakout against a German defence as determined as it was skilful.

The north-west European campaign

In the old newsreels, the eventual breakout and the drive across France in the summer and autumn of 1944 seem a triumph of mobile warfare. In fact, the percentage of British casualties in the north-west European campaign was comparable to that for the Western Front in 1914–18. American losses were similar. In contrast to the Great War, divisions were seldom removed from the line. Instead, replacements were funnelled forward – and there were fewer and fewer of them as the campaign progressed. British manpower was exhausted after five years of total war, to the point where it was necessary to break up fighting formations to keep others in the field. The US decision to create only a necessary minimum of ground formations – the 'ninety-division gamble' – frayed at the edges as combat-arms casualties exponentially exceeded expectations.

Seen in that context the debate over 'broad-front' versus 'single-thrust' strategies becomes something of a red herring. Montgomery, commanding the British 21st

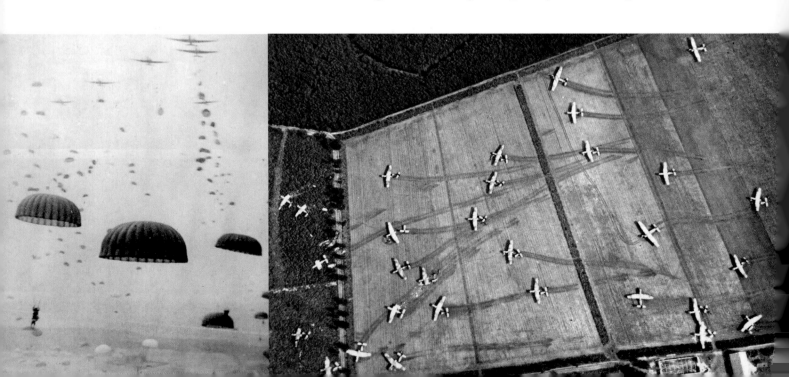

Above US tanks and troops counter-attack through deep snow near Heersbach, Belgium, during the Battle of the Bulge, 1945.

Opposite left Paratroopers landing in the Netherlands during the initial stages of Operation Market Garden, September 1944.

Opposite right Gliders of the 1st British Airborne Division in a landing zone near Arnhem.

Army Group, favoured ending the war by a 'single thrust' north-eastward into the heart of Germany, to include his army group, two American armies and most of the available fuel. Montgomery's American counterpart, Omar Bradley, proposed a drive across the Frankfurt Gap and into central Germany by his 12th Army Group, with the British covering its left flank. If a thrust to the heart of the Reich was what was wanted, that was the most direct route.

Eisenhower's decision to deny both Montgomery and Bradley in favour of a 'broad-front' approach combined political and military elements. Montgomery's proposal might in fact be an Allied operation, but it was unlikely to look like one to an America that had spent four years building a massive army designed to operate as an independent force. More generally, Eisenhower was better aware than his fractious subordinates that the armies at his disposal were neither configured nor equipped for a massive hammer blow. Particularly after the August invasion of southern France, a policy of developing and exploiting local opportunities was congruent with force structures and deployments. A broad-front strategy also reflected the logistical problems inherent in sustaining a high-tech mobile campaign.

By 14 September the Allies had reached a line the quartermasters had not expected until May 1945. The damage done to an originally obsolescent French transport system by weeks of pre-invasion bombardment and years of neglect under German occupation defied rapid repair. The emergency use of trucks on a round-the-clock basis – the American Red Ball convoys and their British counterparts, Red Lion – used up men, vehicles and fuel at unsustainable rates. Montgomery's failure to clear the Scheldt estuary promptly in the autumn of 1944 rendered the harbour of Antwerp temporarily useless. Not supply shortages, however, but increasingly effective German resistance brought the Allied advance to a halt at Arnhem, in the Hürtgen Forest, Lorraine, and all along the frontier of a Germany fighting with a hangman's noose around its neck. At times the Wehrmacht had help – in particular from the overall failure of Montgomery's Operation Market Garden, which had been intended to establish a war-winning bridgehead across the Rhine.

The Ardennes Offensive

The Battle of the Bulge, as the Ardennes Offensive of December 1944 was known, was Hitler's last desperate gamble for a military victory sufficiently impressive to encourage a negotiated peace. Its stated objective of Antwerp was widely recognized as unattainable. The practical aim of the attack was to do as much damage as possible to the US Army and to Anglo-American relations. The first goal was frustrated by a stubborn local defence and by a spectacular counter-attack mounted by General George Patton's Third Army. The second came closer to success when Montgomery boasted of having 'seen off' the Germans, despite minimal involvement of British forces in the sector. It was part of a pattern of increasingly tactless, antagonistic behaviour that meant he came near to being relieved.

Germany shot its Western Front bolt in the Ardennes. By that time both the British and US armies had a solid sense of what they could do well. Their citizen-soldiers were a match for any, and their commanders had honed or acquired high levels of skill. The Rhine river, far from proving a formidable obstacle, was crossed in a half-dozen places, by methods ranging from elaborate set-piece battles, to the inspired seizure of an undestroyed bridge, to paddling across in rubber boats. The rest of the war was a mopping-up operation that met with fierce but episodic resistance, against a background of attempts to avert military and political clashes with the Red Army advancing from the other direction.

ENDGAME

The final Soviet offensive against the Third Reich began in January 1945. Its focal point was the northern sector: East Prussia, Pomerania and Silesia. Sheer numbers overwhelmed the Germans. By 31 January the Red Army was on the Oder river, its progress marked by a wave of pillage, murder and rape that sought to repay four years of German atrocities in a few weeks and came close to succeeding. In the south, Budapest held out until 12 February, thanks in part to a final counter-attack by some of the panzer troops that survived the Ardennes. With its fall, the Soviets fought their way into Austria and reached Vienna on 13 April. The desperate German defence of that city was overshadowed by the struggle for Berlin, where the final attack began on 16 April. By the 25th the city was encircled, the Red Army fighting its way towards the centre. On 30 April the hammer and sickle went up over the Reichstag building. Hitler committed suicide the same day, and on 8 May an unconditional German surrender brought an end to his war.

Japan's signing of the surrender terms on 2 September (see pp. 154–55) concluded the fighting. The Axis had been not merely defeated but crushed: its soldiers dead or in POW camps, its cities devastated, its territory under occupation, its citizens at the mercy of their conquerors. The price had been high and comprehensive. Industrial war spared neither cities nor homes; much of Europe had been smashed to rubble by shells and bombs. Almost as many French civilians died under Allied bombing on D-Day as American soldiers did on the beaches. As many as 27 million Soviet citizens were dead, over half of them civilians – 15 per cent of the pre-war population. Nazi Germany's over 7.25 million dead amounted to over 10 per cent of its 1939 population, and 'only' 1.5 million were civilians. For the United States and Britain, both coming in at a total of under half a million, it had by comparison been a 'good war'.

Russian soldiers fly a Red flag, made from German tablecloths, over the ruins of the Reichstag, Berlin, 30 April 1945.

Citizens attempt to board a crowded tram in Dresden amid the rubble left by Allied bombings, 1946.

Paradoxically, the very completeness of the Allied victory facilitated the postwar collapse of the Grand Coalition. Stalin had from the beginning suspected the goodwill of Britain and the United States, to a point where on several occasions between 1941 and 1944 he considered opening peace negotiations with Hitler. As the war neared its end the Soviet ruler wished to strengthen the geopolitical position of the Soviet state to create a springboard for world revolution. Churchill hoped to preserve as much as possible of the British Empire while establishing Britain as Greece to America's Rome. Roosevelt's vision of a postwar world rendered prosperous by free trade, and regulated by a United Nations underwritten by a consortium of great powers, was generous, but so broad-gauged that it overlooked the reservations of America's coalition partners. Face-to-face conferences – Tehran in 1943, Yalta in 1945 – produced agreement, if not consensus, on specific subjects such as Russia's entry into the war against Japan, or the frontiers and government of post-war Poland. They could not, however, bridge the fundamental gaps in understanding and interest that would lead to the Cold War, whose course and consequences are treated by later essays in this volume.

7 World War II: The Asia–Pacific Conflict

ALLAN R. MILLETT

Opposite Crew members work to put out a blaze on the USS *Belleau Wood* caused by a kamikaze attack, Leyte, October 1944.

The Asia–Pacific conflict (1937–45) had its roots in Japan's determination to be a modern urban-industrial nation capable of replacing the European empires in Asia with its own regional political-economic empire. World War I had created new opportunities for Japan, but bitterness towards the United States and Britain for limiting its conquests during the conflict drove Japanese politics in a more nationalistic, militaristic direction. Aware of the growing inability of the Soviet Union and Europe as colonizers to defend their Asian interests, the Japanese government, now dominated by the army and ultra-nationalist civilian leaders, seized power in Manchuria in 1931–32 and sent an expeditionary force to Shanghai in 1932. The minister of war and foreign minister engineered Japan's first diplomatic coup, the Anti-Comintern Pact of 1936, which in essence was a German–Italian–Japanese alliance against the Soviet Union – and by extension against the USSR's protégé, Nationalist China. Sure that Nazi Germany would paralyse the Western powers by its expansionism in Austria and Czechoslovakia, Japan began a war of conquest in China.

WAR BETWEEN JAPAN AND CHINA

The initial Japanese military campaign (1937–38) seemed to prove that every ultra-nationalist assumption was correct. The Japanese army (*Kaigun*) and navy (*Haigun*), each with its own air force, defeated the diverse warlord, communist and Nationalist forces in north China, and occupied Peiping and the provinces claimed in 1915–19. The critical campaign was the capture of Shanghai and Nanking, which destroyed the best German- and Russian-trained divisions in Chiang Kai-shek's army and drove his government up the Yangtze river to Chungking. Japanese naval supremacy ensured the occupation of all the coastal cities and important economic zones as far as the border with French Indochina. Western enclaves such as Hong Kong fell under virtual siege. Additional Japanese military advances in 1938–39 put the imperial army on the borders of the USSR, up China's river valleys by 1,600 km (1,000 miles), and along its entire coast. Nevertheless, at least half of China's people, economic resources and land remained under the control of some part of the new Nationalist, warlord and communist coalition. Even with the commitment of much of the Japanese army and army air forces, China remained unconquered. The Japanese ruled by fear.

An unlikely and unspoken alliance between the United States and the Soviet Union helped stop Japan's occupation of China. The Red Army, reinforced to a million soldiers with air and armour, guarded the Asian border of the Soviet Union. Much of the Japanese army, including its tank forces, deployed to the same border. Inevitable minor skirmishes eventually led to a short but significant Russo-Japanese war in 1939 over influence in China and Mongolia (see p. 101), in which the Japanese army received a shocking defeat by a Soviet army that had supposedly been ruined by Stalin's military purges. The American intervention was unofficial and much less direct since the Roosevelt administration, whatever its pro-Chinese sympathies, had to obey neutrality laws that prohibited direct military and economic aid. Nevertheless, Chinese and pro-Chinese interest groups used overseas assets to send critical military aid to the Nationalists through Burma and French Indochina. Tokyo correctly concluded that the United States encouraged Allied inattentiveness to international neutrality laws. The Soviet threat, however, discouraged any immediate action.

The outbreak of war in Europe in September 1939 and the fall of France in July 1940 changed the strategic context of the Japanese–Chinese war. The pro-Nazi faction in Tokyo gloried in the Tripartite Pact (September 1940), which created an alliance with Germany and Italy against Britain and the neutral United States. This treaty to some degree offset the shock of the German–Soviet Non-Aggression Pact of August 1939. With Germany theoretically removed as a check upon Stalin's desire to overturn the results of Russia's 1904–5 defeat, Tokyo needed Hitler's reassurance that he would support Japan's imperial interests – if they were directed towards the British, French

Mongolian cavalry during the military action at Khalkhin-Gol, August 1939.

and Dutch colonies of South and South-East Asia. Japan tested the new alignments by negotiating an agreement with Vichy France to place Japanese troops in northern Indochina, which effectively closed one route of Allied aid to China and intimidated Britain into shutting down the Burma route too.

The German invasion of the USSR in June 1941 returned the strategic initiative to Japan, whose strategic planners could now give full attention to the 'southern option' – a campaign to capture Malaya and the Dutch East Indies. Such a campaign capitalized on many Japanese advantages: air and naval supremacy, sympathetic native populations, Allied military weakness, operational surprise, and forward-basing on Formosa and in French Indochina. It would also put strategic materials such as oil, rubber and tin under Japanese control. The Japanese added two other territorial objectives – Burma and the Philippines – that would eliminate two more 'European' colonies and the threat of Allied air and naval forces. Hong Kong joined the target list, as did Guam and Wake Island, isolated American bases in the mid-Pacific. In addition to securing the 'South Seas Resource Area' of oil and rubber for the Japanese Empire, the campaign would shut all the doors for foreign aid to China. Fighting for their survival against Hitler, Britain and the Soviet Union were unlikely to divert troops to a war with Japan. In fact, Japan found its former enemy, Joseph Stalin, happy to sign a non-aggression treaty in April 1941. This arrangement left one unresolved problem: how to dispose of the American threat?

US NAVAL BUILD-UP

With his habitual genial deception, Franklin D. Roosevelt committed his administration to Britain's survival after the fall of France. Sensing crisis, the US Congress produced the 'Two-Ocean Navy Act' of 1940 that emphasized the building of aircraft carriers (11; see box overleaf), fast battleships (9) and cruisers (44), as well as destroyers, submarines and carrier aircraft, a $1.1 billion programme that by 1943–44 would make the US Navy the unchallenged global naval power. The programme found its justification in War Plan Orange (war with Japan), which became Plan Rainbow One, the defence of Western hemispheric waters. If war with the United States appeared inevitable, as many Japanese officers assumed in 1940–41, it should be fought and won before the 'Two-Ocean Navy' arrived.

The Roosevelt administration tried to deter Japanese expansionism through a series of economic sanctions in 1941. Roosevelt also recalled General Douglas MacArthur to active duty and added US Army air and ground forces to his command, the citizen-based Philippine army. This force's mission was to guard the air and naval bases of Luzon, which were in easy reach of Japanese bombers and warships. To support this commitment Roosevelt ordered the navy to shift most of its battleships and three or four of its aircraft carriers to Pearl Harbor in Hawaii from the US west coast. Whatever his intent, Roosevelt's economic coercion failed. It actually gave new urgency to Japan's decision to go to war and to add the US Pacific Fleet to the target list. The commander of the Japanese Combined Fleet, Admiral Yamamoto Isoroku, had reservations about starting a war with the United States, but if there was to be war, he demanded a strike on Pearl Harbor – the base and warships there – in the war's first hours. The army and naval staffs finally agreed to a campaign plan in the late summer of 1941, even though eleventh-hour negotiations were still under way.

Admiral Yamamoto Isoroku, commander in chief of the Japanese Navy Combined Fleet, planning the Midway operation, 1942.

Aircraft Carriers

When aircraft went to sea in World War I, naval aviation pioneers sought a special type of warship that could launch and recover planes in numbers larger than the two to four floatplanes carried by battleships and cruisers. The initial missions for naval aviation were reconnaissance and directing naval gunfire. Other aircraft, however, would have to drive off enemy aircraft with similar missions. Floatplanes would not be numerous or capable enough for this mission. By the end of World War I the Royal Navy, US Navy and Imperial Japanese Navy had prototype carriers at sea. All three navies were envisaging naval operations conducted out of range of land-based naval aviation.

By the 1930s many countries had added carriers of similar characteristics to their fleets. Planes took off and landed from a flight deck; carriers turned into the wind to improve the wind-over-wing effect and thus increase

a pilot's control. Catapults later reduced the risks of take-offs, and arresting cables halted landing aircraft. These innovations allowed carrier aircraft to be heavier in construction, fuel loads and ordnance. By World War II most carrier aircraft had become all-metal monoplanes capable of carrying bombs and torpedoes, radios and aircrews of up to three.

The work of maintaining carrier aircraft most often took place in the hangar deck, the vast machine shop below the flight deck. Aircraft reached the flight deck for fuelling and arming by means of elevators. Explosions in the hangar deck could turn any carrier into a roaring inferno, afloat but useless. To sink a carrier required multiple torpedo strikes below the waterline. When in the 1930s carrier aviation added attacks on ships to their missions, a typical carrier air group included fighters as escorts and

Opposite A SBD scout-bomber lands on a carrier, seeking an arresting wire. Battle of the Philippine Sea, 19–20 June 1944.

Opposite below A F6F Hellcat fighter prepares for launch.

Below USS *Enterprise* – the only US Navy carrier to survive the Battle of Santa Cruz (26 October 1942) – seeks a port in the South Pacific.

interceptors, scout dive bombers and torpedo planes. The size of the air group on a fleet (large) carrier varied between 60 and 90 aircraft.

Powered by oil-fed steam turbine engines, a World War II carrier could reach speeds of 30 knots (55 kph), but its oil consumption determined lower cruising speeds, which increased vulnerability to submarine attack. The under-sea and air-attack threats could be met only with a system of combat air patrols, shipboard anti-aircraft batteries and a squadron of escorting cruisers and destroyers. To save weight, the US Navy and Imperial Japanese Navy

accepted the risk of unarmoured flight decks, and the Japanese designed some carriers without an 'island' and smokestacks. Royal Navy and US Navy carriers remained distinctive for their 'islands' of several levels and stacks on the starboard side of the flight deck amidships. Inside the 'island', the aviation staff, under the command of the air group commander, directed flight operations with visual signals, radar and radios. The captain of a carrier (who in the US Navy was required to be an aviator) remained responsible for all operations and was answerable to a task-force commander.

JAPANESE OFFENSIVES, 1941–42

The West Pacific

The Japanese campaign of conquest in the first five months of 1942 created a new empire for Japan in South-East Asia and established the planned strategic barrier against the United States in the mid-Pacific. The campaign succeeded because of the training and pre-positioning of preponderant air and naval forces, and a barely adequate number of army divisions and naval landing forces from the Home Islands, Formosa, China, Saipan and Indochina. Had the Allies deployed and used greater air and naval forces, the Japanese landing forces might not have succeeded as rapidly and cheaply as they did. Japanese planners focused on air and naval superiority.

In late 1941 the Combined Fleet's carrier force, protected by battleships and cruisers, sailed in silence through winter storms across the northern Pacific. It launched its crack dive-bomber and torpedo squadrons against the tied-up battleships and cruisers of the Pacific Fleet at Pearl Harbor on 7 December. The attack crippled the US Navy, which lost, at least for months, 8 battleships, 3 cruisers and 3 destroyers. Attacks on the island's four airfields put almost 400 aircraft out of action, ensuring air superiority. Having learned that two US Navy carrier task forces were at sea, positions unknown, and concerned about his aircraft losses in his second strike, Admiral Nagumo Chichi cancelled a third strike that would have ruined the base and fuel farms, making any future US Navy operations in 1942 difficult, if not impossible. Around 2,400 service personnel and civilians died in the attacks. The surprise of the attack, coupled with Japanese diplomatic ineptness, enraged the

Five US Navy battleships aflame off Ford Island, Pearl Harbor, 7 December 1941.

American public and deflected criticism away from the Roosevelt administration and US armed forces for their unawareness.

Concurrent Japanese operations in December 1941 focused on air and naval superiority in the western Pacific. The exception was the capture of Hong Kong, Britain's Chinese colony, defended by six Commonwealth infantry battalions, some artillery and local volunteers. Three Japanese divisions, supported by air strikes and heavy artillery, eliminated the colony's tiny air force and naval patrol fleet, making the capture of the mainland enclave and the island only a matter of time, which expired on 25 December. Japanese losses (2,754) were almost two-thirds those of the defenders (4,400). The Japanese air forces on Formosa played similar havoc with the American air and naval bases on Luzon, Commonwealth of the Philippines. Even five hours after he learned of the Pearl Harbor disaster, General MacArthur had not solved a disagreement between his staff and air commander. On 8 December (still 7 December in Hawaii), a Japanese naval air force of 192 aircraft attacked Clark Field on Luzon, destroying 17 B-17 bombers, 56 fighters and much of the base itself, thus eliminating MacArthur's counter-invasion air capability. Follow-up air attacks on the Asiatic Fleet bases at Subig Bay and Cavite crippled the mixed force of surface ships and submarines. The US Navy surface force (the cruiser *Houston* and 4 destroyers) and 30 surviving submarines redeployed south to join Dutch and Commonwealth squadrons to defend the Dutch East Indies.

The fall of Singapore

The resource-rich areas of Malaya and the Dutch East Indies attracted the main Japanese strategic effort and made the Allied bastion of Singapore the critical theatre objective. Multiple small but dispersed landings in upland Malaya and the northern Dutch East Indies on 8 December had the desired effect of drawing Allied air and naval forces into forlorn battle. Deprived of air cover by damage to an accompanying carrier, left in the Atlantic, the Royal Navy battleship *Prince of Wales* and battlecruiser *Repulse* did not survive wave after wave of Japanese bombers from Indochina. They sank on 12 December with 840 officers and sailors still aboard. The Commonwealth–Dutch–American air and naval forces resisted longer but unsuccessfully. Out of an Allied naval force of 5 cruisers and 9 destroyers by the beginning of March 1942, only 4 destroyers survived to escape to Australia. With no fear of air or naval attacks and with Allied reinforcements cut off by sea, the Japanese land forces could advance against only the enemy ground forces, which actually outnumbered them in the Philippines and Malaya.

The Japanese ground campaigns in Malaya and the Philippines had common focuses: the two great cities and strategic political centres of Singapore and Manila. Both had strong seaward defences, but both depended upon mobile ground forces to prevent an assault from their inland sides. Both had large civilian populations to complicate their defence. Both could only buy time to allow Allied naval forces to rescue them, a matter of many months if possible at all. Japanese military planners understood all these problems, having gained experience from similar campaigns since 1904 in Manchuria and China. Neither of the Allied commanders, Air Chief Marshal H. R. Brooke-Popham and General MacArthur, had much choice but to meet the Japanese as far forward as possible and to play for time.

General Sir Arthur Percival and his staff, led by a Japanese officer, march to meet General Yamashita Tomoyuki and to surrender Singapore, 15 February 1942.

The Japanese army of 60,000 veterans took only fifty-four days to force a Commonwealth army of 88,600 to retreat to Singapore. Japanese mobility, flanking amphibious operations and night attacks confounded the defenders. The operational initiative exercised by General Yamashita Tomoyuki confused the Commonwealth army commanders, including General Sir Arthur Percival, who could not even hold Singapore, defended by 70,000 troops, against 35,000 Japanese. Percival surrendered after a two-week battle for the island. Key factors in the surrender on 15 February 1942 were ammunition shortages and the loss of the city's reservoirs, but the demoralization of the soldiers and the fate of the civilians made further fighting appear suicidal. In the entire campaign the British forces lost 39,000 casualties and 130,000 POWs. Yamashita's army, almost out of supplies and exhausted, had won, suffering 15,000 casualties, or 20 per cent of its strength. The Japanese victory was compared to the Battle of Mukden (1905) as a brilliant feat of arms. In the aftermath the Japanese won over many Malayan and Indian POWs to their cause, shipped European POWs and internees off to compounds and work camps, and cowed the Chinese population by the immediate execution of at least 5,000 community leaders.

Invasion of the Philippines

The fall of Manila and the futile defence of the Bataan Peninsula sealed the fate of the Philippines by 9 April 1942, although the defenders of Corregidor Island and some southern islands held out for another month. The defence of Luzon depended upon 110,000 armed Filipinos and 30,000 US Army soldiers. The only real Filipino regulars were the Philippine Scouts and Philippine Constabulary, who amounted in all to 12,000 officers and men on Luzon. Between 10 and 24 December 1941 the Japanese Fourteenth Army, commanded by General Homma Masaharu, had landed on Luzon both north and south of Manila, virtually unopposed. The initial Japanese force numbered only 40,000 officers and men and grew to 100,000, but only half of them were combat troops.

A Chinese child soldier in Burma, 1943.

The failed defence of Luzon doomed all the Philippines and demonstrated MacArthur's shortcomings as a fighting general. Having initially ordered his Filipino divisions, essentially militia, to defend Luzon and sacrificed them to the Japanese 49th Division, MacArthur then reverted to the standing plan to declare Manila an open city and concentrate all his forces on the Bataan Peninsula, but without first stockpiling ammunition, food or medical supplies. Moreover, Filipino refugees swelled Bataan's population to 100,000. Sick, starved and without adequate ammunition, Bataan's defenders surrendered in April 1942. Managing 78,000 POWs confounded the Japanese, who killed or allowed to die more than 6,000 Filipinos and 600 Americans in the infamous 'Bataan Death March'.

Pummelled by air strikes and artillery, the Corregidor garrison held out for almost a month because it was composed mainly of US Army regulars and Marines with adequate rations and supplies, protected by tunnels and concrete emplacements. The Japanese, however, systematically eliminated the coastal artillery and then took the island in a costly amphibious attack. Another 11,000 US military personnel became POWs. Meanwhile MacArthur, under direct orders from President Roosevelt, left Luzon on 11 March by motor torpedo boat and aeroplane for Australia, to organize a relief expedition. He found many weapons and supplies, but few troops and no naval force except a few submarines. He would return, but not soon.

With the Allied forces in the Philippines and Malaya neutralized as a threat to a campaign to seize the Dutch East Indies, the core of the South Seas Resource Area, the Japanese naval forces and the Sixteenth Army opened operations against the Dutch colonial forces on 20 December 1941 and made the Dutch surrender on 8 March 1942. Another 100,000 Allied military personnel and 50,000 civilians went into prison camps. The Japanese campaign featured paratroop drops, multiple amphibious landings and timely air strikes. Many native Indonesians assisted the Japanese, who saw themselves as the liberators of oppressed Asians, excluding the 1 million local Chinese inhabitants of the Dutch East Indies, who were regarded as potential subversives. Chinese and native minority groups, such as the Dyaks of Borneo, became the foundation of British–Australian special operations against the Japanese occupiers. These guerrilla raids, however, did not disrupt oil production and other critical economic activities that fed the Japanese war industry and people.

> '*We built up our enemy into something terrifying, as soldiers will always do to excuse their defeats, and frightened ourselves with the bogey of the superman of the jungle.*'
> General William Slim, assessing the British defeats in Malaya and Burma

Advances in Burma

The final Japanese 1941–42 offensive took the Fifteenth Army to the Indian and Chinese borders by June 1942. The four-division Japanese expeditionary force defeated or outflanked a more numerous coalition of Indian, British, Chinese and Burmese armies. Again Japanese air superiority and naval operations enhanced the combat-effectiveness of the Japanese ground forces, whose skill and ferocity had now reached mythic proportions. The invaders also enjoyed the help of many Burmese nationalists, encouraging Japanese commanders to plan to subvert India itself. The

Burma campaign ensured that the country would not be used as an Allied base area or route for supplies to China. General Joseph W. Stilwell, US Army theatre commander and chief of staff of the Chinese Nationalist Army, summed up the Burma campaign and whole Allied war effort in Asia in 1942: 'I claim we got a hell of a licking.'

THE ALLIED RESPONSE

The Japanese victories, however, only hardened Anglo-American determination to wage an uncompromising war of retribution that would reduce Japan to its pre-1895 territorial status and bury Japanese imperialism. Japan's strategic dilemmas in a long war were self-evident. It did not have a long-range plan – or even the capability – to replace or enlarge its navy and air forces. There was no shipbuilding programme for a larger fleet of oil, food and ore carriers with anti-submarine escorts. The army could not govern the new members of the Greater East Asia Co-Prosperity Sphere without Japanese garrisons and their murderous military police, the *kempetai*. The puppet governments could not suppress Allied-sponsored resistance movements in Burma, Malaya, Indochina, China and the Dutch East Indies. The Chinese armies also remained a threat of sorts, perhaps 10–15 per cent of their 300 divisions improved by American advisers and weapons flown in from India.

Against this background of Japanese weaknesses, Roosevelt and Winston Churchill, without compromising their 'Germany first' strategy, used limited operations in late 1942 to buy the time necessary to build a force that by 1944 would roll back the new Japanese Empire. Allied victories in Africa and the Middle East (see Chapter 6) allowed Churchill to return six Australian divisions home for South Pacific operations, and to rebuild the British Fourteenth Army with veteran, dependable British, Indian, African and Gurkha troops. Roosevelt pressed his military leaders to deploy six army divisions and two Marine divisions to the South Pacific. In early 1943 the United States had as many naval forces deployed to the Pacific as it had sent to Europe. The Pacific Fleet received all of the Essex-class and Independence-class carriers, which were unneeded in the war with Germany.

Japanese reverses

The first Allied offensive operations against Japan followed two sea battles won by the US Navy, both defensive engagements that weakened the *Haigun*'s carrier air force. At the Battle of the Coral Sea (May 1942) the Americans lost a large carrier, but Japan lost more planes and pilots, as well as a light carrier. The Japanese abandoned plans to take Port Moresby, the last Allied enclave on New Guinea. In an effort to complete the Pearl Harbor attack, Yamamoto took four heavy carriers, his battleships and cruisers, and a complete invasion fleet towards Midway, west of the Hawaiian Islands. As he hoped, he lured the only three carriers in the Pacific Fleet to sea for intended destruction by his carrier aircraft or battleships. In two days of battle the actual engagement cost the Japanese all four carriers and the Americans one. The losses staggered the Japanese because not only half their carrier force but most of the veteran airmen of those four carriers were wiped out. This war of attrition continued for a year in the South Pacific, the Japanese sinking replaceable Allied warships and the Americans killing irreplaceable Japanese pilots, as well as sinking warships.

Opposite Carrier operations at the Battle of Midway, 4–7 June 1942.

Below Survivors of the sinking of the aircraft carrier USS *Lexington* are picked up by another ship after the Battle of the Coral Sea, 8 May 1942.

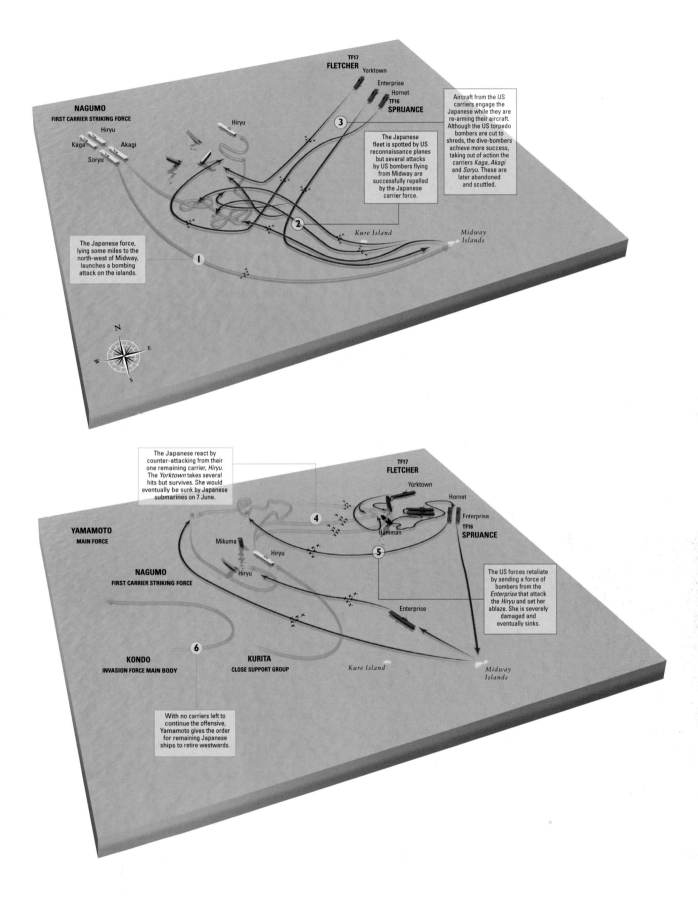

NAGUMO
FIRST CARRIER STRIKING FORCE

Hiryu
Kaga   Akagi
Soryu

Hiryu

TF17
FLETCHER
Yorktown
Enterprise
Hornet
TF16
SPRUANCE

3

Aircraft from the US carriers engage the Japanese while they are re-arming their aircraft. Although the US torpedo bombers are cut to shreds, the dive-bombers achieve more success, taking out of action the carriers *Kaga*, *Akagi* and *Soryu*. These are later abandoned and scuttled.

The Japanese fleet is spotted by US reconnaissance planes but several attacks by US bombers flying from Midway are successfully repelled by the Japanese carrier force.

2

Kure Island

Midway Islands

The Japanese force, lying some miles to the north-west of Midway, launches a bombing attack on the islands.

1

N
W   E
S

The Japanese react by counter-attacking from their one remaining carrier, *Hiryu*. The *Yorktown* takes several hits but survives. She would eventually be sunk by Japanese submarines on 7 June.

TF17
FLETCHER

Yorktown
Hornet
Enterprise
TF16
SPRUANCE

4

Hamman

YAMAMOTO
MAIN FORCE

Mikuma
Hiryu
Hiryu

NAGUMO
FIRST CARRIER STRIKING FORCE

5

The US forces retaliate by sending a force of bombers from the *Enterprise* that attack the *Hiryu* and set her ablaze. She is severely damaged and eventually sinks.

Enterprise

KONDO
INVASION FORCE MAIN BODY

6

KURITA
CLOSE SUPPORT GROUP

Kure Island

Midway Islands

With no carriers left to continue the offensive, Yamamoto gives the order for remaining Japanese ships to retire westwards.

Above US soldiers hunt Japanese infiltrators in an attempt to regain Bougainville Island, March 1944.

Opposite left US Marines land at Cape Gloucester, New Britain, 26 December 1943. The aim of Operation Cartwheel was to isolate the major Japanese forward base at Rabaul and to cut its supply and communication lines.

Opposite right A Japanese freighter sunk by US aircraft off Guadalcanal, October 1942.

The South Pacific, a region of volcanic mountains covered with tropical rainforests and noted for its epidemic illnesses, harsh living conditions and limited ports, hosted a war of endurance. The Japanese had the advantage of the best-developed base, Rabaul in northern New Guinea, and airfields on the southern tip of the nearby island of Bougainville. The Japanese navy wanted to extend the base system to the southern Solomons and the coast of New Guinea, thus cutting the American supply line that ran through French Polynesia to Australia. At MacArthur's initiative, the US Joint Chiefs of Staff approved Operation Cartwheel, the isolation of Rabaul. In seven months of gruelling engagements on land and sea, American and Australian forces captured the Japanese bases on New Guinea's north shore. On Guadalcanal the 1st Marine Division, reinforced by two Army divisions, outfought and outsmarted a larger Japanese force between August 1942 and December 1943. Both sides lost 24 warships; the Japanese won most night-time engagements while the US Navy held its own in daytime battles but lost two more carriers. A series of night-time engagements in November 1942 convinced the Japanese area commanders that they could not prevent American reinforcements from coming to Guadalcanal or sustain their own forces in the southern Solomons or on New Guinea.

At that time the US naval forces in the region had one modern battleship and one large carrier at full operational status. Japanese losses of pilots (1,200) and aircraft, however, had become prohibitive, and the Japanese planners now decided to seek a decisive fleet action in the Marianas area of the Central

'Waiting at the shore, we gently lifted out the soldiers retreating from Guadalcanal one by one and laid them on the sand . . . hardly human beings, they were just skin and bones . . . so light, it was like carrying infants.'
Japanese private who helped unload the survivors of Guadalcanal, 1943

Pacific. The Japanese navy consequently abandoned Rabaul and Truk as major operating bases.

The Marianas campaign

The Allied forces of the South and South-West Pacific continued the parallel advance north to isolate Rabaul, but MacArthur and Admiral Chester W. Nimitz, who commanded the mega-theatre Pacific Ocean Areas, soon shifted their joint and combined forces towards different geographic objective areas. Advancing in 800-km (500-mile) increments – the range of land-based fighter-bombers – MacArthur's forces bypassed some Japanese bases and seized others by amphibious landings and air landing assaults. No landing could be treated as a walk in the surf. The advance led inexorably towards the Philippines. MacArthur justified his campaign on the strategic grounds that US air and naval forces in the Philippines would stop the flow of raw materials and food to the Home Islands. His personal stake was just as compelling. In 1942 he had assured the Filipino people that he would return and liberate them, a pledge supported in Washington for political reasons, for the United States had promised the Philippines its independence.

> *'I feel like a June bride. I know just what's going to happen, but I don't know how it will feel.'*
> One of MacArthur's soldiers on landing on a Japanese island, 1944

The US Navy saw only one mission, the defeat of the Japanese Combined Fleet in the Central Pacific. This incomplete task was seen as an essential requirement to cutting off Japan's economic resources and invading the Home Islands. American planners expected a decisive campaign for the Marianas. Should the Japanese lose Saipan, Guam and Tinian, the US Army Air Forces (USAAF) bombers, specifically the new B-29, could mount a strategic bombing campaign on Japanese cities. The US Navy could redeploy its growing submarine force to the Marianas, which would double the submarine patrols against Japanese oil tankers and food-carrying ships. Sinking Japanese carriers and killing Japanese aircrews came first for the planners at Pacific Ocean Areas headquarters in Hawaii. In 1943–44 the Pacific Fleet would be built around task forces of new carriers, fast battleships and cruisers. The naval aviation establishment would field a new fighter (the Grumman F6F Hellcat) and bomber–torpedo plane (the Grumman TBF Avenger), and a pool of 25,000 well-trained pilots for the carrier force. The hard times of 1942–43 had passed.

The uneasy mix of collaboration and conflict between the two American-dominated trans-Pacific offensives at least shared a common broad strategic goal, to sever Japan from its sources of raw materials by destroying its air-naval forces and base system outside the Home Islands. The tension at the highest level of national leadership involved the merits of land campaigns in Burma and China. The commitment of large American ground forces was never a serious issue; the American commitment of scarce amphibious shipping, tactical and transport aircraft, and vehicles and weapons most certainly was. Winston Churchill and Chiang Kai-shek argued that their armies prevented the redeployment of Japanese divisions to the Philippines and the Home Islands. With reservations, the US War Department accepted this argument. The Navy Department did not, since the Navy believed, with reason, that its submarine force and carrier aircraft reduced the reinforcement risk. When the British Fourteenth Army began its final sustained, successful offensive in January 1945, it did so with limited USAAF support. The one US Army regimental combat team in Burma was there to reopen a road to China; the ten Chinese divisions that fought in northern Burma had the same limited mission. Commanded by General William Slim, one of the greatest field generals of the war, the Fourteenth Army recaptured Burma by war's end to restore one part of the British Empire. It prepared to retake Malaya, another 'jewel in the crown'. Fought at the severest levels of suffering and ferocity, the war for Burma played little part in Japan's ultimate defeat, but remains a model of operational excellence and tactical tenacity.

Indian troops of the British Fourteenth Army clear the Imphal–Kohima road of Japanese, north-east India, 1944. The Japanese were driven back into Burma with heavy losses.

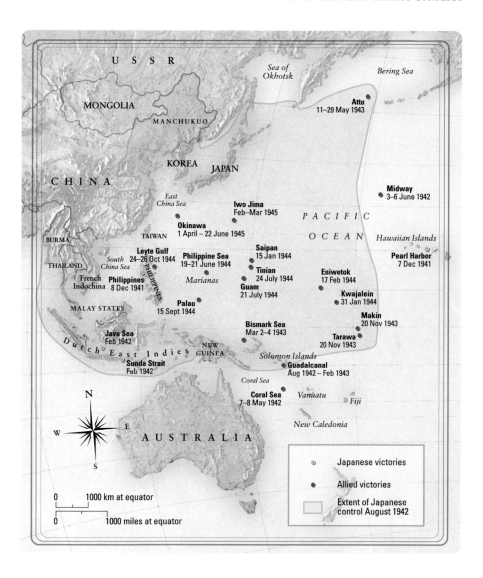

The Asia–Pacific War, 1941–45.

The American–Chinese alliance proved disappointing and more demanding than the Burma campaign. Even when American advisers and weapons reached the Nationalist Army, the Chinese husbanded their arms for the future war with the communists. Their immediate task was defending a series of bases built for the first B-29s deployed to bomb Japanese bases and ports on China's coast. In 1944 the Japanese responded with their own offensive, which forced the bombers and their service units out of range of any important targets. The B-29s redeployed to the Marianas once they had been captured (see below). The remaining aircraft made more limited attacks on targets designated by the Nationalists. Despite the energy of the Chinese lobby in Washington and Roosevelt's hope that China would play a major role in Japan's defeat, the United States did not make the liberation of China an essential objective. The Americans focused on arming and training the Nationalist Army, guarding weather stations, rescuing downed fliers and collecting intelligence.

Waged by an all-American joint expeditionary force commanded by Admiral Raymond A. Spruance, the Marianas campaign of the summer of 1944 sealed the fate

of the Japanese Empire. From November 1943 to May 1944 it had been preceded by smaller but crucial landings in the Gilberts and Marshalls. The lesson learned from Tarawa in the Gilberts was that air and naval gunfire had to improve. The amphibious assault on Saipan provided the Combined Fleet with the opportunity for a decisive naval engagement, which the Japanese lost in June 1944. In every phase of the Battle of the Philippine Sea, the US Navy proved its superiority. Communications intelligence and submarine and air scouting denied the Japanese any surprise. Pre-emptive carrier air strikes removed the threat of Japanese land-based bombers, a key element in Japanese plans. American submarines attacked and sank two enemy carriers, thus forcing Admiral Ozawa Jizaburo to launch his own carrier air strikes at prohibitive ranges and with reduced numbers. Hellcat squadrons turned the battle into the 'Great Marianas Turkey Shoot'. American air groups from 15 carriers shot

'I'm reluctant to say that I was involved in the so-called air support for the landing at Tarawa for it was pretty sorry. We didn't really know what we were doing.'
A US Navy aviator on the Tarawa landing, 1943

> '*It will be extremely difficult to recover from this disaster and rise again. When I think the prospect of victory is fading out gradually, it's only natural that my heart becomes as gloomy as the sky in the rainy season.*'
>
> Admiral Ugaki Matome, reflecting on the Philippine Sea defeat

down almost 300 Japanese planes at a cost of 29 aircraft.

On the battle's second day Spruance shifted to offensive strikes (too late, said his critics) against the Japanese carrier force, now stripped of air defenders. At ranges that ensured one-way trips for many US Navy aircraft, the Americans pursued the Japanese fleet with limited success, sinking or damaging three of the seven remaining enemy carriers. The delayed air offensive cost 100 aircraft and 49 lives, despite heroic efforts by all elements of the task force to rescue downed aircrews. The aircraft and aviation personnel could now be easily replaced by the US Navy. The Japanese could not say the same.

The land battles of the Marianas campaign demonstrated that American ground forces had also become unstoppable, despite Japanese defences and fanatical banzai charges. The final casualties for the capture of Saipan, Tinian and Guam were 23,000 Americans and 80,000 Japanese. Two-thirds of the fallen Americans survived, but only a handful of Japanese became prisoners. The only possible conclusion for Japanese commanders was that their troops could prolong their own annihilation and hope to inflict prohibitive casualties on the Americans, but they could not defeat an American landing force with ground defences alone.

JAPAN FACES DEFEAT

Japan fought on, but for a less unfavourable defeat, not a negotiated victory. It wanted to salvage some of the empire, declared null and void in the Allied Cairo Declaration (November 1943). The Japanese political elite, still military-dominated, removed the government of General Tojo from power, but only to provide more cautious leadership, not to sue for peace. Nevertheless, a 'peace faction' within Hirohito's court rallied to the cause of preserving the institution of the emperor. In a culture where political dissent often led to assassination or execution, the 'peace faction' had every reason to be cautious, since a group of generals and industrialists still controlled the government, the army, the police, and the xenophobic associations that enforced wartime political and economic laws. The change of government simply signalled a new effort at national mobilization for the defence of the Home Islands.

Return to the Philippines

Despite the defeat in the Marianas, the Japanese navy could still be a dangerous adversary because the Combined Fleet's thirty battleships and cruisers remained at sea. MacArthur's return to the Philippines, specifically to Leyte, provided one more chance to ambush the US Pacific Fleet, rendered vulnerable by its division into the Seventh Fleet (Admiral Thomas C. Kinkaid) and Third Fleet (Admiral William F. Halsey) for Philippine operations. In theory the two fleets, which had no common theatre commander, had complementary missions. Kinkaid's force, which included small escort carriers and older battleships, would conduct all amphibious operations. Halsey's Task Force 38 would seek out and destroy the remaining Combined Fleet,

Opposite Officers and sailors of Task Force 58 – the US Navy's principal striking force in the Pacific War – watch the air battle above the fleet, Philippine Sea, 19 June 1944.

Below 'Fight to the Bitter End' – a photograph used for Japanese propaganda purposes, 1943.

US Marine amphibian tractors head for Peleliu in the Palau islands, 15 September 1944. It was estimated that the island would be taken within four days, but the battle raged for more than two months.

thus protecting Kinkaid's force. Anticipating the Leyte landing, the Combined Fleet headquarters designed a novel, dangerous Plan 'Sho-Go' ('Ultimate Victory') aimed at Kinkaid's naval forces off Leyte's east coast. For once Japanese communications security plans worked, ensuring some initial surprise. Nevertheless, human misjudgments and US air and submarine patrols shaped three separate naval clashes (23–25 October 1944): the battles of Cape Engaño, San Bernardino Strait–Samar and the Surigao Strait.

The results of these three engagements, fought with great courage and skill at the tactical level by the US Navy, ended the Japanese navy as a serious threat. In three days the Japanese lost 26 warships; the Americans, 1 escort carrier and 3 escorts. Although a decisive Japanese victory had seemed unlikely because of the lack of air support, the Combined Fleet might have inflicted much greater damage on Kinkaid's force had not the Japanese admirals shown great caution and great rashness at the wrong moments. The Northern Force fulfilled its sacrificial function by luring Halsey's Task Force 38 north to a battleground off Luzon's northern tip; Halsey's air groups sank 4 carriers, almost devoid of aircraft, and 4 escorts with ease. Halsey's charge north to Cape Engaño followed a similar aerial pounding of the main Japanese threat, the Centre Force (Admiral Kurita Takeo) of 5 battleships (including the monsters *Yamato* and *Musashi*), 12 cruisers and 15 destroyers.

Having sunk *Musashi* and four cruisers in a day-long aerial assault on 24 October, Halsey interpreted Kurita's night-time retreat in San Bernardino Strait as a permanent withdrawal. Instead, Kurita reversed course and fell on Kinkaid's escort carrier groups the next morning. The fury of the US Navy's air and surface attacks on Kurita's far superior force, which suffered no major damage, convinced Kurita he had engaged part of Halsey's TF 38. He broke off his attack and sailed away, losing three more cruisers to air and submarine pursuers. In the meantime, the Southern Force tried to force its way through the Surigao Strait on the night of 24–25 October, and ran into a groupment of Kinkaid's shore bombardment force of fourteen battleships and cruisers. Proving its hard-learned skill in surface night battles, Task Force 77.2 sank 11 Japanese warships at the cost of 1 destroyer, lost to 'friendly fire'. In all the battles 10,000 Japanese sailors perished at a cost of around 1,500 for the US Navy. The battles of Leyte Gulf ended the Combined Fleet's capability to stop the American fleet in conventional battle.

Kamikaze strikes and Japanese defence

The Japanese navy found another way to destroy American ships, by plunging aircraft into them. With no official approval, its pilots in October 1944 either bombed at suicidal levels or simply dived into fifteen US Navy ships, sinking them or sending them away for extensive repairs. The US Navy combat air patrols and shipboard anti-aircraft fire could not down every penetrator, a fact quickly recognized by admirals Onishi Takijino and Ugaki Matome, the Japanese navy aviation commanders who organized the Thunder Gods Corps or kamikaze ('divine wind') squadrons. At least 5,000 young, under trained pilots eventually found honourable death in their cockpits. In addition to the ships they sank or damaged – more than 400 – the kamikaze pilots forced American air commanders to substitute fighter-interceptors for fighter-bombers and to rediscover their anti-aircraft batteries, thus reducing fire support for the ground forces in the Philippines. Without naval air cover, the US Fifth Air Force on Leyte found itself victimized by several Japanese Fourth Air Army attacks on the two USAAF airfields on the island. The patchwork air campaign allowed

Below Kamikaze pilots pose at Choshi, east of Tokyo, before a sortie in the Philippines, November 1944.

Below right A kamikaze attack on an American light carrier off Okinawa, April 1945. Suicide attacks reached their peak during this battle, and sank a total of 36 Allied ships.

the Japanese army aviators to cover the flow of Japanese reinforcements to the 35th Army on Leyte, which raised its strength from 23,000 to almost 80,000. Reinforcements from Formosa and China maintained the strength of the 14th Area Army on Luzon (General Yamashita) at 200,000. The US Sixth Army on Leyte, however, increased from four to eight divisions or 200,000 soldiers of all kinds.

The Japanese defence of Leyte did not reflect the new defensive concepts of General Yamashita or his talented contemporary on Iwo Jima, General Kuribayashi Tadamichi. The 35th Army on Leyte fought and died almost to a man (1,000 POWs were taken) in a conventional defend/counter-attack pattern. Rugged terrain alone did not suffice. The contemporaneous defence of Peleliu, an airbase in the nearby Palau island group, showed the potential of a cave-oriented, fortified defence; instead of a Tarawa-like four-day battle, the US 1st Marine Division and most of the Army's 81st Infantry Division took a month (September–October 1944) to destroy 10,000 underground defenders, at a cost of 7,000 casualties. Yamashita's plan to defend Luzon depended on waging war in the mountains, not in the cities and towns of the agricultural valleys. He forced the US Sixth and Eighth armies to fight for crucial reserves and airfields, to limit Allied firepower by defending hill towns occupied by friendly Filipinos, and to hold Allied POWs and internees hostage. In Kuribayashi's case, Iwo Jima (see box overleaf) was an island of volcanic rock made for tunnelling and bunker-building, a mini-Gibraltar for underground fighters with artillery and machine guns.

The campaigns for Luzon, Iwo Jima and Okinawa (December 1944 to June 1945) demonstrated that the new style of Japanese defence might prolong the war and send casualties soaring. The longer the ground campaign went on, the longer the US Navy had to endure kamikaze attacks. Yamashita kept an army in the field until Japan's surrender. The US Sixth Army – aided by perhaps 60,000 Filipino guerrillas – killed or captured 100,000 Japanese soldiers, a lesser number than the Filipino civilians who died in the same period, principally in and around Manila from city fires and American artillery. To be sure, fanatical Japanese sailors and soldiers slaughtered at least 10,000 innocents during the recapture of the city. Yamashita's defensive scheme reduced the US Sixth Army to near ineffectiveness through wounds, disease and emotional exhaustion. With the US Eighth Army committed to liberating the rest of the Philippines, MacArthur commanded two field armies of sixteen of the twenty-one Army divisions sent to fight the Japanese. He exhausted many of them before completing his 'return'.

> *'He had died and no longer moved . . . Others had died with him. He had screamed for them all. The others had died quietly, but he had protested; he had been their advocate. He had argued their cause and had protested the injustice, the cruelty, and the helplessness of the trial they had undergone.'*
>
> A veteran US Marine sergeant recalling the death of a private on Iwo Jima

Iwo Jima and Okinawa

At the battles for Iwo Jima (February–March 1945) and Okinawa (April–June 1945) the three Marine divisions faced an implacable enemy to whom a hopeless cause seemed a chance to prove devotion to the emperor and unique values. Kuribayashi's defenders died almost to a man on Iwo Jima (over 21,000 of them), but ruined the US Marine Corps divisions and their supporting units (over 23,000 casualties, and 6,000 dead).

Tracer fire from shipboard anti-aircraft guns lights the sky during the Battle of Okinawa, April–June 1945.

For the first time a Japanese garrison had inflicted more casualties than it suffered.

In the April–July 1945 battle for Okinawa, the Japanese 32nd Army (110,000 soldiers) defended only the southern third of Okinawa and produced a style of warfare unseen since 1914–18. The battleground included 450,000 Japanese civilians, of whom at least 150,000 died in combat, committed suicide or were executed by Japanese soldiers to avoid 'Yankee atrocities'. Of the American expeditionary force of three Marine and four Army divisions, only one did not become combat-ruined. American ground-force casualties, all causes, numbered 66,000. Moreover, the extended campaign, waged only 560 km (350 miles) from the Home Islands, exposed the supporting Task Force 58 (Admiral Spruance) to ten major kamikaze attacks that cost only 1,500 Japanese lives and aircraft, but that sank or seriously damaged 124 US ships and killed or wounded 12,000 sailors in two months, more casualties than the navy had suffered in the preceding two years. American planners predicted that

The Battle of Iwo Jima

The Battle of Iwo Jima, in which the United States captured the heavily fortified airbase on the route to Tokyo, involved some of the fiercest fighting in the entire Asia–Pacific theatre of World War II. Japanese-held islands in the Marianas and Carolines, further to the south, had already been captured by the Americans, and the Japanese knew that the loss of their airfields on Iwo Jima would facilitate US air raids on the Japanese mainland, disrupting war manufacturing and severely denting civilian morale.

At 2 a.m. on 19 February 1945, the amphibious landing commenced with a naval and aerial bombardment of Japanese positions lasting some seven hours. But this failed to destroy the deep Japanese trenches and tunnels or their well-concealed artillery, leaving the first waves of Marines exposed to unexpected and devastating fire. The loose terrain of black volcanic pebbles made advances particularly difficult, but by the end of the first day, having sustained heavy losses, the critical Japanese positions on Mount Suribachi, with a commanding view of the landing beaches, had been cut off from the rest of the Japanese force. The mountain itself was captured on 23 February.

It would take another month to subdue the entire island: progress was slowed by the extensive tunnel systems that allowed the Japanese to repeatedly escape demolition and flame-thrower assaults on their positions and then reoccupy areas that had apparently been cleared. The United States occupied Iwo Jima until 1968, when it was returned to Japan.

Opposite left US Marines land on a beach of black volcano ash, Iwo Jima, 19 February 1945.

Opposite right A US Marine patrol plants a flag on Mount Suribachi, 23 February 1945.

Below The Battle of Iwo Jima (19 February – 26 March 1945), perhaps the best-known battle of the Pacific War.

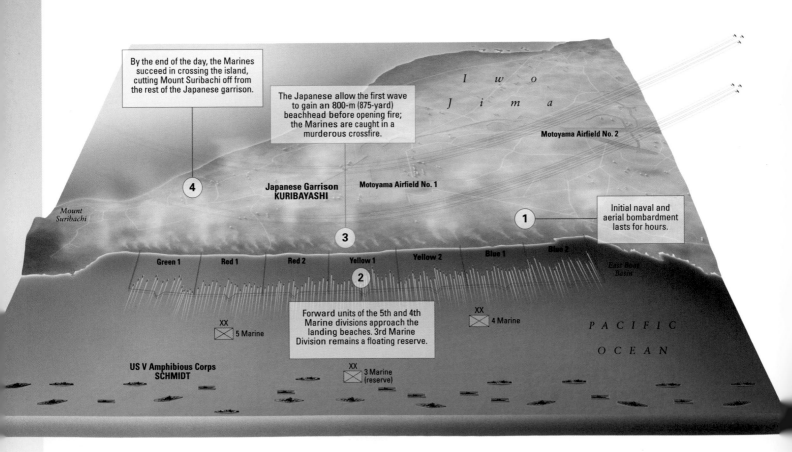

By the end of the day, the Marines succeed in crossing the island, cutting Mount Suribachi off from the rest of the Japanese garrison.

The Japanese allow the first wave to gain an 800-m (875-yard) beachhead before opening fire; the Marines are caught in a murderous crossfire.

I   w   o

J   i   m   a

Motoyama Airfield No. 2

4

Japanese Garrison
KURIBAYASHI

Motoyama Airfield No. 1

Mount Suribachi

1   Initial naval and aerial bombardment lasts for hours.

3

Green 1   Red 1   Red 2   Yellow 1   Yellow 2   Blue 1   Blue 2   *East Boat Basin*

2

XX ⊠ 5 Marine

Forward units of the 5th and 4th Marine divisions approach the landing beaches. 3rd Marine Division remains a floating reserve.

XX ⊠ 4 Marine

P A C I F I C

O C E A N

US V Amphibious Corps
SCHMIDT

XX ⊠ 3 Marine (reserve)

	UNITED STATES	JAPAN
COMMANDERS	Harry Schmidt	Kuribayashi Tadamichi
STRENGTH	*c.* 110,000 ashore	22,786
CASUALTIES	5,931 dead	21,703 dead
	17,372 wounded	1,083 captured

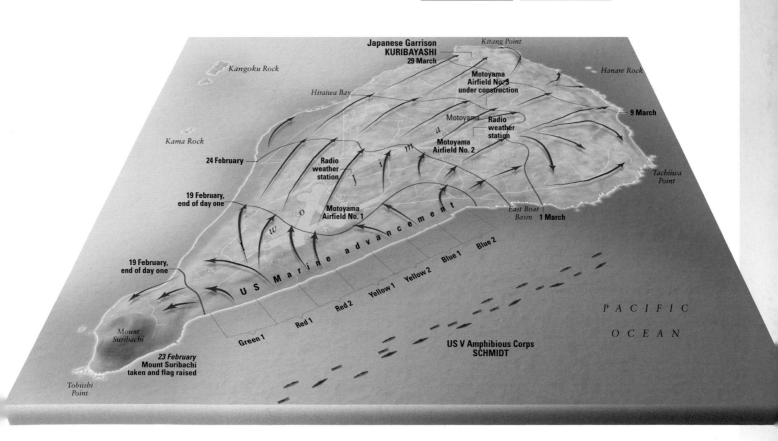

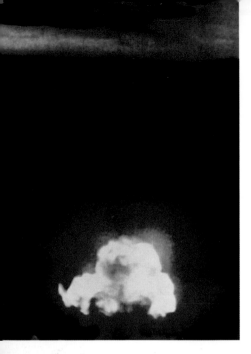

the anticipated invasion of the Home Islands would simply reproduce Iwo Jima and Okinawa on a more horrific scale, as they watched the Japanese army bring aircraft and divisions out of Manchuria and China to defend the sacred homeland.

FINAL SURRENDER

The strategic-bombing advocates of the USAAF and a substantial part of the US Navy's leadership believed the invasion of the Home Islands – Operation Downfall – would be unnecessary. Repeated B-29 strikes, unremitting submarine attacks on the Japanese merchant navy and a naval blockade with mines and carrier task forces would force the Japanese to surrender with no conditions. Another factor was that the Soviet Union had agreed to declare war on Japan ninety days after Germany's surrender. Few doubted that Stalin would reverse the defeat of 1904–5, with interest. American diplomats watched Stalin make an alliance with Nationalist China for prized territorial concessions and to sidestep Japanese efforts to use Russia as a peacemaker. Military observers watched the Soviets create an army of eighty divisions (over 1 million soldiers), which faced a hollow Kwantung Army of 400,000, stripped of its best units and equipment. A privileged few Americans (and Soviets) knew that the US scientific–engineering community had used the discovery of the nuclear chain reaction to develop a bomb of either plutonium or uranium that could produce destruction measured by the tens of thousands of tons of conventional explosives. In July 1945 the Manhattan Project directors watched with pride, amazement and horror as the first atomic bomb turned the New Mexican desert to glass and ash.

The problem with the strategic bombing/economic strangulation approach to Japanese defeat was that its effects were too recent to be measured in political terms. Faulty torpedoes and the patrol distances of US submarines were not solved until 1944, through technical fixes and forward basing. US Navy submarines cut Japanese merchant tonnage in half, with oil tankers the prize target. Japanese anti-submarine forces did not keep pace. The sinkings increased in 1945, and the Japanese merchant fleet was halved again, to 1.2 million tons. An economist could predict the collapse of the Japanese economy, had the Japanese leaders had a Western mindset. The bombing campaign – waged by the 20th Air Force's B-29s based in the Marianas – produced no significant damage between November 1944 and March 1945 because high-altitude formation bombing of specific industrial targets did not work, owing to high winds, Japanese urban patterns and limited time over target. In desperation a new commander, Major General Curtis E. LeMay, adopted the tactics of the RAF Bomber Command's air war on Germany: burn up cities using night-time streams of bombers flying at staggered altitudes. The approach confounded Japanese air defences. From March to August 1945 the B-29s ruined sixty to seventy Japanese cities, notably Tokyo in the fire-bombing raids of March. Before the first atomic bomb exploded, at least 300,000 Japanese had died. The entire campaign lost the USAAF almost 500 bombers and 3,000 lives to weather, distance and Japanese air defences. The air-war planners could measure the level of effort and physical destruction of the bombing, but not its political effect.

> '*I saw blackened bodies, half-burned bodies, people who expired even as they called out "Water! Water!" and firemen dead on trucks. The swimming pool at school was a mountain of corpses.*'
>
> A Japanese teenager who stumbled through the ruins of Tokyo, 1945

Opposite top The first atomic bomb detonation, which took place at the Alamogordo Test Range, New Mexico, 16 July 1945.

Opposite below In March 1945 a series of USAAF fire-bombing raids targeted Japanese cities. The raid against Tokyo on 9/10 March destroyed 16 square miles (41 sq km) of the city centre and killed over 85,000 people.

Right The Japanese surrender on board the USS *Missouri* in Tokyo Bay, 2 September 1945. The Allied delegation was led by Douglas MacArthur.

With only hints of capitulation, the 'peace faction' in the Japanese government manoeuvred to persuade Emperor Hirohito to force the army-led war faction to accept Allied terms. The key issue was the institution of the emperor. If Hirohito, a war criminal under the Allied definition worked out at the Nuremberg trials, accepted the status of limited, constitutional monarch, he might save his office, if not his person. This nuance escaped both Japanese and American diplomats until August 1945. Exactly which shocks of August turned the Japanese government to accept unconditional surrender is arguable. In meetings held on 6–9 August, Hirohito's inner counsellors were divided three/three. The shocks came fast. The first atomic bomb destroyed Hiroshima on 6 August. On 9 August the Japanese learned that the USSR had declared war and invaded Manchuria, and the USAAF dropped a second nuclear bomb on Nagasaki. (The USAAF had a third bomb available.) Hirohito ordered a surrender ('bearing the unbearable') because his counsellors had convinced him that his duty was to save the institution of the emperor, to pre-empt a brewing communist revolution and to protect 5 million overseas Japanese from vengeful slaughter. Hirohito accepted the Allied terms of surrender on 10 August, and his message in turn was accepted by the Allies two days later. The formal surrender took place on 2 September aboard the battleship *Missouri* in Tokyo Bay.

8　Sea Power and Naval Warfare

MICHAEL EPKENHANS

Opposite The aircraft carrier USS *Ronald Reagan* and the fast combat support ship USNS *Bridgeon* on manoeuvres in the Indian Ocean, 2008.

The attacks of terrorists and pirates on world shipping in the early 21st century have once again highlighted the vulnerability of Western societies. Governments and/or fanatics, as well as conventional criminal groups, have begun to threaten the West by waging 'asymmetric' and undeclared wars, driven by nationalist, religious, racial or economic motives. As in the 19th and early 20th centuries, Western reaction has been to turn for protection primarily to the navy. Only naval vessels have the capability both to control strategic lifelines and to deter and, if necessary, fight pirates and terrorists on the oceans and along the shores of unstable countries such as Somalia. Accordingly, many countries are reorganizing their navies and building new naval vessels, following an old tradition of naval defence of their political and economic interests.

FROM THE TURN OF THE CENTURY TO THE OUTBREAK OF WORLD WAR I

In the century before World War I, navies were widely regarded as the most important instruments and symbols of the power of nations. Britain and its Royal Navy, which had ruled the world and its oceans without being seriously challenged by any rival, were the example many nations tried to emulate. As the 19th century progressed, industrial, technological and social changes had a deep impact upon the domestic structures and foreign and economic policies of many European nations, the United States and Japan, and there was a corresponding impact on attitudes to naval power and on naval policy.

In a global context sea power now seemed more important than ever. Highly industrialized countries had become dependent upon the free and constant flow of goods, raw materials and men to secure the power and prosperity of their respective nations. In this context the writings of Alfred T. Mahan of the US Navy became highly influential. Deeply convinced that international politics was basically a struggle over who gets what, when and how, Mahan argued that in history naval forces had always been the decisive instrument.

The transition from the age of sail to the industrial age had had a deep impact upon navies. Ironclads had replaced sailing ships, and the invention of the screw propeller, self-propelled torpedo and explosive shells had both revolutionized and challenged old principles of naval warfare. In the 1880s some naval theorists maintained that in the future modern technology would allow weaker naval powers to successfully fight stronger ones. However, naval manoeuvres had called the feasibility of a *guerre de course* (privateering) strategy seriously into question, and Mahan and his followers believed that a traditional battle was still the only way to achieve and defend naval supremacy. Success would depend on a strong battle fleet. In Mahan's eyes, commerce warfare was no alternative, for neither cruisers nor torpedo boats would ever be able to achieve command of the sea or decisively threaten oceanic communications.

Navies were becoming more professional in every respect. Naval schools and academies had been established at Dartmouth, Annapolis and Kiel (in Britain, the United States and Germany, respectively) to train officers and men in seamanship, naval tactics and gunnery. At the same time, naval staffs and ministries began to develop long-term building programmes and detailed war plans against possible enemies. Modern and efficient shipyards and armament firms became crucial. Without enterprises such as Vickers-Armstrongs in Britain, Krupp and Blohm & Voss in Germany, Schneider in France, Carnegie and Midvale in the US and Witkowitz and Skoda in Austria-Hungary, there would have been no modern battleships, no battlecruisers, no submarines, no armour to protect ships, no heavy guns or torpedoes to sink enemy vessels, no wireless to improve communication between ships, and no turbines or diesel engines to increase their speed.

> '*Control of the sea by maritime commerce and naval supremacy means predominant influence in the world . . . [and] is the chief among the merely material elements in the power and prosperity of nations.*'
> Alfred T. Mahan, US Navy, 1890

Within the space of a decade many states systematically built up battle fleets, with battleships as their backbone. Despite many doubts as to their use in the modern age, technological progress had made this type of ship a formidable weapon once more. New armour developed in Germany by Krupp gave better protection above and below the surface; medium-calibre quick-firing guns introduced as secondary armament could effectively fight attacking torpedo boats; and new boilers increased the speed of battleships.

Although the experiences of the Russo-Japanese War of 1904–5 (see Chapter 1), with its 'classic' battles between navies fought at far greater distances than ever before, supported this rather simplistic view of the importance of sea power and battleships, Mahan's ideas were not shared by all naval theorists. In Britain, for example, Julian Corbett, one of the Royal Navy's chief advisers, argued that 'sea-denial' – preventing the opposing power from using the sea – was also a means of defending Britain's maritime supremacy, and in Germany admirals Curt von Maltzahn and Karl Galster also doubted the validity of Mahan's ideas for the German High

Above The Krupp factory in Essen, *c.* 1900. Until the end of World War II, Krupp was Germany's most important supplier of armour plate, guns and gun mountings.

Opposite above Alfred T. Mahan, whose *Influence of Seapower upon History* (1890) greatly influenced the education of naval officers all over the world in the late 19th and early 20th centuries.

Opposite below Midshipmen at the United States Naval Academy, Annapolis, Maryland, 1922.

Seas Fleet. In London, even the energetic Admiral Sir John Fisher proved unable to 'revolutionize' the Royal Navy by implementing a completely new strategy with all its consequences upon shipbuilding, and the Imperial Navy Office in Berlin publicly rebuked all critics for fear of far-reaching repercussions on its construction policies.

One of the results of the manifold attempts to establish or increase power at sea was naval races. Although the Anglo-German naval race before World War I is probably the best known (see pp. 27–29), since it changed world history, Austria-Hungary and Italy, Turkey and Greece, and even Brazil and Argentina, competed with each other at the beginning of the 20th century. Whereas Germany's political leadership hoped that the build-up of a battle fleet consisting of 61 capital ships, 40 light cruisers, 144 torpedo boats and 72 submarines would force Britain to give up any political or economic inclination to attack, and moreover to concede to its rival sufficient naval presence for the conduct of a grand policy overseas, the other powers tried to safeguard their interests in the Adriatic, the eastern Mediterranean and the South Atlantic by building up navies of their own. The impact of these races upon international politics was profound. On a global scale, Britain and Germany eventually found themselves in two opposing alliance systems armed to the teeth and waiting for the spark to blow up the powder keg. In the Adriatic, Austria-Hungary and Italy, hardly able to disguise their rivalry, watched each other with increasing mistrust, while in the eastern Mediterranean the outbreak of war between Greece and Turkey over the future of a number of small islands was only a question of time in 1913–14. In each case navies played an important role in defending claims or realizing more far-reaching aspirations.

THE WAR AT SEA DURING WORLD WAR I

When war broke out in August 1914, as well as battles between armies, a great naval encounter was expected between Germany and Britain. Surprisingly, such an encounter did not take place until May 1916, and it did not prove decisive.

The development of HMS *Dreadnought* (see box on pp. 30–31) in Britain had eventually caused a change in naval doctrine. Instead of establishing the more usual close blockade and thus risking a battle under unfavourable conditions under the guns of Heligoland, the Admiralty had decided to impose a distant blockade between Scotland and the Norwegian coast. In the end this strategy of sea-denial achieved the same aim, namely the defence of British naval supremacy, and cut off Germany's lifelines at the same time. The German navy, which in 1913–14 had begun to realize that this might be Britain's strategy, and which was well aware of the risk of losing its whole battle fleet in a single encounter, had no viable plan to force the Grand Fleet to offer battle in the German Bight. Initial hopes to whittle down British naval strength through a kind of guerrilla warfare (*Kleinkrieg*) soon proved futile. Instead, on 28 August 1914 superior British forces surprised German vessels guarding the German Bight, sending three light cruisers and a torpedo boat to the bottom. German attempts to retaliate by raiding the British east coast in November and December 1914, and, if possible, by surprising and sinking inferior British forces, also failed.

> '*I am greatly distressed by the affair at Heligoland . . . Our light forces are not sufficient for such skirmishes. If things go on like this, they'll soon be wiped out. The English will enclose us in a great circle of mines; then our fleet will be "bottled".'*
>
> Grand Admiral Alfred von Tirpitz
> to his wife, 28 August 1914

On 24 January 1915 British forces at Dogger Bank surprised German battlecruisers. In the course of the ensuing battle the armoured cruiser *Blücher* was sunk. The result of this new disaster was not only a change in the command of the High Seas Fleet, but also an even more careful strategy. For more than a year the High Seas Fleet

The sinking of the German battleships *Scharnhorst, Gneisenau, Nürnberg* and *Leipzig* at the Battle of the Falkland Islands, 8 December 1914.

VICTOIRE NAVALE DES ILES FALKLAND
QUATRE CROISEURS ALLEMANDS ATTAQUÉS ET COULÉS PAR L'ESCADRE ANGLAISE

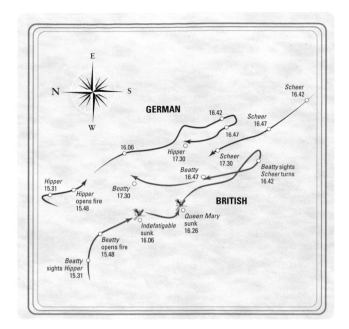

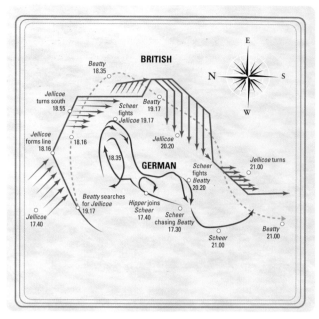

The Battle of Jutland, showing the situation in the afternoon and evening of 31 May 1916.

remained on the defensive. Another change in command in January 1916 and the attempt to prove that the imperial navy was willing to contribute to Germany's victory in the war eventually led to the Battle of Jutland. On 31 May 1916 the High Seas Fleet had left harbour for a raid against the British coast, which, more or less by accident, resulted in an almost classic battle. Though British losses in ships and men were higher than those of the enemy, the 'Glorious First of June', as the Kaiser first wanted to call the Battle of Jutland, was no German victory. Strategically, the battle had changed nothing. As a result the High Seas Fleet remained on the defensive, carefully avoiding any battle that might end in total destruction. A subsequent plan, developed in early October 1918, for a raid against the British coast had no strategic aim at all: it was nothing but a suicide mission to save the honour of the German naval officer corps. Weary of the war, the navy's ratings mutinied, overthrowing the order in less than a week.

'*There can be no doubt that even the most successful outcome of a fleet action in this war will not force England to make peace.*'

Admiral Reinhard Scheer, 'victor' of the Battle of Jutland, to the Kaiser, 4 July 1916

Although the North Sea and eventually the Atlantic were the main theatres of submarine warfare, other areas were also of importance. In the Baltic the Imperial German Navy fought the Russian navy. By infesting the eastern parts of the Baltic with mines, and supported by British submarines, the Russian navy, though inferior in strength, unexpectedly inflicted heavy losses on the German navy and on German shipping between Sweden and the Baltic ports right from the outbreak of war. The German conquest of Poland and parts of the Russian Baltic coast in 1915–16 improved the situation only slightly. Only in September 1917, after the Russian Revolution, did the German navy eventually conquer the Bay of Riga and the Russian Baltic Islands in its first amphibious operation. Plans for a similar operation against the Russian port of Kronstadt to fight Bolshevism in late 1918 had to be given up for lack of army support.

In the Adriatic the Austro-Hungarian and Italian navies were at war from May 1915. There was no real victor until the end of the war. Apart from some minor battles, both sides somehow achieved their aims, namely to protect their own coasts from invasion. However, Italy and its allies were eventually more successful, since, by preventing the Austro-Hungarian navy from breaking the blockade of the Strait of Otranto, they defended their naval superiority in the Mediterranean, just as they had done in the North Sea.

In the eastern Mediterranean and in the Black Sea the situation was very similar. Although two German warships, the battlecruiser *Goeben* and the light cruiser *Breslau*, had escaped their British pursuers by running into Turkish waters and had been put under Turkish command, they were not strong enough seriously to threaten British and Russian superiority in the Mediterranean or the Black Sea. This effectively cut Turkey's lines of communication with Europe. The seconded cruisers did, however, help to strengthen the Turks in their defence against the Allied attempt to force the Dardanelles in 1915. A futile naval attack was followed by an amphibious operation that soon became a full-scale disaster for Britain and its allies.

The only serious threat to British naval superiority came from submarines (see box overleaf). Realizing by late 1914 that a Mahanian blue-water strategy – attempting to gain and use control of the sea – would bring no success, the German naval command slowly began to revert to a completely different strategy: submarine warfare. The submarine had been invented in the mid-19th century, and since the turn of the century, in a slow process of trial and error entailing many accidents and setbacks, all navies had developed this new type of vessel.

> '*The submarine is the coming type of war vessel for sea fighting . . . The ultimate purpose of the Fleet was to make blockade possible for us and impossible for the enemy . . . Surface ships can no longer maintain or prevent blockade . . . All our old ideas of strategy are simmering in the melting pot!*'
>
> Sir John Fisher, British First Sea Lord, 1904

On the eve of war Britain had the largest submarine fleet, 72 vessels, while the German navy had only 28.

The success of the German U-9 submarine in sinking three old British armoured cruisers within an hour off Dover in September 1914 was something of a turning point. Attempts to introduce submarine warfare on a larger scale, however, met with severe opposition from Germany's political leadership, mindful of the danger of provoking the United States into entering the war on the Allied side. Only in February 1917, when victory on land was still not in sight and when hunger and lack of raw materials had become serious domestic problems, did Germany's leadership decide to put everything on one last card to force Britain to submit. Though German submarines inflicted heavy losses on Allied shipping in the first months of 1917, the introduction of the Allied convoy system soon helped to improve the situation. Moreover, new forms of anti-submarine warfare and a large-scale mining offensive effectively blockading their exit routes proved successful in fighting German submarines, which soon suffered increasing losses, totalling 178 (and 4,474 men) out of 335 vessels in service.

Cruisers played no important role in the naval war. The lack of bases and coaling stations had been one reason why Admiral von Tirpitz had always emphasized the need to build a battle fleet and not a fleet of cruisers waging commerce warfare on the oceans. Subsequently Germany's cruisers were doomed to be sunk sooner or later. On its way home the German East Asiatic Squadron defeated a British squadron off the coast of Chile in November 1914, only to be sunk a month later off the Falkland Islands by superior British forces. The remaining German light cruisers, such as the famous *Emden* (sunk in November 1914) and the *Dresden*, waging commerce warfare in the Atlantic and Pacific oceans, were all hunted down by spring 1915, and so were most of the German auxiliary cruisers laying mines or attacking Allied merchant vessels in distant waters.

THE INTERWAR YEARS, 1919–39

The experiences of World War I had a deep impact on the role of navies and on the principles of naval warfare. From the Allies' point of view, the situation had improved. Following Germany's surrender and the scuttling of its High Seas Fleet at Scapa Flow in June 1919, the German menace did not exist any more. Britannia, it seemed, ruled the waves again with her fleet of 58 capital ships, 103 cruisers, 12 aircraft carriers, 456 destroyers and 122 submarines. In the Treaty of Versailles, signed in June 1919, the Allies, moreover, limited not only the number but also the type of warship Germany would be allowed to possess in the future. The Austrian navy had vanished with the collapse of the Dual Monarchy, and so had the Russian navy in the turmoil of revolution.

However, against the background in Britain of scarce financial resources, an ailing economy and the need to provide money for improved social services instead of new battleships, cuts in defence spending were inevitable. Moreover, hoping to avoid a naval race with the United States, which, in 1916, had declared its desire to build up a navy second to none, the British government in 1922, in spite of harsh complaints by the Admiralty, entered into negotiations with its former allies. These led to an

The German battlecruiser *Hindenburg* in shallow water at Scapa Flow, 21 June 1919. By scuttling their ships, officers of the former Imperial High Seas Fleet hoped to save their honour after a humiliating end to the Great War.

Submarines

A typical *Gato*-class submarine was armed with ten 21-inch (533-mm) torpedo tubes, six forward and four aft.

With engine rooms both aft and forward, *Gato*-class vessels had top speeds of 20.2 knots (37 kph) on the surface and 8.7 knots (16 kph) submerged.

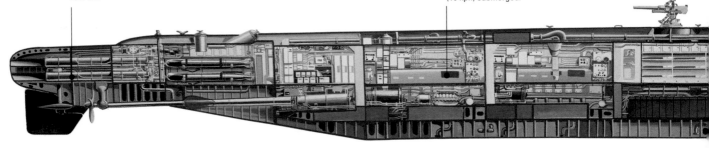

Top Sailors take cover around the conning tower of a German Type XIC U-boat as it comes under attack from the air, *c.* 1943. U-boats of this type inflicted heavy casualties upon Allied shipping in the Atlantic between 1941 and 1943.

Above A USS *Gato*-class submarine. Built between 1940 and 1944, this type of vessel, along with its two successors, made up the vast majority of US submarines in World War II.

Opposite Russian seamen line up on a nuclear-powered Akula-class submarine, Vladivostok, 2008.

Submarines, which were developed in the 19th century and first used successfully in the American Civil War, fundamentally changed the character of naval warfare. Capable of fighting the enemy both above and below the surface, they could either attack or interdict enemy shipping all over the world. At the beginning of the 20th century all navies gradually began to introduce this new type of weapon, even though capital ships were regarded as the most important means of gaining and defending naval supremacy.

Soon, however, greater ranges, increased speed, better armament with torpedoes and guns mounted on deck, and improved pressure hulls, which allowed greater depths, turned the submarine into a formidable weapon in the war at sea. World War I saw a breakthrough in the development of both strategy and tactics. Though often regarded as a negligible weapon of weak naval powers, the submarine displayed its capability as a most dangerous weapon against warships and commercial shipping. The German High Seas Fleet, realizing that it had no chance of winning an open battle against the Grand Fleet, and in retaliation against Britain's distant blockade of German commercial shipping, reverted to different forms of submarine warfare from late 1914 onwards. In 1917 a new offensive against Britain's lifelines inflicted severe losses upon Britain's trade and supply lines without, however, changing the course of the war.

The long range and good habitability of the *Gato*-class submarine made it especially suitable for patrol endurance.

During World War II the submarine again played an important role in German naval strategy. Based on World War I designs, these vessels infested all the world's oceans. They now attacked in groups ('wolf packs') in order to increase their effectiveness. In many ways Germany's submarine strategy proved the model of the naval strategy of other navies, which, like the US Navy in the Pacific War, also used submarines widely to interdict enemy shipping. But in spite of the heavy losses suffered by Allied shipping once again, the development of new countermeasures and the breaking of the German Enigma code helped to win the battle, which was mainly fought in the Atlantic Ocean.

After World War II submarines soon became the most important weapon in the Cold War. The replacement of conventional diesel engines with nuclear power increased submarine speed tremendously, from 8 knots (15 kph: the German U-9 in 1914) to 24 knots (44 kph: the USN Ohio-class submarine). Steel or even titanium hulls, which have increased from a modest 493 tons (U-9) to 16,500 tons (Ohio class), have allowed submarines to reach ever greater depths to evade detection, and to carry twenty-four ballistic missiles instead of only a small number of torpedoes. Today both nuclear and conventional submarines still play an important role in the defensive as well as the offensive naval strategies of all major navies.

The Japanese *Yamato* was the most powerful battleship in history. In spite of its strength, it was sunk by US naval planes on 7 April 1945, during the Battle of the East China Sea.

agreement (the Washington Naval Treaty) effectively limiting capital ship tonnage. In the next ten years the British and American navies would possess only 525,000 tons of capital ships; Japan, 315,000 tons; and France and Italy, 175,000 tons. The tonnage (10,000 tons) and the calibres (20 cm; 8 inches) of other ships were limited as well. In the history of sea power this was indeed a remarkable event.

Although this agreement did not, as Britain had demanded, include submarines, because of French and Italian objections, it was a step forward as far as arms limitation was concerned, at least for the time being. In 1930 at the London Naval Conference the agreement was renewed, with some changes regarding cruisers. However, the refusal of Japan's demand to increase its capital ship-building ratio at the second London Naval Conference in 1935 led to the agreement's collapse. The Anglo-German Naval Agreement, signed in the same year, which limited German naval strength in capital ships to 35 per cent of that of the Royal Navy but granted parity in the building of submarines, seemed a success at first sight, but in the long run the Kriegsmarine had no intention of sticking to it longer than necessary.

Although many battleships had to be scrapped following the Washington agreement, the battleship remained the backbone of the fleets of all naval powers in the interwar years. Of course, many politicians, admirals and naval theorists had begun to realize that air power might have a far-reaching impact upon naval warfare. As early as 1917 a special subcommittee of the British War Cabinet had forecast the rise of aerial operations at the expense of the military and naval.

However, in spite of much controversy and many trials – the US Air Force sank the former German dreadnought SMS *Ostfriesland* in 1921, thus testing the effect of aerial bombing on battleships – for the time being most admirals were convinced that battleships, especially if armed with a sufficient number of anti-aircraft guns and if strengthened with thicker armour, could defend themselves successfully against attacking aeroplanes. Moreover, the 1930s even saw a revival of battleship building all over the world instead of a decisive shift towards new types of ships. Like their predecessors at the turn of the century, the rulers of Nazi Germany, communist Soviet Russia and Fascist Italy regarded battleships as both the most important symbols of power and the most effective weapons in a naval war. Subsequently and secretly ignoring all international agreements limiting battleship tonnage, they began to build a new generation of battleships, much larger and more powerful than those constructed before. The *Bismarck* and the *Tirpitz* displaced 45,000 tons, the planned Soviet *Sovetskii Soyuz* an estimated 46,000 tons or even more, and the Italian *Vittorio Veneto* 37,000 tons. The Japanese *Yamato* and *Musashi*, ordered in 1937, reached an incredible 72,000 tons of displacement. Their main armament of 38-cm or even 46-cm guns (15 and 18⅛ inches respectively) was similarly powerful. Far bigger ships with even more powerful guns were planned or even laid down in Germany and Japan, before the course of the war ended all naval construction. Compared with these battleships, those of the King George V class built for the Royal Navy under the new construction programme of 1936, displacing only 35,000 tons and armed with only 35.5-cm (14-inch) guns, were slower, smaller and less well armed than their rivals.

'The day may not be far off when aerial operations with their devastation of enemy lands and the destruction of industrial and populous centres on a vast scale may become the principal operations of war, to which the older forms of military and naval operations may become secondary and subordinate.'
Imperial War Cabinet subcommittee, 1917

The continuing emphasis on the need for battleships did not preclude the development of new aircraft carriers in Britain, the United States and Japan. These were faster, larger and better protected than their predecessors, and new aeroplanes, such as the dive and torpedo bomber, as well as special operational policies and air-to-sea doctrine, increased their capabilities in wartime.

The aircraft carrier HMS *Ark Royal*, completed in November 1938. After some near misses, it was ultimately torpedoed and sunk on 13 November 1941.

Above At 45,000 tons, the *Bismarck* was Germany's most powerful battleship. Having left German waters on 19 May 1941 to attack Allied convoys in the Atlantic, it was sunk eight days later by British naval forces.

Right The Battle of the Atlantic in the spring of 1942 – a critical period in which U-boats inflicted severe damage on Allied shipping in the Caribbean and along the east coast of the United States.

WORLD WAR II, 1939–45

On a far greater scale than the previous world conflict, World War II was a naval war. It was, ironically, an old German pre-dreadnought battleship, the *Schleswig-Holstein*, that fired the first shot of the new war on 1 September 1939, when German troops invaded Poland. As far as the Kriegsmarine was concerned, it had learnt its lessons from the experiences of World War I. Being inferior to the Royal Navy, it demanded the occupation of Norway and Denmark in an attempt to avoid another blockade with all its consequences for both the German war effort and the population, and to get open access to the Atlantic. Moreover, right from the outbreak of war the Kriegsmarine launched attacks on Allied shipping all over the world with submarines and a small number of pocket battleships and battleships such as the *Graf Spee*, the *Scharnhorst* and the *Gneisenau*. Unlike in World War I, however, the German *Seekriegsleitung* (Supreme Naval Command) avoided any battle between surface ships because of the overwhelming strength of the Royal Navy. In the event, Germany's most powerful warship, the battleship *Bismarck*, surprisingly sank HMS *Hood*, the most powerful British vessel, on its way into the Atlantic, where it was supposed to attack Allied convoys, in May 1941. Within days, however, it was hunted down by its British pursuers and sunk. As a result the *Tirpitz*, the sister ship of the *Bismarck*, hardly left its hiding place in the Norwegian fjords until it was sunk by British aircraft in November 1944. As early as July 1941 the German naval command had openly admitted its dilemma as far as fleet action was concerned.

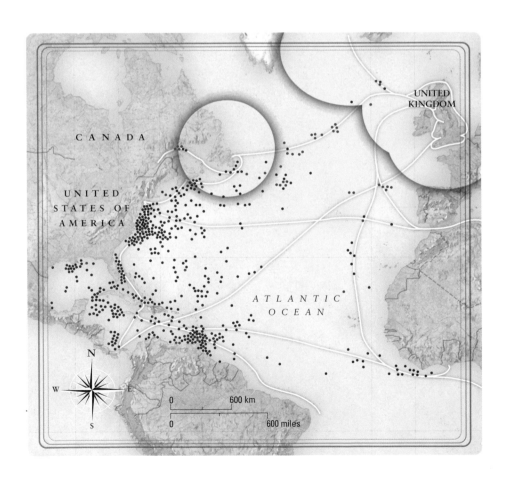

- Allied ships lost in convoy, 1 January – 31 May 1942
- Allied ships lost in independent sailings, or stragglers from convoys, 1 January – 31 May 1942

Maximum range of effective air escort

Major convoy routes

Coast Guardsmen on board the USS *Spencer* watch as a depth charge hits a German U-boat, 17 April 1943.

The remaining big surface ships, such as the *Scharnhorst* and the *Gneisenau*, were either also withdrawn to home waters or sunk in 1942–43. From 1940–41 the most important German weapon against the Allies was, once more, the submarine. Technological developments and new tactics had turned submarines, which operated in wolf packs, into deadly devices threatening Allied lines of communication across the Atlantic, including US and Canadian coastal waters, but also in the Indian and Pacific oceans and in the Mediterranean.

Although German submarines inflicted heavy losses upon Allied shipping (2,610 vessels, roughly 13 million tons, were sunk), they nevertheless lost the important Battle of the Atlantic. Britain could not be starved into submission or deprived of military supplies. New technologies played an important part in this fight against the U-boats. High-frequency direction finders enabled warships to get much more accurate triangulation fixes on U-boats transmitting from over the horizon, beyond the range of radar. This allowed them to be dispatched at high speed in the direction of the U-boat well before it could come within effective torpedo range of the convoy. More significantly, however, the German naval cipher code was broken by the British (see pp. 116–17) using the first digital program-controlled electronic computers. Cryptoanalysts at Bletchley Park

> '*While in World War I we had the second strongest battle fleet in the world but no appropriate operational base, we now dispose of a strategically favourable operational base; however, we do not have the required battle fleet to operate in the Atlantic.*'
>
> Memo from the German Supreme Naval Command, 21 July 1941

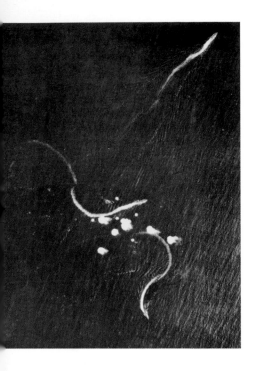

Although a tactical Japanese victory as far as ship losses were concerned, the Battle of the Coral Sea (4–8 May 1942) was a strategic victory for the Allies, since it prevented the Japanese from taking Port Moresby.

'With our sea power making possible the use of all our other resources we gave Japan the choice of surrender or slow but certain death.'

Admiral Chester Nimitz, US Navy

provided the Admiralty with summaries that enabled it to redirect convoys just in time and thus save them from U-boat attacks. Churchill later told King George VI it was thanks to this intelligence that the war had been won. New tactics of anti-submarine warfare, the growing impact of air surveillance of important sea-lanes and, above all, the enormous industrial capacity of the US, which allowed the building of more ships than the Germans could sink, also contributed to the victory of the Allies in the Battle of the Atlantic in 1943. The German submarine arm suffered terrible losses (757 out of 859 U-boats, with almost 30,000 men). More importantly for the Allies, despite their heavy casualties in the defence of naval supremacy in the Atlantic and the Mediterranean, this achievement proved decisive for the successful amphibious landings in Africa, Italy and Normandy in 1942–43 and 1944, and for the Russian war effort.

Compared with the European theatre of war, the war in the Pacific (see Chapter 7) was a naval war to a much greater extent. In its fight against Britain, the US and the Dutch, Japan relied upon its navy. With its carriers, battleships and cruisers the Japanese navy, which was the culmination of a remarkable process of modernization and industrialization, inflicted heavy losses on the Western Allies in the initial phase of the war by using new tactics and unscrupulous methods of aggression. Moreover, Japanese success in the naval war paved the way for its armies to conquer huge parts of the Pacific world in the following months. In return, as soon as the Allies had recovered from their initial shock and regained their strength, their success over the Japanese fleet in a number of battles – beginning with the Battle of Midway in June 1942, as well as the US strategy of island-hopping – led to the surrender of Japan in September 1945. Although carriers escorting convoys with supplies of men and war materials also played an important role in the war against Germany, they proved the backbone of naval forces on both sides in the huge areas of the Pacific. However, the naval war in the Pacific also saw the last large-scale encounters between big ships, which clashed several times off the Philippines and in Japanese home waters; the sinking of *Musashi* and *Yamato*, the biggest battleship ever built, by US aircraft in 1944 made it clear that the end of the battleship era had arrived. While carriers and big ships pushed back the Japanese navy and army, US submarines successfully cut their lines of communication by waging a commerce war against Japanese shipping.

THE COLD WAR, 1949–89

The first nuclear bombs dropped in the final days of the war against Japan in August 1945 helped to end the war in the Pacific; however, they also indicated that future wars might be completely different, whether on land or at sea. Moreover, the experiences of the war and the impact of air power on warfare definitely ended the era of Mahanian battle fleets. Even though the Soviet Union toyed with the idea of building up such a navy in the Stalin era, most battleships in Western navies were scrapped in the late 1940s. HMS *Vanguard*, launched in 1946 and scrapped in 1960, was the last British battleship and the only European one built after World War II; the

'The use of carrier aircraft and Marines in the projection of military force can be an absolute requirement in insuring our control, or continued safe use, of areas of the high seas essential to our national needs.'

Admiral J. Holloway, US Navy, 1976

Jean Bart was the last French battleship to see action, during the Suez Crisis in 1956. The US Navy had more battleships in active service – some of which, such as USS *Wisconsin* and USS *Missouri*, even served in the Gulf War of 1991. By that time, however, they were launching cruise missiles instead of using their main heavy artillery against enemy positions on land.

Carriers, cruisers, destroyers and submarines seemed better able to perform the duties they were assigned in the Cold War era: to deter the Soviets, to safeguard US supplies to Europe in the event of war, to project power in major or minor conflicts, or to support amphibious landings, as in the Korean, Vietnam, Falklands and Gulf wars. Though nuclear-powered carriers and missile cruisers soon expanded the strategic capabilities of Western navies, from the early 1960s on, nuclear-powered submarines became the most important weapon in the nuclear arms race between East and West. Hiding in the oceans or below the North Pole, armed with ballistic missiles and very difficult to detect, they were both the most sophisticated and most dangerous weapon for both sides, allowing them either to deter an enemy attack or to successfully launch a second strike in a nuclear conflagration.

In spite of the strategic importance of nuclear submarines, both sides in the Cold

US aircraft carrier in the Korean War, January 1952. Aircraft carriers played an important role, supporting Allied land forces in their attempt to push back communist troops.

War also maintained, and soon enlarged, their surface fleets. Led by Admiral Gorshkov, the 'Red Tirpitz', the Soviet Union, deeply shocked by US naval superiority during the Cuban missile crisis in 1962, built up its naval forces in the 1960s. Instead of being a navy operating in coastal waters in order to support the army, to undertake amphibious landings or to keep open strategic sea lanes into the Baltic, the Mediterranean or the Atlantic, the Red Navy openly challenged Western naval supremacy on all oceans by acquiring bases wherever possible to extend its spheres of influence in peacetime and in times of crisis, such as the wars in the Middle East. Moreover, enormous funds were channelled into the build-up of bases such as Murmansk or Baltiisk, from which it could threaten NATO supply lines in the Atlantic and the Baltic with its enormous number of submarines of all types, and with modern weaponry such as sea-to-sea missiles launched from cruisers or fast patrol boats. The Soviet navy also copied the United States in seeking to construct aircraft carriers. In the 1970s and 1980s the United States and its allies continued to enlarge and modernize their navies in response . The new aircraft carriers of the Nimitz class and a series of new and far more powerful nuclear submarines of the Ohio and Los Angeles classes – which were part of a new programme intended to create a US navy of 600 ships – thus eventually contributed to the collapse of the Soviet Union, which, despite numerical superiority in many ship classes, simply could no longer afford a quantitative and qualitative race against NATO.

NEW CHALLENGES: THE WAR AGAINST TERRORISM

When the Cold War ended with the fall of the Berlin Wall in 1989 and the unexpected collapse of the Soviet Union in 1991, it was hoped that this would be the end of a century of conflicts and arms races whether on land, in the air or at sea. However, the break-up of Yugoslavia and the increasing number of civil wars in Africa and, of course, in strategically important areas in the Middle East soon made it clear that this was a vain hope. Instead, whereas the fear of a nuclear war had helped to deter the use of force to some extent, Western powers in particular now had to consider intervention in order to stop mass killings among hostile ethnic groups or in defence of their own interests against dictators such as Saddam Hussein and terrorist groups such as al-Qaeda (see Chapter 13). As in all the wars since World War II, air power and land power also proved important in the quick deployment of troops, the massive bombardment of strategic targets and the waging of war on land itself.

However, without sea power success would have been more difficult and more costly. Navies secured supply lines and projected power in areas where neither aeroplanes nor armies could operate for political, military and financial reasons, or simply through a lack of forward bases. Moreover, navies also provided an enormous amount of firepower, from the aircraft on their carriers and the cruise missiles launched from old-fashioned battleships, modern missile cruisers and even submarines. Missiles fired from positions in the Red Sea, the Arabian Sea, the Indian Ocean and the Adriatic hit distant targets in Sudan, Afghanistan, Iraq and Serbia.

In all these conflicts navies displayed their military capabilities both in establishing blockades of hostile countries, such as Serbia in the Adriatic in the 1990s, and in the attempts to restore peace and to defend Western values and interests in strategically important but unsafe areas all over the world. This seems even more

Opposite Chinese sailors march through Tiananmen Square during the National Day parade in Beijing, 1 October 2009.

Below In the Gulf War of 1990–91 and the invasion of Iraq in 2003, the US Navy contributed to military success by launching hundreds of cruise missiles from vessels in the Persian Gulf and the Red Sea.

'*The potential and relevance of maritime power in today's world is as great as ever . . . Maritime forces are mobile, versatile and resilient . . . their ability to poise makes them powerful tools of diplomacy, and a capacity for leverage particularly in the context of expeditionary operations is of greater importance than ever.*'

Principles of British Maritime Doctrine, formulated in 1995

important in a globalized market in which 90 per cent of all goods are transported on the oceans, and in which political and social stability is dependent upon economic prosperity to a large extent. That is why India and China, two incipient superpowers of the 21st century, have decided to modernize and to enlarge their respective navies. While by 2020 the Indian navy is expected to operate three aircraft carriers – currently the most important indicator of naval strength – China has not only built nuclear submarines, but is also toying with the idea of either building or acquiring aircraft carriers.

Recent incidents have further emphasized the pressing need for naval staffs and politicians all over the world to develop new doctrines for fighting enemies that have fundamentally changed in character; to build ships capable of fighting in littoral waters rather than safely escorting troops and all kinds of supplies from the United States to Europe, as in the Cold War era; and to win political and public support for the purchase of new equipment and for naval operations that many once thought would never be seen again.

9 War in the Air

JOHN BUCKLEY

Opposite A US F-15E Strike Eagle deploys flares over Afghanistan, 2008. Counter-insurgency warfare remains air power's biggest challenge in the 21st century.

When NATO's aerial bombardment of Yugoslavia came to an end in May 1999 and victory was achieved without the deployment of ground forces, it appeared that a campaign had at last been won by air power alone. For some, this was a great revelation, and even such sceptics as the distinguished military historian John Keegan acknowledged that air warfare had at last come of age. This followed the apparent success of Allied air power in forcing Saddam Hussein's armies out of Kuwait in 1991. In both cases, however, although air power had laid the foundations for victory, success had been attained through a variety of measures, political and diplomatic, and through the use – or indeed the threat of application – of land forces.

Nevertheless, the success of air forces in these two campaigns appeared to vindicate to a significant degree those air-power theorists, advocates and practitioners who had jealously guarded the independence of air forces around the world in the expectation that one day their prophecies would come to fruition. Ultimately theirs was a search for the ability of air forces to win wars largely independently of other arms and services, and to deliver strategic-level victory quickly and decisively without recourse to long and ruinous land and maritime campaigns. At times this aim blinded air-force leaders to the realities of national strategy and ongoing conflicts, but there is no doubt that over the course of the 20th century air power increasingly came to dominate warfare. Today it is inconceivable that a state would be able to contemplate war without first grappling with the demands of air power.

THE EMERGENCE OF AIR POWER

The first use of aircraft in warfare took place in North Africa in the conflict between Italian and Turkish forces battling over Libya in 1911–12, but the much grander concept of employing air forces at the strategic level – that is, attempting to win wars independently of other arms – had already appeared in novels and short stories, where writers took to imagining, often in fanciful terms, how air forces would shape and dominate future wars. *The War in the Air* (1908), by the noted British author H. G. Wells, fused the growing great-power rivalry in Europe with the emergence of powered controlled flight. His vision was of civilization brought to the point of collapse through the ruinous damage and upheaval caused by air attack.

> '*Aviation is fine as a sport. But as an instrument of war it is worthless.*'
> General Ferdinand Foch, 1911

'When my brother and I built the first man-carrying flying machine, we thought that we were introducing into the world an invention which would make further wars practically impossible.'
Orville Wright, 1917

Growing interest in flight fuelled concern over air power and how it should be integrated into strategic planning, particularly since by 1910 the great powers in Europe appeared to be on a collision course. All the major powers' armed forces seriously investigated the possibilities of employing aircraft in war, although for the most part this centred on reconnaissance and observation, for there were innumerable technological issues facing the offensive use of air power: on the outbreak of war in 1914 there was no effective method of dropping bombs or shooting down enemy aircraft. Indeed, throughout World War I the most important role played by air power was in providing intelligence on the enemy and in directing artillery fire. Even these roles proved troublesome since communications technology was in its infancy, and for much of the war the best and most immediate observational information was relayed from static balloons, which provided excellent if vulnerable platforms for gathering intelligence on the enemy's lines and rear zones.

As the war progressed, however, and reconnaissance aeroplanes became more robust and commonplace, investigation began into methods for destroying such aircraft; there would be considerable advantage in being able to gather information on the enemy's positions while denying the same to them. Nevertheless, it took until late 1915 for the first effective interceptor to be introduced – the Germans' Fokker Eindekker – and it was 1916 before large-scale aerial dog-fighting began. Ironically, although aerial combat was seen as modern and far removed from the attritional slaughter of the trenches, loss rates in air warfare mirrored those of the ground forces. Aero-technology was crude and often poorly tested, and caused huge numbers of flying accidents, while pilots and aircrew had little time to train properly in their unreliable and temperamental aeroplanes. By 1918, although aircraft were being employed in sophisticated ground-attack missions as part of coordinated all-arms operations, loss rates were still running at over 30 per cent.

A Friedrichshafen G.V bomber. Germany employed large bomber aeroplanes for long-range operations, most notably against cities such as London in the summer of 1917.

Right Illustration from 1917 showing a German Albatros aeroplane downed by a French Spad. Aerial combat during World War I was brutal and bloody, far removed from the popular image of the chivalrous aces.

Below Poster warning of the threat posed by German Zeppelins, 1916. Airships provided the first real means of mounting long-range bombing raids, bringing civilians fully into the firing line for the first time.

Air power was also employed at the strategic level in World War I, and it was this that drew most attention from air-power advocates. In 1914 the only aircraft capable of conducting long-range operations and of carrying worthwhile payloads of bombs were airships, and in this field the Germans led the way, principally with their famous Zeppelins. In 1915 Germany began targeting England in the first sustained bombing campaign, but weather, navigational difficulties and improving air defences increased airship loss rates, and by 1916–17 long-range aeroplanes, such as the Gotha, were being used by the Germans. Once again, however, technical issues and mounting loss rates caused the campaign to lose impetus, and results were poor. The psychological impact, however, was much more profound than the physical, and in 1918 the British government was moved to form the first independent air arm, the Royal Air Force, with a key task of air defence, in

> '*Air warfare is a shot through the brain,*
> *not a hacking to pieces of the enemy's body.*'
> Major General J. F. C. Fuller, 1935

response to the public outcry over the manner in which the Germans were apparently able to drop bombs with impunity on London. Although the reality was much different, it appeared to some analysts that the morale-sapping effects of bombing on civilian populations were more important than the actual physical damage, and this was underscored during the Allies' postwar investigation of their own 1918 bombing campaign.

As the Great War came to an end, it was clear that there had been great leaps forward in air warfare: almost all the major roles and duties conducted by air forces in later wars were presaged by operations in World War I. Nevertheless, it was also apparent that that war had done much more for air power than air power had contributed to the outcome of the conflict.

THE SEARCH FOR A ROLE, 1918–39

In the aftermath of World War I, despite the cries of 'never again' and the war being labelled as the war to end all wars, political leaders realized that war was still a distinct possibility in the future; what they did not want, however, was a repeat of the Western Front and a long, four-year attritional struggle. Air power appeared to offer an alternative, through the policy of strategic bombing (see box on pp. 182–83). The effects of bombing on civilian populations, and the possibilities of direct attack on enemy cities and industries, provided the opportunity to deliver a quick victory. Moreover, there appeared to be no defence against bombing: by the time defending fighter aircraft were scrambled and in a position to intercept, the enemy bomber fleet would have already done its work. Air-power theorists and advocates such as the Italian Giulio Douhet emphasized that the first strike would be crucial and should be as destructive as possible in order to shock an enemy state into a rapid capitulation. He even advocated the widespread use of poison gas. Such a

'Would not the sight of a single enemy airplane be enough to induce a formidable panic? Normal life would be unable to continue under the constant threat of death and imminent destruction.'

General Giulio Douhet, 1921

German aircraft such as the Junkers Ju 52 were used by Nationalist forces during the Spanish Civil War. The German Air Force was also able to learn lessons from the fighting.

'*The cavalry, in particular, were not friendly to the aeroplane, which it was believed, would frighten the horses.*'
Sir Walter Raleigh, official RAF historian between the wars, 1922

campaign would be brutal, but it would end the war quickly, short-circuiting the slide into a long struggle that would ultimately cost far more in lives and resources.

Such a vision of war had little widespread political appeal in the 1920s, but all the major air forces examined the possibilities of strategic bombing. The USSR, Britain and the United States were particularly enamoured of the idea: for the Soviets it appeared to be a modern and revolutionary way to fight a war, while for the British it offered the chance to avoid having to commit its manpower to the trenches of the Western Front again. There was, however, little funding available to support the development of strategic air forces until the 1930s and, when Europe again slid towards war, much was changing both politically and technologically. Germany and France, committed to possible continental land warfare, channelled their air resources towards this role and away from long-range bombing, despite the protests of air-power advocates, while in the USSR Stalin's purges decapitated the Red Air Force. From being the largest strategic air force in the world, by the outbreak of war the Soviet air arm was firmly focused on army support. Only in Britain and the United States, distanced from continental Europe both physically and politically, did strategic air power develop. Yet many of the practical aspects of how to conduct such a campaign – navigation, targeting, endurance, defence – were too quickly glossed over, particularly in the RAF.

'*The bomber will always get through. The only defence is in offence, which means that you have to kill more women and children more quickly than the enemy if you want to save yourselves.*'
Stanley Baldwin, British prime minister, 1932

There were also growing technological developments that served to raise concerns over the viability of strategic bombing, most notably in the mid-1930s the emergence of radar (see box on p. 105) and heavily armed, high-performance interceptors.

On a global scale mastery of the air also began to change the power relationships between the industrialized countries and their imperial possessions. Air forces provided a much cheaper method of controlling and containing colonial regions and peoples than deploying large numbers of troops and resources. Aircraft also carried a psychological presence that demonstrated imperial power and technological superiority over non-industrialized populations. If necessary, air power could prove effective enough in some cases to actually enforce imperial power, as demonstrated by the British in Iraq and Palestine, the French and Spanish in North Africa, and the United States in Central America. By 1939 air forces around the world had developed and demonstrated independence both in attitude and capability. Air warfare was viewed by all as crucially important in any future conflict, and, in the case of aerial bombardment of civilians with high explosives and poison gas, appeared to be a horrifying and potentially devastating prospect.

WORLD WAR II

The mid-1930s through to the early 1950s, a period that included World War II, was an age of mass air power, one in which vast fleets of aeroplanes were developed, capable of delivering devastating attacks and dominating warfare. Aero-technology

'The Nazis entered this war under the rather childish delusion that they were going to bomb everyone else, and nobody was going to bomb them. At Rotterdam, London, Warsaw, and half a hundred other places, they put their rather naive theory into operation. They sowed the wind, and now they are going to reap the whirlwind.'

Air Marshal Arthur Harris, RAF, 1942

had taken a great leap forward in the years prior to the outbreak of war in 1939, as older biplanes of limited speed, firepower and payload capacity were replaced by faster, sleeker and more dynamic all-metal monoplanes carrying greater arrays of weaponry. Yet the aircraft were not so advanced and expensive as to preclude mass production, as was the case in the subsequent Cold War – a result of technological developments such as the jet-propelled aircraft, which became operational in the last year of the war.

When war came in 1939, although the potential for devastating strategic bombing was emerging, no one was prepared to carry it through or was capable of doing so. As the Germans swept all before them they employed their air forces to win control of the airspace over a military theatre, in order to seize and retain the initiative, before conducting a variety of operational and occasionally tactical-level duties in support of the campaign's aims. In part this concept, known as the 'operational air war', included close air support, but less than 10 per cent of the Luftwaffe was designated for direct army support. Better prepared than their opponents and able to grasp the necessity of using air power to support immediate campaign necessities, the Luftwaffe proved remarkably effective until deeper weaknesses were exposed, such as their inability to sustain losses for any length of time and the paucity of their long-term planning and resources.

View into the hall of a Soviet aircraft factory, where Ilyushin Il-2 Shturmovik ground attack aircraft are being assembled, 1941. Soviet production of aircraft alone outstripped that of Germany.

Over Britain in 1940 the Luftwaffe failed to suppress the RAF, a force deliberately designed to mount a sustained strategic air-defence campaign. Against the Soviet Union in 1941 and 1942, when called upon to fight a much larger campaign than had been planned for, and with fewer resources than they had admitted possessing, the Luftwaffe soon began to haemorrhage to death, especially in the harsh operating conditions of Russia's bleak winters. By the mid-point of the war it was confronted by Allied air forces that matched it in quality and surpassed it in quantity, and from early 1944 onwards German air power went into a sharp decline. Pilot training, for example, had to be curtailed in order to make good front-line losses, which in turn increased casualty rates and thus propelled the Luftwaffe into a vicious downward spiral, despite the development of cutting-edge aero-technology such as the Messerschmitt Me 262 jet fighter-bomber.

The Soviets rapidly recovered from the heavy losses of 1941, when some 90 per cent of the Red Air Force was lost, but stuck slavishly to a model of army support and paid little attention to long-range bombing operations, which accounted for less than 5 per cent of their air activity. Nevertheless, the Soviet model, which aimed to guarantee air superiority and battlefield support over the key operational areas in any given campaign, worked well enough. The Soviets had not set out to attain air supremacy, by which the German air force would have been swept from the skies across the entire theatre, and indeed the scale of such an undertaking would have been immense. Nevertheless, by 1945 Soviet air power was robust and in many ways a match for Western air power.

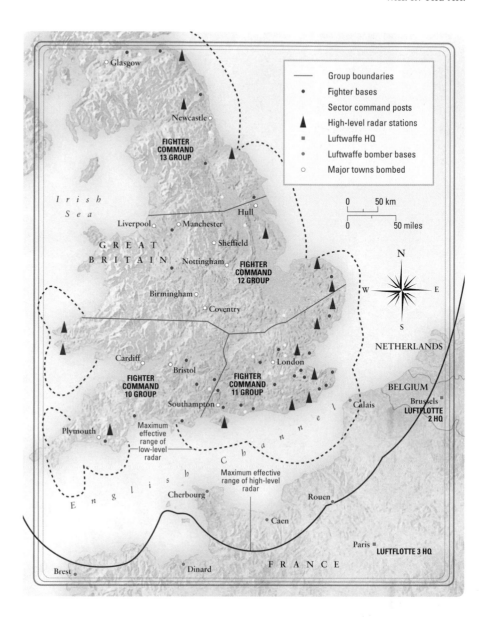

Group boundaries
• Fighter bases
• Sector command posts
▲ High-level radar stations
■ Luftwaffe HQ
• Luftwaffe bomber bases
○ Major towns bombed

0   50 km
0   50 miles

Right The Battle of Britain (July–September 1940), in which the Luftwaffe tried, and failed, to seize vital air superiority.

Below The Messerschmitt Me 262 jet fighter-bomber was ground-breaking in design, but suffered from technical weaknesses. In addition, dwindling numbers of trained pilots and diminishing fuel supplies limited its impact.

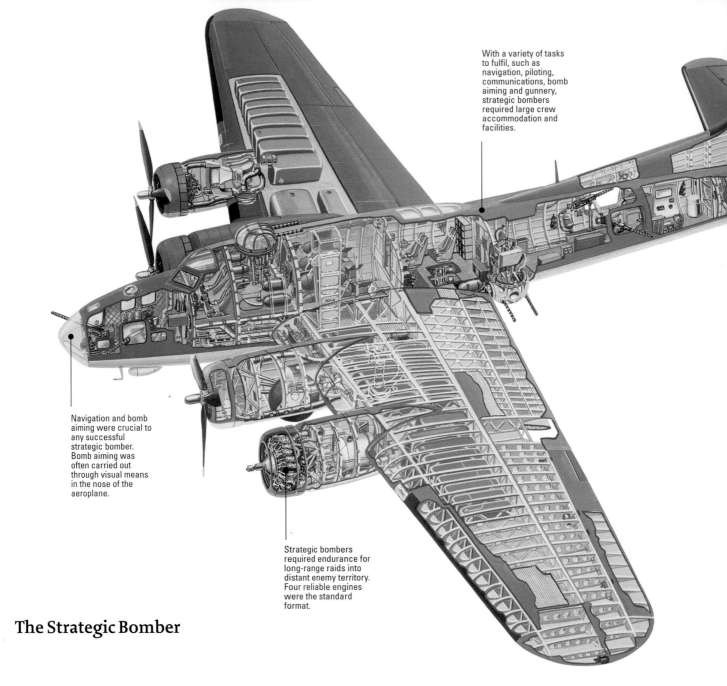

With a variety of tasks to fulfil, such as navigation, piloting, communications, bomb aiming and gunnery, strategic bombers required large crew accommodation and facilities.

Navigation and bomb aiming were crucial to any successful strategic bomber. Bomb aiming was often carried out through visual means in the nose of the aeroplane.

Strategic bombers required endurance for long-range raids into distant enemy territory. Four reliable engines were the standard format.

The Strategic Bomber

The most iconic representation of destructive air power is the strategic bomber, a weapon that dominated air-power theory in the first half of the 20th century. The first true strategic bombers were airships, but, as orthodox aeroplanes began to appear with sufficient range and payload capacity, the unwieldy and expensive airship soon began to be replaced. Many technical issues such as bomb aiming and navigation remained unresolved,

however, even by the start of World War II; until technologically advanced aircraft such as the Lancaster and B-17 Flying Fortress were coupled with effective radar equipment, the results of bombing remained disappointing. Even in the 1942–45 era bombers had to be backed with vast resources and escort fighters to reap the best rewards.

Nevertheless, by the last year of the war the Allies' strategic air fleets projected the power to devastate cities,

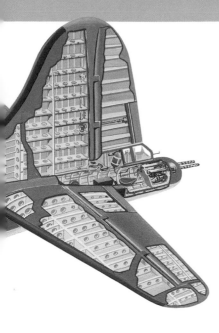

Opposite The Boeing B-17 Flying Fortress. First flown in the 1930s, this iconic long-range bomber was used in great numbers in Europe and the Pacific theatres.

Above right The Boeing B-52H Stratofortress, the last of the classic strategic bombers. Although tested and developed in the early 1960s, it was still in operation in the 21st century.

Right Two F-22 Raptor fighters and one B-2 Spirit bomber – the key strategic stealth platforms in the US Air Force inventory – flying in formation over Guam, Western Pacific.

the most infamous example being the controversial raid on Dresden in February 1945 – commanded by the RAF's Arthur 'Bomber' Harris and the USAAF's Carl 'Tooey' Spaatz – in which as many as 80,000 people may have perished. Such actions brought into question the whole concept of civilian losses in war as a result of aerial bombardment. The most famous postwar strategic bomber, the American B-52, remains in service in the 21st century. However, in the late 1950s the large multi-engined bomber was supplanted by the missile as the principal strategic air weapon, and only with the development of the 'silver bullet' concept – exemplified by the B-2 – in which a high-tech precision-delivery platform can offer the highest possible chance of a successful attack, has the larger bomber found a continuing role, albeit as a precision weapon.

Above British Lancaster bombers on a night-time raid over Germany. Although less accurate, such raids reduced bomber losses. British poster, 1943.

Above right The American P-51 Mustang Mk IA. It was initially something of a disappointment, but later versions of the Mustang, fitted with British-designed engines, changed the face of the strategic air war in Europe.

The Western Allies, however, had taken a different path, one that was governed by the need to dominate the airspace over a theatre completely. Over the Atlantic air power provided a crucial weapon in the battle to secure the shipping lanes. The Allies also had to mount a variety of amphibious landings from 1942 onwards, and these were fraught with difficulties. Against Japan in the Pacific, it was vital to American prospects that the Japanese navy's air arm was eliminated as a threat prior to any major Allied amphibious offensives, and in a series of major battles this was achieved by June 1944. Air support was also crucial in bolstering amphibious operations in the Mediterranean theatre, and experience there resulted in the drive to win complete air supremacy, a strategy that would serve the Allies well in the invasion of France in 1944. Through the massive investment made in building and training vast air fleets, and because of the attrition imposed upon the Luftwaffe when defending German airspace against the Allied strategic bombing fleets, Allied air supremacy was attained in 1944 to such an extent that the Luftwaffe virtually ceased to exist as a major fighting force. The support provided by the Allied tactical air forces in ground operations from D-Day onwards was considerable, and German troops complained bitterly that they were never able to function properly in 1944–45 because of the suffocating effects of Allied air power.

Despite these achievements, however, it is the strategic bombing campaigns of World War II that stand out as being the most significant air-warfare developments of the age. Although in 1940 RAF Bomber Command could stage only pitiful and near-fruitless bombing raids, mounted by inadequate and under-resourced squadrons,

> '*Hitler built a fortress around Europe, but he forgot to put a roof on it.*'
> US President Franklin D. Roosevelt, 1941

'We saw terrible things: cremated adults shrunk to the size of small children, pieces of arms and legs, dead people, whole families burnt to death . . . and fire everywhere, everywhere fire, and all the time the hot wind of the firestorm threw people back into the burning houses they were trying to escape from.'

Lothar Metzger, survivor of the Dresden bombing, February 1945

by 1944 the Allies, with the RAF and USAAF's combined bombing offensive fully under way, were able to mete out punishing air raids that could devastate cities. Difficulties in targeting, navigation and bombing accuracy were slowly overcome in the face of heavy losses, but the real breakthrough came when Allied air chiefs finally recognized that, in order to maximize the effectiveness of the bombing fleet, control of the airspace over Germany needed to be won. This could only be done by deliberately targeting the Luftwaffe's fighter defences, and from mid-1943 onwards this became Allied strategy. When high-performance long-range fighters such as the Mustang began to escort bombers into Germany in daylight, the bombing campaign turned decisively in favour of the Allies. In the Pacific, Japanese resistance to American long-range bombing was less well organized, and when the United States switched to area bombing with incendiaries in March 1945, the effects on Japan's population were dramatic: some 100,000 civilians were killed in one night's bombing of Tokyo, for example.

The strategic effects of bombing were significant indeed, and German production was limited and distorted by the raids to an extent that severely afflicted the country's ability to wage war, though it was never enough to force the collapse of the German state, as some arch-advocates had hoped. Against Japan the strategic benefits of bombing were less obvious: Japanese military production was collapsing anyway in the spring of 1945, and, as in the case of Germany, the belief that devastating attacks would force Japan's military leadership to throw in the towel appears to have been mistaken. To this day there rages a controversy over the necessity of dropping the atomic bombs on Japan, and some have even argued that it was Cold War politics more than military factors that dictated the use of the weapons. This latter point is dubious, but there can be no doubt that the atomic bombings heralded a new age in warfare, one in which mass destruction from the air began to dictate strategy and diplomacy in a way hitherto unseen with any other weapon.

'The very streets were rivers of fire. . .while the people themselves burned like match sticks.'

Japanese survivor of the Tokyo bombing, March 1945

THE COLD WAR

As the United States and the Soviet Union began to square up to each other in the aftermath of World War II, in a confrontation now widely described as the Cold War (see Chapter 11), the role of air power began to change. Indeed, once it was linked with the devastating force of nuclear weaponry, air power actually threatened to change the dynamics of war for ever. If war could result in near total destruction for both sides, as was to become distinctly possible in any superpower conflict from the late 1950s onwards, then major war itself became almost redundant as a political tool other than as a deterrent. Such considerations were to shape the place and nature of air warfare markedly in the post-1945 era.

Most obviously, in order to ensure that one side did not consider the use of force to be viable, that side had to be convinced that its enemy had the capacity and will to deliver a massive attack using atomic weaponry. By the 1950s air forces were therefore driven to develop the ability to drop mass area blast weapons such as atomic bombs on the enemy in order to maintain this balance. Obviously both sides endeavoured to gain advantages, and neither the United States nor Soviet military ever openly admitted that a winnable war could not be prosecuted, but politicians usually regarded the threat of destruction from the air as too great a risk to warrant open war. This was to become more overt still when missiles replaced aeroplanes as the strategic delivery method for nuclear weapons in the 1960s. In particular, the advent of the intercontinental ballistic missile (ICBM) – a weapon with which the two superpowers could hit each other within minutes, and a long-term product of rocket designs dating back to World War II – made the threat of nuclear holocaust so much more immediate. The threat was brought even closer with the development of submarine-launched ballistic missiles, with which the USSR could cancel out the advantage held by the United States in the form of missiles based in Europe aimed at the heart of the Soviet Union.

The secondary effect of the Cold War was that the priority given to confronting enemies with air-launched nuclear weapons undermined other aspects of air power.

*'We're going to bomb them
back into the Stone Age.'*
General Curtis E. LeMay, US Air Force, 1965

Accuracy was deemed less important, and conventional forms of air power were often relegated in value because strategists believed that a war would 'go nuclear' very quickly anyway, so tactical operations would play a limited role. In addition, technology was advancing so quickly

that unit costs of modern, sophisticated jets, weapons and training programmes were such that the price of first-class air-power status soon grew exponentially. There were only limited resources, and indeed conventional air forces were more expensive to build and maintain than nuclear weapons. Consequently there were political and economic driving forces behind the emphasis on strategic air forces designed to meet the threat of superpower confrontation.

Even though the United States and the Soviet Union effectively avoided direct conflict, they nevertheless indulged in proxy wars around the globe, hoping to shape the world to their ends. This eventually drew both into employing air forces in support of conventional operations, and indeed into types of conflict such as counter-insurgency wars – for example Vietnam for the Americans (1965–73) and Afghanistan for the Soviets (1979–89). Here, political constraints and new ground-to-air weapons technology undermined the efforts of supposedly modern air forces against an enemy that could not be directly and overwhelmingly crushed from the air for political reasons, or that hid within a civilian population. The large-scale use of indiscriminate air bombardment in low-intensity conflicts or when an enemy could not be clearly identified was simply unwarranted, and US air power for much of the Vietnam War was unable to contribute as fully as it surely would have done in a more obviously high-intensity inter-state conflict, despite the fact that more bomb tonnage was dropped on South-East Asia than had been dropped in World War II.

By the 1970s military thinkers had begun to re-evaluate NATO's strategy for meeting a Warsaw Pact (see p. 217) threat in Europe. Since the Korean War (see Chapter 11) there had been little stomach for the scale of high-maintenance and costly conventional forces necessary to stop a Soviet-led attack in Central Europe; the

Opposite A US B-52 drops a bomb load onto Viet Cong positions during the Vietnam War, March 1968. Despite the heavy bombing, the strategic effect of air power was limited in South-East Asia.

Below Aerial view of damage inflicted by a US B-52 bombing strike north of Dai Tieng, Vietnam, 1968.

Below right A naked girl and others escape an accidental napalm bombing of their village by South Vietnamese government planes, Trang Bang, South Vietnam, 8 June 1972.

cheaper option was to rely on tactical nuclear weapons to balance things out. This, however, would almost certainly have escalated into a major strategic nuclear exchange with resulting devastation. In order to make a campaign in Central Europe viable, therefore, a new doctrine for defence was required, which eventually became the 'AirLand Battle'. This foresaw an integrated war-fighting area in which precision weapons, directed by cutting-edge technology, would more than counterbalance the Warsaw Pact's superiority in numbers. The development of precision-guided munitions, such as the Tomahawk cruise missile in the 1980s, ratcheted up the cost of first-class air-power status to a level that only the United States could meet. Air forces played an integral role in this concept as they carried the ability to project fast-manoeuvring firepower deep into the enemy's rear zones. New emerging high technology in the United States presented the opportunity to make AirLand Battle a reality, and, though the Cold War came to an end before it became truly viable, the mere threat of it contributed to the Soviet Union's desire to bring an end to the confrontation with the West sooner rather than later.

THE SPACE RACE

The emergence of new technology like the ICBM also propelled the Cold War into space from the 1950s onwards. Rocket technology developed from the Third Reich's programmes aided the push for artificial satellites by the Cold War powers, and in 1957 the Soviets won the first round with *Sputnik*. They followed this with the first man in space in 1961; the US response, following hefty investment, was a man on the moon by the end of the decade. Further US lunar expeditions placed the Americans clearly in the lead in space, but it was the desire to make military use out of this lead that particularly threatened the balance of power in the Cold War.

The test launch of a *Bumper* V-2 at Cape Canaveral, Florida, 1950 – an ambitious two-stage rocket programme.

In the 1980s Ronald Reagan put in place a programme that became known rather disparagingly as 'Star Wars'. The aim was to develop new high-tech weapons such as lasers and particle beams that could stop a nuclear missile attack on the United States. As previous deterrent strategy had assumed that an attack could not be prevented, Star Wars potentially created a destabilizing effect and might have forced the Soviets into a pre-emptive strike or action before their nuclear arsenal was rendered redundant. In the event, Star Wars came to very little in the 1980s because the technological problems were too great, and in any case from the middle of the decade onwards the Soviet Union began to disintegrate. Under the administration of George W. Bush the concept re-emerged, known as 'Son of Star Wars' or 'Star Wars II', in an effort to make the United States impervious to any missile threat, whether launched from an enemy such as Russia or by a rogue state or group. Such an umbrella system of anti-missile high-technology weapons is still some way off, however.

AFTER THE COLD WAR

In the aftermath of Vietnam, US air-power theorists began a major rethink about the structure of their air forces and the nature of their air-power doctrine. How should air forces be used in the future? By the end of the Cold War new thinking had emerged, best encapsulated in the writings of Colonel John Warden of the US Air Force. He refocused the purpose of air power back onto the delivery of a clear and relevant politico-strategic benefit, not just brute force intended to pummel an opponent into submission. The greatest impact would probably be a direct hit on the enemy's leadership in an effort to decapitate the state, induce shock and paralysis, and force a quick resolution. In addition, this strategy would target those who had most likely precipitated the war, and consequently there would be less public anguish about the use of force, especially since civilian casualties would be kept to a minimum. Political restraints on the use of quick, shattering air strikes have hindered the full employment of Warden's vision, but the invasion of Iraq in 2003 has been its closest approximation (see Chapter 13).

Many campaigns since 1991 have in truth proved much too messy to allow such a direct and obvious employment of air power. Indeed, perhaps the greatest challenge facing air forces since the end of the Cold War has been the growth in low-intensity conflicts and in peacekeeping and implementation operations. Although greatest attention has been paid to the conduct of the two Gulf wars (1991 and 2003), in reality such styles of war, involving heavy attacks by air forces against enemy states and their armed forces, have become less likely: few have the military force, bravado and desire to confront the United States in such circumstances. More likely are low-intensity campaigns in which dissident and insurgent groups provide the threat, perhaps in a civil war context. In such circumstances surgical strikes become vitally important, and the drive towards precision targeting and attacks by weapons such as the cruise missile has had both military and political benefits. Nevertheless, these operations are difficult and awkward to conduct, and do not conform easily to modern air-war theory. How air power meets this challenge in the age of the so-called War on Terror will determine how relevant it remains to warfare.

A US soldier examines the impact point of a precision-guided 5,000-lb (2268-kg) bomb that entered through the dome of a government building in Baghdad.

'What's the sense of sending $2 million missiles to hit a $10 tent that's empty?'
US President George W. Bush, September 2001

10 End of Empire

François Cochet

KEY DATES

Late 1930s Growth of independence movements in many colonies

1942 Formation of PETA army in Indonesia under the occupying Japanese

September 1945 Start of the Indonesian Revolution against the Netherlands; the Viet Minh declare unilateral Indochinese independence; beginning of the First Indochina War; the Palestinian Jews begin a war of independence against the British

1947 The Cold War begins; the Eastern bloc supports insurrectionist movements against colonizing nations

1948 Emergence of the Mau Mau rebel movement in Kenya; start of communist insurrection in Malaya

15 May 1948 Proclamation of the state of Israel

27 December 1949 Indonesia becomes independent

1952–56 Mau Mau uprising

7 May 1954 Viet Minh communist revolutionaries defeat French forces at Dien Bien Phu

1 November 1954 – 19 March 1962 Algerian War of Independence

4 February 1961 Angolan War of Independence begins

15 January 1975 The Alvor Agreement grants independence to Angola and ends Portuguese colonization

Opposite French soldiers surrender to the Vietnam People's Army in a carefully prepared propaganda picture, 1954.

After World War II the colonial powers were confronted by a wholesale questioning of the colonial system, which resulted in many wars of varying intensity. The causes were diverse and profound. The 1930s saw the development of nationalist movements throughout the colonies, many going back to the 1914–18 war, when those peoples made significant investments of manpower to support their ruling countries, and from then on felt entitled to a more equitable distribution of power between colonizers and colonized. This was particularly so in the British and French empires, which recruited large numbers of soldiers from their subject nations. World War II played an equally important role in this change of attitude. The Japanese waged an intensive propaganda war against the white populations in the countries they conquered in 1942, especially against the Dutch, and the Americans added fuel to the fire by becoming a mouthpiece for anti-colonialism. All these factors, together with the atmosphere created by the Cold War after 1947, led to a wide variety of 'wars of decolonization'.

Strictly speaking, it is difficult to categorize these as 'wars', because the term does not quite fit. The daily lives of the soldiers involved consisted more often than not of searching people, houses and areas; and there were police operations, ambushes and skirmishes when, for example, new roads were being opened up. But as in all such revolutionary episodes, it was difficult to identify an enemy that could swiftly merge with the rest of the population. In any case, the scale of these conflicts varied considerably, and in fact it was only in the French Empire that one could talk of war in the true sense of the word, above all in Indochina.

GUERRILLA WARFARE AND SMALL-SCALE CONFLICTS

Kenya

Britain, which presided over the largest empire in the world, was affected by many different kinds of revolution, which obliged it to maintain a system of National Service until 1960. The Mau Mau rebellion in Kenya (1952–56) was not a true war of independence, but it anticipated the ethnic conflicts that have continued to cause bloodshed throughout Africa right up to the present day. The secret society of the Mau Mau was formed about 1948, to gain increased access to the land north of Nairobi. In 1952 it unleashed violent attacks on white farmers and their employees. But this was also an intertribal war, with the Kikuyu rebels trying to dominate other tribes in Kenya. Mau Mau gangs attacked Naivasha and Lari on 26 March 1953, and in May the same year General Sir George Erskine took overall command of the security

'When the Missionaries arrived, the Africans had the Land and the Missionaries had the Bible. They taught us how to pray with our eyes closed. When we opened them, they had the Land and we had the Bible.'

Jomo Kenyatta, future Kenyan prime minister, on colonialism, 1932

forces (British and African soldiers, members of the police and Kikuyu loyalists), some 55,000 men in total, supported by air and artillery. The Mau Mau warriors were believed to be about 15,000 in number, and were poorly armed.

In 1954 General Erskine launched an operation code-named 'Anvil', in which about 17,000 suspects were rounded up and put in detention camps, where they were not particularly well treated; this gave rise to fierce controversy. Conventional military operations failed to quell the Mau Mau rebellion, and it was Erskine's successors, General Gerald Lathbury and General Frank Kitson, who introduced an effective tactic of anti-subversion by opposing the Mau Mau with loyalist African troops, including former members of the Mau Mau itself. It was during one of these counter-guerrilla campaigns that the Mau Mau leader, Dedan Kimathi, was captured, in October 1956; he was hanged in 1957. Police operations, which ended in 1960, finally drove the insurgents into the Aberdare Mountains, and their leader, Jomo Kenyatta, was arrested. The revolution resulted in the deaths of some 10,000 Mau Mau, 1,888 civilians and 612 members of the security forces.

Malaya

The Malayan Communist Party already existed before World War II, but it changed its name to the Malayan People's Anti-Japanese Army to wage guerrilla warfare against the invaders. In August 1948 Chin Peng, Maoist leader of the Malayan Races Liberation Army (MRLA), launched a rebellion against the authorities in Kuala Lumpur, who appealed to the British for help. Some 5,000 communist partisans, armed with weapons taken from the British and the Japanese, developed techniques of harassment and terrorism, with an increasing number of surprise attacks on the 40,000 soldiers sent to suppress the revolt. Following Mao's 'fish in the water' tactics, which based guerrilla operations on civilian support and cover, the Malayan communists used local people – especially the Chinese community – to supply them with provisions and launched raids on convoys, as well as carrying out assassinations, including that of the British high commissioner, Sir Henry Gurney, in 1952.

A British military team then waged an anti-guerrilla campaign that proved to be extremely efficient. General Gerald Templer reorganized the Malayan security forces. Anticipating the tactics of the French army in Algeria, he relocated rural communities into 'New Villages', which were meticulously demarcated and controlled. A strict check was kept on food supplies, to ensure that they were not used to fuel the rebellion. General Sir Harold Briggs and General Sir Walter Walker implemented a complex, coherent strategy, which entailed winning over the local people. It was supported, however, by a network of posts fortified with artillery, which acted as a magnet to the guerrillas of the Malayan Races Liberation Army but could be rapidly reinforced with troops transported by helicopter. This operational link between troops on the ground and back-up from the air was an extraordinary new tactic, which the French copied in Algeria and the Americans in Vietnam. Its success was spectacular. Malaya gained its independence in 1957, and by 1960 terrorist activities had virtually ceased. This was the only genuine victory by a former colonial power over communist subversion. Between 1948 and 1960, 509 Britons were killed, 1.27 per cent of the forces deployed, but losses among the civilian population during the same period were reckoned to be in the region of 13,000.

Above British troops of the Special Air Service (SAS) are dropped off in the jungle to search for bandits, Malaya, 1953.

Opposite The Kikuyu Home Guard show their prowess with bow and arrow as they prepare to fight Mau Mau rebels, Kenya, 1953.

'The jungle has been neutralized.'

Sir Gerald Templer, high commissioner of Malaya, 1952

Palestine

Another region that lay under British control was Palestine, and there the situation was very different and far more complex. The Arabs wanted emancipation from British rule, which had been ratified by the League of Nations in 1920, while at the same time the Jewish community, which had rapidly increased from the 1930s onwards, wanted to establish its own state, particularly to provide a home for the survivors of the Holocaust. Even before World War II, the Haganah, an organization dedicated to the formation of a Jewish state in Palestine, had secretly created a fighting force, along with branches for medicine, intelligence and the procurement of weapons. A more radical organization, called the Irgun, was formed in 1932, and on 1 January 1944 it decided to take armed action under the command of Menachem Begin. Prominent British figures, such as Lord Moyne, were assassinated.

September 1945 saw the true beginnings of a 'war of independence'. Faced by a British force of about 100,000 men, the Zionist groups numbered just a few thousand

Troops inspect the wreckage of the King David Hotel in Jerusalem – headquarters of the British Mandate – shortly after it was bombed by the Zionist Irgun group, 22 July 1946.

militants. They launched military-style operations against the British, for instance attacking the camp at Atlit to release immigrant internees. There was increasing sabotage of railways and air bases such as Qastina and Kefar Syrkin, while the prison at Acre was taken and the Jewish prisoners released. On 22 July 1946 Irgun blew up the headquarters of the British authorities in Palestine, located at the King David Hotel in Jerusalem, and 91 people were killed. In April 1948 the Haganah launched the first major operation within the framework of 'Plan D', the aim of which was to control the borders of the Hebrew state as laid down by the United Nations Partition Plan. This operation entailed the seizure of Arab villages and the expulsion of their inhabitants in order to gain access to the sea. On 15 May 1948 the British evacuated Palestine.

Although the first Arab–Israeli war cannot really be said to belong to this discussion, one extremely important element of the military plan must nevertheless be emphasized. The first war of 1948, following the creation of the state of Israel on 15 May, was itself a conventional infantry battle, supported by artillery and armoured cars. The Israel Defence Forces (Tzahal) were formed on 31 May. This gives a clear indication of the speed with which the Israelis were able to consolidate their power. The experience gained by the 30,000 Palestinian Jews who had fought for the Jewish Brigade as part of the British army during World War II proved to be decisive. This marked the beginning of the still unresolved Palestine problem (see Chapter 12).

Indonesia

The Dutch experienced a genuine war of decolonization in Indonesia, which had been conquered in the 17th century and partly provided the basis for the Netherlands' wealth. During World War II the Japanese had seized the two main islands of Java and Sumatra, in March 1942, and in the early days of their occupation encouraged the theme of independence through virulent anti-white racism. They authorized the establishment of a small Indonesian army, PETA (Volunteer Army of Defenders of the Homeland), which undoubtedly served as a testing ground for the freedom fighters. At the end of the war, the Dutch thought they could restore their traditional ties with their Indonesian colony. On 17 August 1945, however, Sukarno – leader of the pro-independence party – unilaterally declared independence. In mid-September 1945 the British landed at Surabaya to give support to the Dutch, and PETA went into action. Very soon the allied Dutch and British forces were forced to cede the interior of the country to the insurgents and to retreat to the coast.

The Dutch army was extremely weak in 1945, having undergone total reconstruction after its heavy defeat in 1940 and five years of occupation by the Nazis, and there was an acute shortage of transport – particularly shipping. The *pemuda* gangs, the poorly armed young freedom fighters who harassed the Dutch troops in Java between 1945 and 1949, became a symbol for the Indonesian nation's armed rebellion against the colonial powers. Under Hubertus Johannes Van Mook, the Dutch launched two 'policing operations', the first in summer 1947. The United Nations imposed a ceasefire on 4 August 1947, bringing the military success of Dutch forces to a halt. But this ceasefire was very weak, and conflict broke out anew in February 1948. The second operation, in December 1948, with a large force of 160,000 soldiers and heavy armour, including US Sherman tanks, did enormous damage to

Guerrilla Warfare

Techniques of guerrilla warfare vary considerably according to time, place, and the weapons and equipment that are available. Immediately after World War II, the Jewish Haganah, Irgun and Stern Gang groups invented urban terrorism, which attacked the symbolic power centres of the British. At the same time, the Viet Minh put into practice the principles of 'revolutionary warfare' as devised by Mao Zedong at the beginning of the 1930s. This was a South-East Asian version of rural Marxism-Leninism; the aim was to control local communities by establishing a dual political and military organization – tactics also used in other parts of the world, notably Algeria.

One common factor of guerrilla warfare was the need for a 'sanctuary' to which a group that found itself in trouble could go for help. The Viet Minh had China after 1949, and the Algerian ALN found refuge in Tunisia and Morocco, both of which were already independent.

For the armies that opposed the guerrillas, these wars of decolonization were not very conducive to technological innovation. Napalm was one relatively new weapon, used in Indochina and then later in Algeria and Angola. The British used helicopters for the first time in Malaya, and they were also employed by the French as tactical weapons in Algeria – an experiment repeated by the Americans in Vietnam and, on a smaller scale, by the Portuguese in Angola and Mozambique.

Above A helicopter arrives to evacuate US troops wounded in the battle for A Shau Valley, South Vietnam, 30 April 1968.

Below Israeli Haganah fighters in the Arab Quarter of Haifa, 1948.

British tanks passing through Surabaya, Indonesia, 1945. The British were supporting Dutch attempts to re-establish ties with their former colony.

the international image of the Netherlands, which was accused of massacring the Indonesians. Many Indonesian leaders were captured during Operation Crow, as it was known, although republican forces refused to surrender. But the failure of the Dutch forces to control the countryside and villages was complete. Attacks on the cities of Surakarta and Yogyakarta in December showed that military defeat was very near. American pressure (notably by way of the Marshall Plan) led the Dutch to recognize their defeat, and in January 1949 they accepted the reinstatement of the Indonesian government.

The Indonesian War of Independence was in fact the most significant ever fought by the Dutch forces. The campaign was far from being as straightforward as had first been imagined: the troops were far from home, and the chain of logistics was an extremely complex one. The conflict proved very expensive for a country that had just emerged from World War II, and conditions soon made it necessary to introduce conscription – which in itself was a problem, since it ran contrary to the convictions of the younger generation in the Netherlands, who did not understand the purpose of the war. Of the 160,000 soldiers fighting in Indonesia in 1947, 100,000 were conscripts. The estimated loss of life was 2,500 Dutch, or 1.56 per cent of the fighting force, and about 5,000 Indonesians.

Angola

The Portuguese wars of decolonization – in Angola, Mozambique, Guinea-Bissau and Cape Verde – take us to a different level of military action. Angola had been Portuguese since the 16th century, but the country did not come under complete Portuguese control until 1920. As in many other regions throughout the world, independence movements after World War II developed along lines dictated by the Cold War of the period. The Marxist MPLA (Popular Movement for the Liberation of Angola) emerged in 1956, and the war for independence began on 4 February 1961, when its members attacked the prison in Luanda to release their fellow freedom fighters. At the same time, they massacred some 2,000 Portuguese colonials. The

Portuguese already had armed forces in Angola, and these were joined by units of volunteers. Lisbon dispatched more and more troops, so that by 1973 there was an army of almost 140,000 men. Opposing them were some 7,000 members of the MPLA. In Cape Verde and Guinea-Bissau there were about 5,000 rebels, while in Mozambique Frelimo (the Mozambique Liberation Front) under Samora Machel was about 4,000 strong. All these movements used ambush tactics against the Portuguese troops.

For the colonial power itself, the war effort became more and more expensive, until finally it accounted for no less than 40 per cent of the annual Portuguese budget. Some of the equipment used by the Portuguese troops was French, in particular the armoured cars (the AMX-13 and eight-wheeled Panhard EBR reconnaissance vehicles). To meet the need for additional soldiers, the Portuguese dictatorship brought in four-year military service, which was extremely unpopular among the youth of the country, who had no desire to go and fight for the remnants of a remote empire.

The end of Portuguese colonization was chaotic, and was undoubtedly hastened on 25 April 1974 by the seizure of power in Portugal itself by a group of militant left-

A platoon of the Angolan National Liberation Army moves through bush country, 14 September 1964.

wing army captains. They relinquished the empire through the Alvor Agreement on 15 January 1975, which immediately sparked off a massacre of white colonials and at the same time unleashed a bloody civil war. Like the Organisation de l'Armée Secrète in Algeria, the white population put up brief resistance to the independence process, but the subsequent military evacuation was like a stampede. In a gigantic air operation 300,000 colonials fled the country as it plunged inexorably into a civil and ethnic war that did not end until 1991 and was punctuated by the interventions of South Africa, the Soviet Union, Zaire and Cuba. After 1975 the USSR supplied massive quantities of arms to the MPLA in order to ensure victory over the non-Marxist FNLA (National Front for the Liberation of Angola) and UNITA (National Union for the Total Independence of Angola). Over a period of fifteen years a total of 3,500 Portuguese lost their lives in Angola and Mozambique, 2.5 per cent of the fighting force. Civilian losses were estimated at around 90,000 in Angola (1961–75), 15,000 in Guinea-Bissau (1962–75) and 30,000 in Mozambique (1965–75).

REAL WARS AND REAL BATTLES

Indochina

In Indochina the French found themselves involved in a genuine war, in which the Viet Minh (the League for the Independence of Vietnam) became increasingly well equipped. The war was as complex as any such conflict could be. It was a civil war; until 1949 a war of colonial reconquest; from 1950 on a 'hot' war in which East confronted West; and in many ways it was also a conventional war. Unlike other independence movements, the Viet Minh had at its disposal a large number of freedom fighters, estimated at around 50,000 from 1945 onwards, having already begun to organize before World War II. Eventually its numbers rose to about 400,000.

Opposite French troops cross delta country on a self-propelled howitzer during their campaign against the Viet Minh, *c.* 1950.

Above French heavy artillery in action in Tien Lang, Indochina.

Above right French paratroopers armed with MAT-49s capture a guerrilla of the communist Viet Minh forces, 2 December 1952.

The question of the French colony's future arose in September 1945, when the Viet Minh unilaterally declared independence after four years of partial and then total Japanese occupation. The French response was to deploy the prestigious 2nd Armoured Division under General Philippe Leclerc – the division that had liberated Paris – which arrived at the end of October and set about recapturing the south of Indochina, Cochinchina. The operation was successfully completed in February 1946, and the Viet Minh found itself isolated, with its influence in decline. But the French triumph was short lived. Within a year the Viet Minh had secretly reformed, and on 19 December 1946 it went on the attack. The lull now exploded into open warfare, and the new Fourth Republic in France, established in 1946, could not make up its mind about the Indochinese problem. Should it negotiate with the Viet Minh or try to suppress it? In any case the French soldiers in Indochina – consisting largely of the Foreign Legion and colonial troops from black and North Africa – were outnumbered by their Viet Minh adversaries, a situation that made the defeat of the revolutionary movement highly unlikely.

The French troops were equipped mainly with weapons from World War II, such as US M1 Garand rifles. The MAT-49 submachine gun, based largely on the American M3 'grease gun', became the close-combat weapon par excellence. With a capacity of 600 shots a minute, its firepower was immense, and since it was also robust and easy to maintain it became the soldiers' favourite gun. The French also had armoured units (Sherman, Honey and later Chaffee tanks) and artillery that again was predominantly American (4-inch [105-mm] howitzers). While the armoury on land may have been substantial, means of transport – particularly by air – were woefully inadequate. The enemy, on the other hand, went from strength to strength. After 1950 the Viet Minh, which had

> *'Give me 500,000 men and I will win the war in Indochina.'*
> General Philippe Leclerc, 1947

been equipped initially with reclaimed weapons, was increasingly supplied with more modern arms from communist China.

In 1947 the tide turned in favour of the French. The Viet Minh was driven back into Upper Tonkin, the northern county of Indochina, and the Chinese border was recaptured by General Raoul Salan, but he still did not have enough men to finally defeat the Viet Minh. In June 1948 the latter formed its first large-scale unit, Division 308, and attacked fortified French positions. By the end of 1950, which had begun well for them, the French had suffered their first major military disaster – the Battle of RC4 (Route Coloniale 4) along the Chinese border. The Viet Minh launched twenty-seven battalions against two French columns, which were virtually annihilated. Some 5,000 French and Moroccan soldiers were killed, wounded or taken prisoner. The RC4 debacle made visions of French victory in Indochina increasingly unlikely. Viet Minh re-education camps were now introduced, and 2,000 of the 3,000 prisoners from the Far East Expeditionary Corps succumbed during the first few months of their captivity.

> '*Be men. If you are communists, join the Viet Minh: there are people there who are fighting well for a poor cause . . . But if you are patriots, fight for your homeland, because this war is yours.*'
>
> French commander-in-chief Jean de Lattre de Tassigny, speaking to young people at a school in Saigon, 11 July 1951

However, the arrival on 17 December 1950 of a new French commander-in-chief, Jean de Lattre de Tassigny, brought a boost both in morale and in equipment. The forces in Indochina now knew that in 'King Jean' Indochina had a ruler, and for a while this raised their spirits. He also took delivery of weapons from the United States. By now, the latter was fully aware that the conflict in Indochina was part of the Cold War, and so was less reluctant to give aid to the French, even going as far as to assume most of the financial burden for 1954. But Jean de Lattre de Tassigny died of cancer in 1952, and the politicians were already looking for a dignified way out of the war. A military success would allow them to enter into negotiations – arranged for spring 1954 in Geneva – from a position of some strength, and this was the thinking behind the planned operation at Dien Bien Phu (see box on p. 202).

The idea was to draw in as many of the Viet Minh fighting forces as possible in order to cripple them and cut off their supply lines from Laos. On 20 November 1953 the first parachutists from the French 6th Battalion descended on Dien Bien Phu, and these were reinforced by men and equipment to construct a fortified base that could be supplied only through total domination of the air. In January 1954 the Viet Minh took up the challenge, since it, too, needed to go to the Geneva conference table with a victory behind it. China provided it with massive supplies of trucks, heavy artillery and anti-aircraft guns, which made life impossible for the French pilots.

Even today there is great controversy over the real architects of the Viet Minh victory. Did General Vo Nguyen Giap, the famous commander of the Viet Minh, simply follow the 'advice' of the Chinese generals Ye Jianying and Chen Geng? Some of the Viet Minh's actions at Dien Bien Phu were also reminiscent of Soviet tactics – in particular those used at Stalingrad, with Giap concealing his firepower, notably that of the artillery, from his adversaries. Also like the Soviets at Stalingrad, the Viet Minh was prepared to suffer human losses disproportionate to military requirements,

Vietnamese President Ho Chi Minh and General Vo Nguyen Giap (left, behind) during a military campaign, 1950.

'*The conclusion is that you were given a mission that was impossible to carry out.*'
General Georges Catroux speaking to General Christian de Castries, commander at Dien Bien Phu, 25 June 1955

for above all else – again like Stalingrad – this battle was political and emblematic. Assault followed assault, from 13 March until the fall of the garrison on 7 May 1954, in Dantesque conditions not unlike those seen in the trenches at Verdun.

French losses were heavy – 3,000 dead out of a force of 14,000. Of the 11,000 prisoners, 8,431 died during a few months of captivity. On the Viet Minh side, precise figures have never been given, but they must have amounted to something like 12,000 dead and 30,000 wounded. The French government finally faced up to the fact that it must leave Indochina – a decision made all the more inevitable by public opinion, which had never been much in favour of the conflict. The French army may have lost about one in thirty of its troops, but the Viet Minh was hit very hard. What mattered, however, was that the political repercussions of Dien Bien Phu were far greater than the battle's military significance, as the communist leaders of the Viet Minh had always been aware. In all, between 1945 and 1954, the war in Indochina cost the lives of 20,700 French soldiers, 11,600 legionnaires, 15,300 Africans and 46,000 Indochinese. These figures alone testify to this having been a 'real' war.

Dien Bien Phu

In 1954 the Viet Minh succeeded in defeating the French in position warfare – fighting that focused on defensive positions – at Dien Bien Phu, a forward base about 320 km (200 miles) by air from Hanoi, near the border with Laos. This position had been developed from November 1953 by French parachutists in Operation Castor, in order to protect native allies and the opium crop, to threaten an invasion route into northern Laos, and to lure the Viet Minh into a major battle, which it was hoped would enable the French to negotiate from a position of strength.

The French parachutists who arrived on 20 November 1953 rapidly overcame the small garrison at the airstrip in Dien Bien Phu, and by March 1954 the French had a force of close to 11,000 men in the valley, dug in in a series of strong points. General Henri Navarre, the French commander in Indochina, had assumed that, if the Viet Minh attacked, they would choose to use only one division, but in the event Vo Nguyen Giap, the Viet Minh commander, deployed four divisions. During the battle the French added another 4,000 men to the garrison, but Giap was able to commit even more reinforcements.

Viet Minh attacks began on 13 March 1954, and were helped by the French failure to occupy the high ground from which the Viet Minh bunkers could be bombarded; by the folly of the French

Below left Vietnamese soldiers assaulting French positions at the airstrip, Dien Bien Phu, 14 April 1954.

Below French paratroopers land at Dien Bien Phu, 20 November 1953.

	FRANCE	VIET MINH
COMMANDERS	Christian de Castries	Vo Nguyen Giap
STRENGTH	14,000	49,500
CASUALTIES	c. 3,000 dead c.. 11,000 captured	c. 12,000 dead c. 30,000 wounded

assumption that their artillery could overcome Viet Minh guns; and by the weakness of French air power. The Viet Minh had American 4-inch (105-mm) cannon, captured by Chinese communists in the Chinese Civil War, and also Chinese anti-aircraft weapons and Soviet Katyusha rockets. During the siege the Viet Minh fired 350,000 shells. Artillery bombardment of the airstrip prevented the French from landing planes after 27 March, and instead they were dependent on reinforcements dropped by parachute. The outgunned and poorly chosen French strong points were successively stormed, even if, owing to their mass infantry attacks, the Viet Minh suffered far more casualties in combat. The cost of this human wave tactic led Giap to shift to the use of advancing trench positions.

The last assault was launched on 6 May. By then the net had been drawn so tight that air supply drops could bring scant relief to the French garrison; indeed, most fell into Viet Minh hands. The remains of the isolated French force finally surrendered on 7 May, their bases overrun. A total of 11,000 troops were captured.

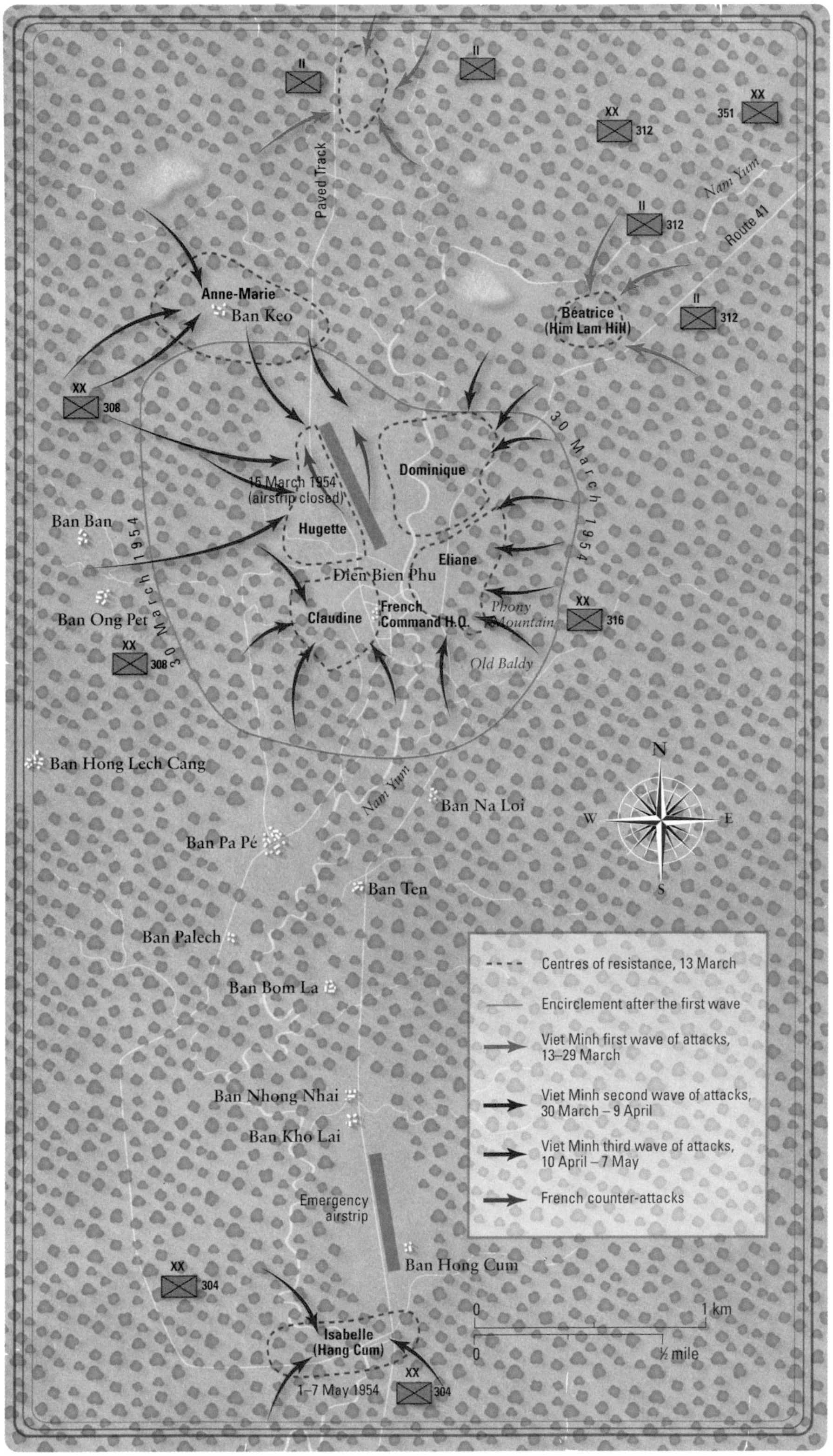

Battle of Dien Bien Phu,
20 November 1953 – 7 May 1954.

Map labels:
Paved Track
Nam Yum
Route 41
Anne-Marie
Ban Keo
Beatrice (Him Lam Hill)
351
312
312
312
308
Ban Ban
15 March 1954 (airstrip closed)
Dominique
Hugette
Eliane
Ban Ong Pet
Điên Biên Phu
Claudine
French Command H.Q.
Phony Mountain
316
30 March 1954
Old Baldy
308
Ban Hong Lech Cang
Nam Yum
Ban Na Loi
Ban Pa Pé
Ban Ten
Ban Palech
Ban Bom La
Ban Nhong Nhai
Ban Kho Lai
Emergency airstrip
Ban Hong Cum
304
Isabelle (Hang Cum)
1–7 May 1954
304

Legend:
Centres of resistance, 13 March
Encirclement after the first wave
Viet Minh first wave of attacks, 13–29 March
Viet Minh second wave of attacks, 30 March – 9 April
Viet Minh third wave of attacks, 10 April – 7 May
French counter-attacks

0 1 km
0 ½ mile

Algeria

It was not until 10 June 1999 that the National Assembly in France recognized the fact that there had been a war in Algeria. Until then, the conflict had been officially referred to only as 'peacekeeping operations'. Algeria had been conquered by France as long ago as 1830; the difference between here and Indochina lay in the fact that the French moved in to form a genuine colony of settlers. It was also divided up into departments, just like metropolitan France. And so, as people said at the time, 'Algeria is France' – and one must understand the nature of these ties in order to grasp just why the war was so fierce and so bitter.

Throughout the conflict, the French army – in contrast to the situation in Indochina – maintained a significant numerical advantage over the FLN (National Liberation Front) and its military arm, the ALN (National Liberation Army). Thanks to conscription – again unlike the situation in Indochina – French forces reached a maximum of 450,000 in 1957–58, whereas at the beginning of 1958 the ALN never had more than 50,000 men. But this numerical superiority never attained the ratio of 1:15 considered essential by specialists in revolutionary warfare to ensure victory in a guerrilla war.

'Shoot down any European, from 18 to 54.
No women, no children, no old people.'
Algrerian leader Larbi ben M'hidi to his troops, June 1956

Above General Charles de Gaulle in Algiers, June 1958.

Opposite French paratroopers in the old Casbah of Algiers: a scene from the film *The Battle of Algiers* (1966), a controversial retelling of the conflict.

The weapons used by the French were mainly the same as those deployed in Indochina. The artillery consisted for the most part of American HM-2 4-inch howitzers, while 40-mm (1½-inch) Bofors anti-aircraft guns were also used on land as back-up. Only light armoured vehicles were used in Algeria: the M24 Chaffee and then the AMX-13. Since there were no battles involving armoured cars, the value of these vehicles lay in their 75-mm (3-inch) guns, which gave valuable support to the infantry. Nevertheless, there were some new developments: the 'peacekeeping' forces had at least 50 large helicopters at their disposal, which increased to more than 300 in 1962. The opposing ALN drew its armoury from a variety of countries – Germany, Czechoslovakia, Britain – but the longer the war went on, the greater its firepower became.

The war was fought on two fronts, with fighting in the cities and also out in the open country. The Battle of Algiers was the best-known example of the first category. In January 1957, in order to counter the terrorist strategy of the FNL, which had control of the Casbah, the government handed over to General Jacques Massu the power to police the department of Algiers. He succeeded in dismantling the FNL/ANL networks by arresting several FLN leaders and finding many hidden arms and explosives depots, and he reduced considerably the number of attacks (from 120 in December 1956 to none at all in October 1957). The price paid, however, was heavy in both human and moral terms. A small section of the French army, in a manner very much against its honourable traditions, found itself compelled through the cowardice of politicians to do a great deal of 'dirty work' in order to obtain results – most notably by using torture.

On open ground, military operations assumed various forms. Apart from its pursuit of the ALN units, it was an important part of the French army's strategy to seal the borders. The object was to prevent the ALN from obtaining reinforcements of men and equipment from outside by blocking off access to Morocco in the west and Tunisia in the east. The Morice Line was built, named after the French minister of defence, André Morice: it consisted of cannons that fired automatically when set off by radar, parallel networks of mines, and electrified barbed-wire fences. The ALN tried to fight back after January 1958 but suffered crippling losses, especially in the east, where in four months the 'battle of the borders' cost nearly 4,000 lives, with 600 men taken prisoner. The biggest operational success for the French, however, came with the so-called 'Challe Plan'. Air Chief Marshal Maurice Challe was put in general command of the French forces in Algeria in 1959. He set out to eliminate all the ALN areas of refuge in the interior of the country, since their very existence was an obstacle to the more peaceful goal of 'reconquering hearts'. From February 1959 to April 1961 he launched 13 military campaigns. The results were spectacular: the military strength of the ALN was halved. The French were on the verge of winning the war, but it was finally lost through increasing United Nations opposition to French rule and through a radical change of attitude towards Algeria adopted by General de Gaulle, who returned to power after the French political crisis of May 1958.

In total, nearly 2 million Frenchmen were involved in the fighting in North Africa. French losses amounted to 21,291 army soldiers, who were either killed in action or died from other causes, 371 sailors and 487 airmen. The statistics are completed by 1,000 men who were unaccounted for (mainly prisoners who died in captivity). The ALN lost between 140,000 and 150,000 men. The number of civilian casualties is uncertain; after independence, the ruling FLN tended to inflate the figures considerably in order to cover up the massacres that its adherents had committed. Estimates range anywhere from 137,000 to 1.5 million – figures that even today the FLN continue to base on fantasy. The most likely statistic is somewhere between 200,000 and 250,000 civilian casualties. In addition, after independence was declared on 19 March 1962, 3,018 Algerian Europeans were abducted, of whom 2,124 were executed, often in horrific circumstances.

CONCLUSION

It should be noted that in most cases these colonial wars were ended by appeals to the international community or by a negotiated solution. In spring 1947 the British asked the UN to settle the issue of Palestine, and from summer 1947 onwards the UN also tried to intervene in the conflict in Indonesia, which ended in the Dutch granting independence. In 1962 the UN condemned the Portuguese massacres that took place in Angola, which implicitly drove the Portuguese to decolonize, and likewise it was international pressure that forced the French to leave Indochina and Algeria. Thus, despite differences in form and geography, these wars of decolonization all had in common their settlement by negotiation. It is not always the strongest who finish victorious.

A young member of the National Liberation Front during independence ceremonies in Algiers, 1962.

The Kalashnikov AK-47

The AK-47 (Avtamat Kalashnikova-1947) or AKM ('modernized' version, 1959) is the most widely used gun in the world today. Production of the rifle is estimated at between 80 and 100 million, and it is manufactured by dozens of countries, mainly under licence. It was first used as standard equipment by the Soviet army in 1947, and was largely influenced by the first real assault rifle, the German Sturmgewehr 44. The AK-47 weighs 3.8 kg empty and 4.3 kg loaded (8.4 and 9.5 lb respectively), and is gas-operated. Its original ammunition was 7.62 × 39 mm (0.3 × 1.5 inch) cartridges, also copied from the German 7.92 × 33. The gun can fire either single shots or 600 shots a minute in automatic mode, with a range of 300 metres (330 yards). The Kalashnikov owes its worldwide success to the fact that it is both cheap and easy to make, but its real advantage lies in its all-round practicality: it functions in all conditions, including the most extreme, whether in the hands of an expert or an amateur. Unlike much more sophisticated weapons, it is also easy to use and to maintain. Its

relatively short range was quite sufficient in wars of decolonization, where contact with the enemy usually took place at close quarters. Soviet, Chinese, Yugoslavian and East German versions have been ubiquitous in many different conflicts since 1947.

Above Women soldiers of the National Liberation Army of Iran train with AK-47s, 28 April 1988.

Below The AK-47's success is due to its simple design, low cost, reliability and ease of maintainance.

The detachable box magazine contains either 20 or 30 rounds.

Using the 7.62 × 39 mm cartridge, the AK-47 has a maximum effective range of around 300 metres (330 yards) when fully automatic.

11 The Cold War

WILLIAM MALEY

KEY DATES

5 March 1946 In a speech at Fulton, Missouri, Churchill refers to an 'iron curtain' dividing Europe

24 June 1948 Stalin cuts off rail and road links with Berlin, thus beginning the 318-day Berlin Blockade

25 June 1950 Outbreak of the Korean War

5 March 1953 Death of Stalin

25 February 1956 In his 'Secret Speech', Khrushchev condemns Stalinist repression

23 October – 4 November 1956 Uprising in Hungary against the Soviet-installed communist government

13 August 1961 Construction of the Berlin Wall begins

16–28 October 1962 The Cuban missile crisis marks the height of Cold War tension

20 August 1968 Soviet invasion of Czechoslovakia

17 November 1969 Strategic Arms Limitation Talks between the United States and the Soviet Union begin in Helsinki

27 December 1979 Soviet invasion of Afghanistan

11 March 1985 Selection of Mikhail S. Gorbachev as Communist Party general secretary

9 November 1989 Fall of the Berlin Wall

Opposite An East German soldier looks through a hole in the Berlin Wall, November 1989.

Between the end of World War II in Europe and the fall of the Berlin Wall in November 1989, the dominant pole of tension in international relations was between the United States and its allies, and the Soviet Union and its satellites. This was by no means the only serious strategic and political fault-line during this period, but it carried by far the greatest risk of a strategic nuclear exchange that could have wrecked a large portion of the earth's surface. The Cuban missile crisis of October 1962 represented the high point of this tension. Yet in one obvious sense, the expression 'Cold War' is somewhat misleading. While direct military confrontation between the United States and the USSR was avoided, the Cold War witnessed a large number of peripheral conflicts between forces that were either allied to or inspired by the Cold War principals. The Korean, Vietnam and Afghanistan wars, the Hungarian Revolution, and conflicts in Third World theatres of confrontation such as Angola cost vast numbers of lives. Furthermore, fear of communist penetration provided a rationale for the use of coercion against perceived internal enemies in countries as diverse as Chile and Indonesia.

ORIGINS OF THE COLD WAR

When Nazi Germany invaded the USSR early in World War II, the Soviet Union was driven into an immediate relationship with the United Kingdom. The British prime minister, Winston Churchill, had previously been an active supporter of efforts to destroy the Bolshevik regime that had come to power in Russia in October 1917, but the exigencies of the time dictated a common effort to overthrow the Nazi regime, a struggle that became truly global following Germany's declaration of war against the United States after Japan's bombing of Pearl Harbor on 7 December 1941. Towards the end of the war the three main Allied war leaders – Churchill himself, Soviet leader Joseph Stalin and US President Franklin D. Roosevelt – met face-to-face in Yalta in the Crimea in February 1945. Roosevelt was dying of congestive heart failure, which claimed his life only two months later, but Churchill and Stalin battled vigorously in the working sessions over the distribution of influence in postwar Europe.

The central problem was that the ultimate shape of Europe would largely be determined not by leadership negotiations, but by the specific geographical areas that the different parties controlled at the moment when the Nazis were defeated. By the time of Yalta, the Nazi regime was close to its death throes, and the huge Soviet assault from the east that was launched in early 1945 ensured that much of Eastern Europe – including Poland, in defence of which the British had actually gone to war with Germany in 1939 – was Soviet-dominated. It was this that led to

209

'From Stettin in the Baltic to Trieste in the Adriatic, an iron curtain has descended across the Continent.'

Winston Churchill, Fulton, Missouri, 5 March 1946

Churchill's famous speech given in March 1946, at Westminster College in Fulton, Missouri, in which he warned that an 'iron curtain' had descended across the continent of Europe.

However, if it is relatively easy to identify a moment at which a sense of looming confrontation set in, it is markedly more complex to determine why such a confrontation occurred at such a time. Explanations in terms of ideology, very popular in some Western circles during the Cold War, asserted that the USSR was driven by the logic of Marxism-Leninism to a confrontational world view. Other explanations saw the Cold War as rooted in a Soviet sense of insecurity, driving it to establish a glacis of subordinated states in Eastern Europe that would protect it against future threats. Others cited opportunism, maintaining that the USSR – through organizations such as the Comintern, the international organization of the Communist Party, which had existed from 1919 to 1943 – had long supported communists from Eastern Europe, and in 1945 seized the chance to put them in positions of power.

Above Children eagerly await a plane bringing supplies into blockaded West Berlin, 1948.

Opposite Churchill, Roosevelt and Stalin meet in Yalta, Crimea, to determine spheres of influence in postwar Europe, February 1945.

PHASES OF THE COLD WAR

The initial phase of the Cold War ran from Churchill's Fulton speech in 1946 to the death of Stalin in 1953. This was marked by a number of dramatic developments: the Soviet consolidation of control in Eastern Europe; the Berlin Blockade – the Soviet attempt in 1948–49 to force the Western powers out of West Berlin by preventing the movement of supplies on the ground; the Soviet test of a nuclear device in 1949 (see box on p. 212); the occupation of Beijing, led by Chinese communists under Mao Zedong, and the establishment in 1949 of the People's Republic of China; and the Korean War. However, it also witnessed the first major split in the communist world, namely the rift between the Soviet leadership and Yugoslavia under Josip Broz Tito, in whose capital of Belgrade the new Communist Information Bureau ('Cominform') had been established in 1948.

A second phase lasted from 1953 to 1962, running from the death of Stalin to the Cuban missile crisis. This period on the one hand was marked by a certain optimism, since Stalin's successor as first secretary of the Presidium of the Communist Party of the Soviet Union, Nikita Khrushchev, set out a doctrine of 'peaceful coexistence' between capitalist and socialist systems, and even paid a visit to the United States. On the other hand, it witnessed a number of severe upheavals: the 1953 uprising in East Berlin; the Soviet invasion of Hungary in 1956; the slow-burning Berlin crisis that culminated in the building of the Berlin Wall; the shooting down of a US U-2 surveillance aircraft over the USSR in 1960; and of course the Cuban Revolution of 1959 and the missile crisis itself.

The 1962 missile crisis inaugurated a third phase of the Cold War that lasted until the end of the 1960s, marked by the replacement of Khrushchev in a 'palace coup' in October 1964; domestic toughening in the USSR, as demonstrated by the trial of the writers Andrei Sinyavsky and Yuly Daniel in 1966; a significant Soviet arms build-up under the new leadership headed by Leonid Brezhnev; and, perhaps most dramatically, the invasion of Czechoslovakia in August 1968 by the Soviet Union and by Eastern European forces it controlled in order to crush a flowering of unorthodox opinion that had gone by the name of the 'Prague Spring'. Yet this was also a period in which the United States and other Western countries were increasingly preoccupied by events seemingly more remote from the immediate US–Soviet relationship, such as the Vietnam War and the Six-Day War in the Middle East in June 1967 (see Chapter 12), while the Soviet Union was faced with clashes on the border with China, and the latter was preoccupied with the massive disruptions caused by the 'Great Proletarian Cultural Revolution'.

The fourth phase of the Cold War, classically associated with the diplomacy of US President Richard M. Nixon (in office 1969–74) and his close adviser Henry Kissinger, secretary of state from 1973 to 1977, as well as with the Ford administration and the early years of the Carter presidency, was dominated by the concept of détente ('relaxation'). This witnessed the successful negotiation of a major Strategic Arms Limitation Treaty (SALT I) in 1972. Nevertheless, it also witnessed the victory of communist forces in the Vietnam War, as well as the bloody advent of the Khmer Rouge regime in Cambodia that resulted in genocidal slaughter of perceived 'enemies' within the Cambodian population.

The fifth phase of the Cold War was inaugurated by the Soviet invasion of

Nuclear Weapons

Nuclear weapons create vast explosive force through the fission of atoms in a chain reaction. The idea of a nuclear weapon arose from fundamental developments in theoretical and experimental physics in the 1930s, and the actual development of a US atomic bomb, inspired by the fear that Nazi Germany might be pursuing such a capability, was the task of the so-called 'Manhattan Project', on which physicists such as Enrico Fermi, Leo Szilard, Ernest O. Lawrence, J. Robert Oppenheimer, Hans Bethe and Richard Feynman worked under the military leadership of Brigadier General Leslie R. Groves. The first atomic bomb was tested in New Mexico on 16 July 1945, at a site known as Jornada del Muerto ('Journey of Death'), producing a yield equivalent to 18,600 tons of the conventional explosive TNT; atomic bombs subsequently destroyed the Japanese cities of Hiroshima and Nagasaki on 6 and 9 August.

The Soviet Union, benefiting from information conveyed by its agent Klaus Fuchs, tested a nuclear weapon in 1949, and both the United States and the USSR proceeded to develop ever more destructive thermonuclear weapons. The development of these capacities, and then of intercontinental ballistic missiles as means of delivery, was seen by some analysts as enabling each side to deter the other from mounting an attack on its core interests.

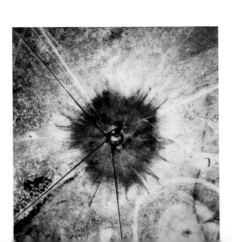

Above In 1960, the US Air Force began constructing 1,000 underground sites for the Minuteman nuclear intercontinental ballistic missile. They would remain on alert for nearly thirty years.

Left Aerial view of the crater left by the first test explosion of a nuclear weapon, Alamogordo, New Mexico, 16 July 1945.

A young woman, accompanied by her partner, stands precariously near the top of the Berlin Wall to talk to her mother on the East Berlin side, 1961.

Afghanistan in December 1979 and lasted until Gorbachev became general secretary of the Central Committee of the Communist Party of the Soviet Union in March 1985. This was a period of high tension, marked not only by the chill in relations that the invasion of Afghanistan produced, but also by the collapse of meaningful strategic arms control negotiations between the United States and the Soviet Union, and by a near-catastrophic crisis following the latter's shooting down on 1 September 1983 of a Korean Airlines passenger aircraft, with 269 people on board, that had strayed into Soviet airspace in the far east of the country.

The final phase of the Cold War followed Gorbachev's elevation, and was marked by a public de-ideologization of Soviet foreign policy in favour of a doctrine of 'new thinking' (*novoe myshlenie*) that emphasized the imperative of avoiding nuclear confrontation for the sake of the common interests of humankind. This culminated in the breaching of the Berlin Wall and the collapse of the Soviet sphere of influence in Eastern Europe in 1989. Two years later the Soviet Union had disintegrated.

THE COLD WAR AND SOVIET–AMERICAN RELATIONS

The United States and the Soviet Union emerged as the two strongest powers at the end of World War II, but they varied enormously in their specific attributes. The United States, which had a surprisingly small army when the war in Europe began, emerged afterwards as the sole nuclear power, in a world in which deterrence was poised to displace classic notions of power-balancing as the key organizing principle of strategic relations. It had also largely escaped the direct ravages of the war, with

A German poster promoting the 'European Recovery Program', otherwise known as the Marshall Plan, c. 1948.

only Hawaii and the Aleutian Islands experiencing direct attack. The USSR, by contrast, suffered enormous direct damage as a result of the German invasion, with casualties in the many millions. Nonetheless, at the end of the war it was the largest land power that the world had ever seen, and in a dominant position in a range of Eastern European states. Furthermore, while the US nuclear monopoly might have appeared to give it the capacity to dictate the terms of postwar international relations, this was not really the case. On the one hand, any threat to use nuclear weapons unilaterally would have been at odds with the provisions of the new Charter of the United Nations, which the United States had actively supported and which prohibited the threat or use of force in any but strictly limited circumstances. On the other hand, the Soviet Union had a convenient hostage in the form of the French, British and American sectors of the divided city of Berlin, which constituted an isolated enclave deep within Soviet-controlled territory.

The broad US posture towards the Soviet Union came to be known as 'containment', given the physical difficulties of 'rolling back' Soviet control of Eastern Europe. This had been traced out in what came to be known as the Truman Doctrine, which President Truman (in office 1945–53) outlined in an address to the US Congress on 12 March 1947. While in an immediate sense Truman's address was concerned with aid to beleaguered Greece and to Turkey, the principles underpinning it, namely the need to bolster states that could be vulnerable to communist penetration, were of broader import, and shaped Washington's approach for nearly two decades. Just months later, it was reinforced by Secretary of State George Marshall's famous promotion of a 'European Recovery Program' that came to be known universally as the Marshall Plan.

The adoption of a policy of containment was not without its costs for Truman and his Democratic Party colleagues, especially Dean Acheson, secretary of state from 1949 to 1953. Republican hardliners, coalescing around a populist junior senator from Wisconsin, Joseph R. McCarthy, accused the administration of having 'lost China', and McCarthy made frenzied charges that the upper echelons of the State Department had been penetrated by Soviet agents. McCarthy caused enormous grief to Truman, and it was only when he foolishly continued his campaign of smears following the inauguration of the Republican Dwight D. Eisenhower in 1953 that the Senate finally censured him. There was an interesting parallel on the Soviet side: Stalin in his last years was increasingly gripped by paranoia, reputedly remarking 'I trust no one, not even myself.' This led to great fear of further purges on the eve of his death, and even to lingering suspicions as to whether he had died of natural causes.

The Truman Doctrine proved highly durable, but it was given a new twist in 1969 by President Nixon, who had been Eisenhower's vice-president from 1953 to 1961. Facing significant constraints because of the quagmire the United States confronted in Vietnam, he enunciated what became known as the 'Guam Doctrine' or the 'Nixon Doctrine', which foreshadowed key roles for major US allies as guarantors of regional security with US support. A principal beneficiary was Mohammad Reza Pahlavi, shah of Iran, whose regime became the recipient of substantial US aid. However, the overthrow of the shah in the Iranian Revolution of 1979 was to expose the central conceptual flaw of this approach. Superpowers cannot easily or safely engage in outsourcing.

THE COLD WAR IN EUROPE

Europe was the first theatre in which the rivalries of the Cold War were played out. At Yalta the competing claims to authority of the Polish government-in-exile and the communist Lublin Committee were promoted by Churchill and Stalin respectively. The situation on the ground resolved the struggle in favour of the latter. In various territories occupied by Soviet troops, communist groups were able to work their way into positions of power. This was most readily accomplished in the Soviet sector of occupied Germany, which became the German Democratic Republic, but it was agonizingly played out in both Hungary and Czechoslovakia. In the former, the Stalinist leader Mátyás Rákosi employed what he called 'salami tactics' to eliminate his opponents slice by slice, and in Czechoslovakia pre-war figures such as Edvard Beneš and Jan Masaryk were targeted, with Masaryk ultimately dying in very dubious circumstances.

It is hardly surprising that these autocratic (and some might say totalitarian) systems, imposed under Soviet pressure, caused a great deal of suffering for their subject populations. Only months after the death of Stalin, there was an uprising in East Berlin in June 1953 that was crushed with tanks. A far more dramatic development occurred in Hungary in October 1956. In February 1956 Nikita Khrushchev, at the 20th Congress of the Soviet Communist Party, had delivered a speech entitled 'On the

A protester shot during the Berlin Uprising of 16–17 June 1953 is helped by German police. The Russians had imposed martial law, using tanks and shooting on demonstrators in order to break up the workers' rebellion.

'Today at daybreak Soviet forces started an attack against our capital, with the obvious intention to overthrow the legal democratic Hungarian Government. Our troops are fighting. The Government is in its place. I notify the people of our country and the entire world of this.'

Hungarian prime minister Imre Nagy,
4 November 1956

Cult of Personality and Its Consequences', which denounced in vivid terms some of the excesses of Stalin's rule. This, of course, undermined the position of a whole raft of East European leaders who had been promoted while Stalin was alive, and struck particularly hard at the Hungarian party leadership. The result was a revolutionary uprising against the whole system of state socialism, in which, paradoxically, a long-time communist, Imre Nagy, came to play a leading part. After a certain amount of agonizing within the Soviet leadership, the revolution was brutally suppressed, with thousands of Hungarian refugees fleeing to neighbouring countries and the cardinal archbishop of Esztergom, József Mindszenty, seeking asylum in the US embassy; he remained there for the next fifteen years, a symbol of the way in which the aspirations for freedom in his country had been snuffed out.

Just over a decade later Czechoslovakia found itself in a somewhat similar position, although without a revolutionary situation developing on the ground. In this case a new leader from within the Slovak party organization, Alexander Dubček, sought to articulate a gentler vision of 'socialism with a human face', allowing freer

> '*All free men, wherever they may live, are citizens of Berlin. And therefore, as a free man, I take pride in the words "Ich bin ein Berliner".*'
>
> US President John F. Kennedy, Berlin, 11 June 1963

discussion of political issues than the Soviet leadership found appetizing. The result was the invasion of Czechoslovakia in August 1968 and the articulation in Moscow of the so-called 'Brezhnev Doctrine', which maintained that a threat to the gains of socialism in any one socialist state was a threat to the gains of socialism in all, justifying intervention to prevent such an outcome. But as things worked out, this was the last invasion to be defended in such terms: in 1981 in Poland, a country where the domination of the communist Polish United Workers' Party had been challenged by the emergence of the Solidarity free trade union, the threat of a Soviet invasion was averted by a declaration of martial law by the military under General Wojciech Jaruzelski.

Confronted with these events, there was relatively little that the United States and its allies could do; if anything, encouragement to the Hungarian revolutionaries through the broadcasts of the US-funded Radio Free Europe did more harm than good, stimulating the naive belief that Western powers might come directly to their aid. What the United States was able to do was act robustly to defend territories not under Soviet domination. A 1948 Soviet blockade of West Berlin was broken by an airlift of supplies transported through Tempelhof airport, and in June 1963 President John F. Kennedy memorably expressed solidarity with its citizens by standing in the heart of Berlin, near the Wall, and proclaiming 'Ich bin ein Berliner'. In institutional terms, the establishment of the North Atlantic Treaty Organization (NATO) in 1949 committed the United States to the defence of Western Europe. In parallel, the USSR established the Warsaw Treaty Organization, more commonly known as the Warsaw Pact, to provide a framework for common military action with its East European satellites, an arrangement reinforced with the establishment of the Council for Mutual Economic Assistance, known more commonly as the CMEA or COMECON.

Opposite Soviet tanks line a street in Prague, 28 August 1968. The invasion was intended to halt the democratic reforms instituted during the 'Prague Spring'.

Below Chairman Mao proclaims the birth of the People's Republic of China, 1 October 1949.

THE COLD WAR IN ASIA

Making sense of the Cold War in Asia is somewhat complicated by the entanglement of ideological and power-political questions with the wider issues of decolonization and nationalism. In China the communist takeover was proclaimed by Mao with the assertion that China had 'stood up'. In Indochina (modern Vietnam, Laos and Cambodia) the experience of French domination, decisively terminated by the defeat of French forces at Dien Bien Phu in 1954 (see pp. 202–3), had shaped the orientations of a generation of Vietnamese communists. Even in Korea, a sense of Korean consciousness existed alongside the undoubted desire of Stalin to strike a blow against an American presence in Asia that had been burgeoning ever since the occupation of Japan in 1945.

Nonetheless, it was in Asia, on the Korean peninsula, that the Cold War entered one of its hottest phases. The victory of the communists in China, together with the USSR's successful nuclear test in Kazakhstan on 29 August 1949, created a potentially more rewarding environment for muscle-flexing. The North Korean offensive across the 38th parallel of latitude on 25 June 1950, which triggered the Korean War, did not, however, deliver the swift victory hoped for by Stalin, and the

Above The USS *New Jersey* fires a six-gun salvo of 16-inch (41-cm) shells into enemy troop concentrations near Kaesong, Korea, 1 January 1953.

Above right A weapons squad leader points out a North Korean position to his crew, north of the Chongchon river, Korea, 20 November 1950.

Opposite A Russian-built MiG-15 – delivered by a defecting North Korean pilot – awaits testing by the US Air Force, October 1953. The Korean War was the first conflict in which jet aircraft played a significant role.

United States, backed by a resolution of the UN Security Council passed while Moscow was boycotting the council's deliberations, swung into action to defend South Korea. While initially the forces of the North enjoyed considerable success and occupied Seoul on 28 June, the Inchon landings, brilliantly executed from 15 September by forces under the command of General Douglas MacArthur, led to the North Korean army being driven out of Seoul and back to the north of the Korean peninsula. But when UN forces pursued North Korean forces across the 38th parallel in early October 1950, China entered the war, and new phases of the see-sawing struggle commenced. Seoul fell to communist forces once more in early January 1951, but was recaptured in March. From mid-1951 the conflict was effectively stalemated, which set the scene for truce negotiations. However, a 1953 truce left much unresolved, and the Korean peninsula remains divided to this day.

The sobering experience in Korea was one of the factors that prompted the United States to promote an additional set of global alliances for the containment of communist power. One of these was the Central Treaty Organization (CENTO), dating from 1959, which was a successor to the earlier Baghdad Pact (a regional security treaty formed in 1955, involving Turkey, Iraq, Pakistan, Iran and Britain). With indirect US assistance it sought to shore up the so-called 'Northern Tier' states of Turkey and Iran, as well as Pakistan to the east. It was formally dissolved in 1979, in the aftermath of the Iranian Revolution. Another was the Southeast Asia Treaty Organization (SEATO), established in February 1955 in the wake of a treaty signed in Manila on 8 September 1954. Initially the only South-East Asian members were Thailand and the Philippines. However, with the outbreak of war in Vietnam, first with Viet Cong raids from North Vietnam into South Vietnam from 1957, and from 1960 with the so-called National Liberation Front providing a

'Can you imagine Donald Duck going on a rampage without Walt Disney knowing about it?'

Edward Barrett, US assistant secretary of state, on Soviet involvement in the North Korean attack, June 1950

political framework for communist action, some SEATO member states (although not formally SEATO itself) became more heavily involved – especially as the Johnson administration escalated US involvement following the 1964 Gulf of Tonkin incident. This saw actual and perceived attacks on a US destroyer by North Vietnamese torpedo boats, and helped justify large-scale American engagement in the conflict.

The Vietnam War became a curse for Democrat President Lyndon B. Johnson and the Republican Richard M. Nixon. Both encountered strong domestic opposition to the price of American participation in the war. Neither had a credible strategy for success – beyond the exceedingly dubious notion of 'Vietnamization', which posited that ramshackle and corrupt South Vietnamese forces would in time be able to stand in for those of the United States and its allies – and the January 1968 'Tet Offensive', which saw even the US embassy in the South Vietnamese capital of Saigon come under attack, further sapped the conviction of the US public that Vietnam was the right theatre in which to be engaged. Fitful peace talks in Paris between 1968 and 1973 finally led to the Paris ceasefire agreement (23 January 1973) signed by Henry Kissinger for the United States and Le Duc Tho for North Vietnam. The terms of the agreement left the North in a strong position, and the fragility of the South – combined with President Nixon's weakened position in 1973–74 because of the Watergate scandal, and the exhaustion of the patience of the US Congress with a messy and divisive war – meant that when the final North Vietnamese thrust to take over all of the South began in 1975, it proved irresistible. Saigon fell on 30 April 1975.

The rationale for the heavier involvement in Vietnam of SEATO member states – which ultimately exposed the limits of SEATO's capacity and led to its dissolution on 30 June 1977 – was what came to be known as the 'Domino Theory', positing that, if South Vietnam were to fall, the remaining non-communist states of South-East Asia could (or would) fall like dominoes, constituting a catastrophic strategic failure to contain communist expansion. The weaknesses of such a deterministic theory were exposed in 1975, when Laos and Cambodia indeed succumbed to communist

Above A US Marine with a Viet Cong suspect, 24 km (15 miles) west of Da Nang air base, Vietnam, 3 August 1965.

Right Locations struck during the communist Tet Offensive in January 1968.

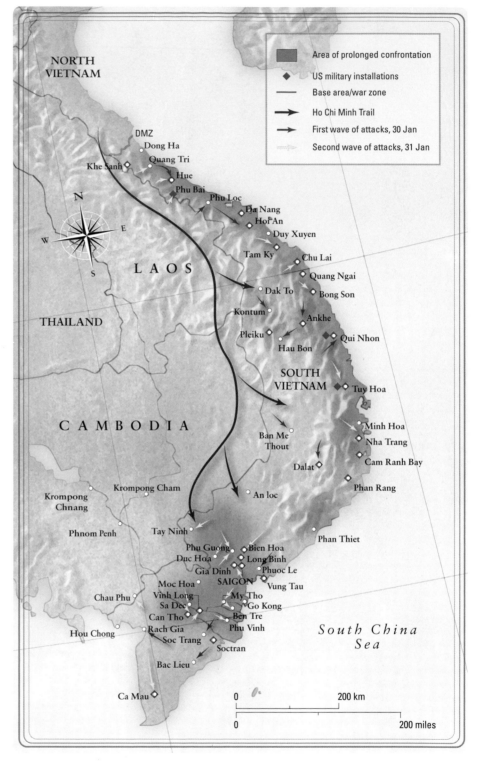

Vietnamese civilians try to scale the walls of the US Embassy in Saigon, hoping to claim refugee status as the North Vietnamese Army advances on the city, 30 April 1975.

rule along with South Vietnam, but states such Thailand, Malaysia, Singapore, Indonesia and the Philippines did not.

Here, one significant complicating factor was the spectacular 1960 Sino-Soviet split. The communist leadership in China had found Khrushchev's post-Stalinist revisionism very difficult to swallow, and ridiculed his 'goulash communism', which sought to ground the legitimacy of socialism in an ability to guarantee basic material prosperity. Domestic developments such as the economic failures of the Great Leap Forward and the leadership crisis that surfaced at the 1959 Lushan Plenum of the Chinese Communist Party also did little to improve the mood of the Chinese. To see differences between Moscow and Beijing flaring into the open was perplexing to many observers, but it gave the Cold War a fundamentally new twist: the idea of a unified world communism made little sense any more, and increasingly the Chinese and the Soviets became competitors for influence, especially in developing states.

THE STRUGGLE FOR THE THIRD WORLD

What China termed the 'Third World' was increasingly the venue for competition for influence between Moscow, Washington and Beijing. A sense of distinctive consciousness in developing countries had begun to surface in the 1950s, a decade marked by extensive decolonization in Africa and increased political assertiveness on the part of post-colonial elites. This was reflected in the 1955 Bandung conference in Indonesia, which led directly to the founding of the Non-Aligned Movement (NAM). This brought together leaders as diverse as Jawaharlal Nehru of India, Yugoslavia's Tito and Fidel Castro of Cuba, who in 1979 was to host a Non-Aligned Summit in Havana. This pointed to one of the peculiarities of the NAM: some of its most prominent members were anything but 'non-aligned'.

It was the overthrow of the Batista regime in Cuba in 1959 and its replacement by a Marxist regime under Castro that set the scene for the political dramas of the following three years. Such a development was extremely unwelcome in Washington: it struck at the very heart of one of the key doctrines of American foreign policy, namely the Monroe Doctrine of 1823, directed against the establishment of European colonial outposts in the Western hemisphere. A Cuba committed to supporting the USSR and enjoying Soviet backing seemed to be just such an outpost. In the early months of the Kennedy administration, in April 1961, this development led to the Bay of Pigs fiasco, in which a US-backed landing by Cuban exiles intent on overthrowing Castro failed disastrously. The exposure of this ill-judged operation severely embarrassed the new president. Even more dramatic, however, was the missile crisis of October 1962, certainly the point of gravest tension in the entire Cold War. Intelligence that the Soviet Union was building missile sites on Cuba from which nuclear-armed missiles could be launched against US targets led President Kennedy to proclaim a 'police action', to be enforced by US naval vessels, directed at preventing missiles from reaching the sites. Vigorous behind-the-scenes diplomacy complemented these public steps, and the crisis was defused when the Soviets

backed down, a decision that left Castro thoroughly infuriated. While the handling of the missile crisis was by no means the only black mark against Khrushchev in the eyes of his colleagues, it was certainly one of the factors that contributed to his removal in 1964, which was accompanied by tart references in the Soviet press to the negative consequences of 'hare-brained schemes'.

Khrushchev's departure did not in any sense put an end to Soviet interest in the Third World. In part, it was required by the threat of expanding Chinese influence, especially in the light of Chinese Marshal Lin Piao's 1965 article 'Long Live the Victory of People's War', which some analysts saw as a blueprint for national liberation movements. However, it was also driven by a sense of opportunity, in the light of grievances of various Third World populations that began to surface in the 1970s. Developments did not follow a linear pattern: in Egypt, for example, President Anwar Sadat in 1972 ordered the withdrawal of Soviet advisers – a mighty setback for Soviet influence in the Arab world. On the other hand, the USSR was able to expand its influence in the Horn of Africa, where the pro-Western regime of Emperor Haile Selassie in Ethiopia was overthrown by a leftist regime under Mengistu Haile Mariam; in southern Africa, where support was given to the MPLA in the aftermath of the 1974 Portuguese Revolution; and later in Central America, where the Sandanista movement, which came to power in Nicaragua in July 1979 after the flight of the dictator Anastasio Somoza, received Soviet support, much to the chagrin of the Reagan administration (1981–89). The US response came partly in the form of support for alternative forces; only rarely did the United States intervene directly, as it did with some success in Grenada in 1983 to prevent the leftist New Jewel Movement from coming to power.

DÉTENTE AND 'COLD WAR TWO'

Despite this rivalry in many parts of the Third World, the 1970s saw better relations between the two superpowers than had hitherto prevailed. The Soviet Union, having completed a huge build-up of its strategic nuclear arsenal in the aftermath of the

Opposite above A women's activist group demonstrates for peace at the height of the Cuban Missile Crisis, October 1962.

Opposite below A Sandinista flees fighting in Leon, Nicaragua. The civil war, fought between the Sandinista government and US-backed Counter-Revolutionaries (Contras) lasted from 1981 to 1989.

Right US President Richard Nixon at a banquet with the Chinese premier Chou En-lai (left) in Shanghai, 27 February 1972. Nixon's visit to China was a significant attempt to establish normal relations between the two countries.

missile crisis, had no reason to feel particularly vulnerable to the United States. The rise of China, indeed, created a certain commonality of interest between Washington and Moscow, and in the early 1970s unconfirmed rumours circulated that the USSR had approached the United States to mount a joint strike against Chinese nuclear facilities (China having tested a nuclear device in 1965) but had been turned down. At the same time the United States had significantly improved its relations with China, most notably through President Nixon's visit in 1972. This in turn sent a positive signal to Moscow: if such an ardently anti-communist figure as Nixon could reach an accommodation with the Chinese leadership, then surely there was scope for better US–Soviet relations as well. Nixon, whose entanglement in the Watergate scandal was to force his resignation in July 1974, was unable to carry this new approach forward, but Kissinger, who remained secretary of state under President Gerald Ford (in office 1974-77), succeeded in doing so.

While 1975 will go down in US history as the year of final defeat in Vietnam, it also represented perhaps the high point of the era of détente. The Helsinki Conference on Security and Cooperation in Europe (July 1975) in a sense constituted a post World War II 'peace conference' as well. Its Final Act represented a bargain of sorts between East and West. The boundaries of European states, and more broadly the spheres of influence in Europe, secured acceptance in exchange for Soviet agreement to a range of human rights guarantees, which provided ballast for the small but courageously articulate dissident movement in the USSR that secretly circulated self-published (*samizdat*) texts celebrating the virtues of democracy and the freedom of the individual.

> '*We have lost the battle for the Afghan people.*'
> Marshal Sergei Akhromeev, Soviet Army,
> 13 November 1986

Nevertheless, by the late 1970s some of the enthusiasm about détente had wilted. Despite the achievements of Helsinki, the dissident movement was under increasing pressure, with key figures at risk of incarceration in psychiatric institutions. This was at odds with the explicit emphasis on human rights that President Carter (in office 1977–81) made a centrepiece of his foreign policy. Furthermore, the Soviet deployment of SS-20 intermediate range ballistic missiles in Eastern Europe led to a decision by NATO on 12 December 1979 to deploy cruise and Pershing-II missiles in response. On the same day a small clique within the Soviet leadership decided to invade Afghanistan, which Soviet forces proceeded to do on 27 December 1979. The consequences were to prove momentous.

Afghanistan had experienced a communist coup in April 1978, but the two main communist factions, Khalq ('Masses') and Parcham ('Banner'), were soon at each other's throats, undermining the new regime's position. Pressure in early 1979 from the Afghan capital, Kabul, for the Soviet Union to become more heavily involved were wisely blocked by the chairman of the Soviet Council of Ministers, Aleksei Kosygin, but by late 1979 ill health had removed him from the scene, and the party leader, Brezhnev, increasingly infirm and erratic in his decisions, was beside himself at the murder in October 1979 of the Afghan communist Nur Muhammad Taraki, who had been Brezhnev's guest barely a month before. The invasion of Afghanistan was entirely successful in removing the loathed Afghan leader Hafizullah Amin, but it had the effect of turning isolated revolts into a widespread insurgency. It also sent

Opposite above Afghan mujahideen stand on a destroyed Russian helicopter, 18 January 1980.

Opposite below Mujahideen attack Kabul by night, 14 May 1983.

East–West relations into a deathly chill. While with hindsight it is clear that the aim of the Soviet invasion was basically to save a client regime, in the wider world it was open to being interpreted as an expansion of the Brezhnev Doctrine and a manifestation of expansionism in general. As Soviet forces became bogged down in Afghanistan, and as the new Reagan administration, pursuant to the Reagan Doctrine, supported the arming of the Afghan resistance (the mujahideen), the Soviet Union staggered through a series of failing leaders – Brezhnev himself, who died in November 1982; Yury Andropov, former Soviet ambassador to Hungary in 1956 and thereafter head of the Committee for State Security (KGB), who held office from November 1982 until his death in February 1984; and finally the feeble Konstantin Chernenko, who died in March 1985. Failure in Afghanistan dogged their steps.

GORBACHEV, 1989 AND THE END OF THE COLD WAR

With the crushing of the Prague Spring in August 1968, it was clear that, if fundamental change were to come peacefully to the Soviet bloc, it would have to be through the emergence of a Dubček-like leader not in a capital of one of the satellites, but in Moscow itself. This finally happened when Gorbachev rose to the position of general secretary. Born in 1931, he had joined the Communist Party in 1952, while Stalin was still alive, but had his most formative political experiences during the thaw under Khrushchev. He had spent much of his career outside Moscow; it was only in 1978 that he moved to the capital, and only in 1980 that he became a full member of the ruling Politburo. While it took him a little while to buttress his position as general secretary through the promotion of some like-minded associates, he soon managed to put his stamp on policy, labelling the Afghanistan experience a 'bleeding wound', and exploiting the 1986 disaster at the Chernobyl nuclear plant to push for more candour (*glasnost*), as well as for broader economic restructuring (*perestroika*) and for a new foreign policy approach. He found unlikely allies in US presidents Reagan and George Bush senior, and in the British prime minister Margaret Thatcher.

Right US President Ronald Reagan and Soviet general secretary Mikhail Gorbachev meet for the first time, to discuss diplomatic relations and the arms race, Geneva, November 1985.

Opposite Germans from East and West stand on the Berlin Wall in front of the Brandenburg Gate, November 1989.

The two decisive developments that marked the path to the end of the Cold War came in 1989. The first was the completion of the withdrawal of Soviet troops from Afghanistan, following the UN-brokered Geneva Accords of April 1988. While this did not solve Afghanistan's grave problems, which were to persist for decades thereafter, it marked a decisive break from a principle once crudely enunciated by Brezhnev to the Czechoslovakian leaders: 'What we have, we hold.' The second was even more dramatic. In November 1989 East Germans visiting Hungary discovered that the reformist Hungarian authorities were prepared to allow them to travel to the West. This made the Berlin Wall redundant, and finally, in scenes that would have been unthinkable even a year earlier, East Berliners were allowed to cross the Wall, and for good measure began to demolish it. Gennady Gerasimov, a prominent Soviet spokesman, proclaimed a new 'Sinatra Doctrine' of peoples and states following their own ways. The effect was to demolish the foundations on which the Eastern bloc stood. Gorbachev lasted only two years more, but he will undoubtedly go down as one of the most decisive figures of the 20th century. Like Samson in the Book of Judges, he pulled down the pillars that held the Temple in place. In doing so, he also brought the Cold War to an end.

'Mr Gorbachev, open the gate!
Mr Gorbachev, tear down this wall!'
US President Ronald Reagan, 12 June 1987

12 Contested Lands: The Middle East, 1945–1993

AHRON BREGMAN

Opposite An Israeli Air Force Phantom jet fighter flies over the Lebanese capital of Beirut, 21 August 1982.

Conflicts in the Middle East took many different shapes in the era after World War II. They were fought between Israelis and Arabs, Arabs and Iranians, Arabs and Arabs; they ranged from battles between conventional armies, to civil wars, to asymmetrical clashes between regular armies and insurgency groups. Many were fights to gain resources such as oil and territory, but others occurred for less tangible reasons, such as religious or political ideology.

ARAB–ISRAELI WARS

Palestine, an area that was under British control from 1917 to 1948, experienced a changing demography brought about by the growing influx of Jewish immigrants, particularly following the rise of Nazism in the 1930s. Jews had made up only 4 per cent of the total population of Palestine in 1882; by 1947 there were 608,230 Jews in Palestine compared with about 1,364,330 Arabs. This demographic transformation was accompanied by a geographical change as the new arrivals purchased large tracts of Palestinian land. Tension between Jews and Arabs increased.

On 29 November 1947 the United Nations proposed to partition Palestine between the two peoples, allowing each community to form its own independent state on some of the land; it offered the Jews 55 per cent of Palestine and the Arab majority 45 per cent. The Jews accepted the offer, but the Arabs objected and threatened that any attempt to divide Palestine would lead to war. The UN proceeded anyway, and passed the partition resolution; the next day a civil war broke out in Palestine and continued until 14 May 1948.

The 1948 war

On 14 May 1948 the British left Palestine and the Jews declared independence, and thus the state of Israel was born and the Jews of Palestine became 'Israelis'. In response, the Arab armies of Egypt, Syria, Lebanon, Iraq and Transjordan, supported by units from Saudi Arabia and Yemen, invaded. Thus what started as a civil war between Jews and Arabs within Palestinian boundaries now became an all-out conventional war between the Israeli Defence Forces (IDF) and neighbouring Arab armies. For the Israelis, this was their 'War of Liberation' or 'War of Independence', while for the Arab Palestinians, some 750,000 of whom became refugees as a result of the war, it became *al Nakba* ('the Catastrophe').

The IDF managed to contain the Arab onslaught, to counter-attack and to seize some of the lands the UN had partitioned off to the Palestinians in 1947. Of the rest of this land allotted to the Palestinians, Egypt managed to capture the Gaza Strip,

and Transjordan took the West Bank. Thus, by the end of the first Arab–Israeli war in March 1949, Palestine was partitioned between Israelis, Jordanians and Egyptians.

In terms of warfare, the 1948 war was quite a primitive encounter in which the single soldier played a leading role while large formations – battalions, regiments, divisions – played little part. Sophisticated weapons, tanks and aeroplanes were hardly used at all. Contrary to popular belief, this war was not one between the 'few' Israelis and 'many' Arabs: careful analysis shows that the number of Israeli troops committed to the battle on the eve of the Arab invasion was roughly equal to that of the invaders, but by the end of the war Israel's fighting force was larger in absolute terms than that of the Arab armies put together. It was not a 'miracle', as is often claimed, that led to Israeli success in halting the Arab invasion, but numerical advantage, better organization and sheer determination.

The 1956 war

Unlike 1948, when war was imposed on Israel, in 1956 it was Israel, in collusion with Britain and France, that went on the offensive. On 26 July 1956 President Gamal Abdel Nasser of Egypt nationalized the Suez Canal Company, of which France and Britain had been the majority shareholders, and the two colonial powers began considering the use of force to regain control. Israel was secretly invited to join the coalition against Nasser, which would provide an opportunity for the young nation to achieve some of its own aims, mainly to gain control of the Straits of Tiran. These waters,

'We are not at war with Egypt. We are in an armed conflict.'

Anthony Eden, British prime minister, on the 1956 attempt to recapture the Suez Canal from Egypt

at the foot of the Gulf of Aqaba, were Israel's primary trade route to East Africa and Asia but had for several years been blockaded by Egypt.

A simple plan emerged: Israel would provide a pretext for French and British intervention by attacking Egypt from the east, approaching the Suez Canal. The British and French governments, as if taken by surprise, would appeal to the governments of Israel and Egypt to stop the fighting. They would demand that both Egypt and Israel halt all acts of war and withdraw all troops 16 km (10 miles) from the canal; Egypt was also to accept temporary occupation by Britain and France of key positions on the canal. Israel, which of course would know the terms in advance, would then accept the terms, and it was hoped that Egypt would follow suit, allowing French and British troops to regain effective control of the canal without bloodshed. However, if Nasser were to refuse the terms, France and Britain would seize the canal by force.

Opposite Palestinian Jews flee from an explosion, Jerusalem, 24 February 1948. This was a time of civil war in Palestine, when Jews and Arabs, often neighbours, attacked each other.

Below British soldiers sit on a captured gun outside Port Said, Egypt, during the Suez Crisis, 1956. They failed to achieve their stated aims, however, as international pressure to stop the operation mounted.

'Soldiers of Israel, we have no aims of conquest. Our purpose is to bring to naught the attempts of the Arab armies to conquer our land.'

Israel's defence minister, Moshe Dayan, on the eve of the 1967 war

'I looked down and saw the Egyptian MiGs shining, sparkling with the pilots sitting inside the cockpits. I looked to my right and saw fire and smoke coming up from all the other bases near Inshas. It was then that I realized that we had managed to surprise them.'

Ronen Peker, an Israeli Mirage squadron commander, on the air assault that opened the 1967 war

Opposite above Israeli tanks lead the drive of Ben Gurion's forces across the Sinai Peninsula, 29 October 1956.

Opposite below Egyptian planes destroyed in a pre-emptive strike by the Israeli Air Force at the start of the Six-Day War, 5 June 1967. With its air force in ruins, the Egyptian army stood little chance against the Israelis.

The IDF struck on 29 October 1956, when aircraft dropped 385 parachute troops at the Israeli end of the Mitla Pass, some 48 km (30 miles) east of the Suez Canal. Egypt then moved forces to face the invaders and, on 30 October, Britain and France issued their ultimatum. When Egypt refused to accept the terms, the Anglo-French coalition struck from the air the following day, and on 5 November sent in ground troops to seize key positions along the Suez Canal. In the meantime, as planned, the IDF moved south and removed the blockade at the Straits of Tiran. In the course of this operation Israel occupied the entire Sinai Peninsula, destroying Egyptian forces and killing hundreds of enemy troops at a cost of 172 Israeli soldiers killed and 700 wounded.

There was international outrage, particularly from the United States, at this blatant action, which smacked of old-fashioned colonial arrogance. The Eisenhower administration forced France and Britain to halt operations, accept a ceasefire, withdraw their troops and agree to UN monitors replacing them along the canal. In March 1957 the Israelis, also under international pressure, withdrew from the Sinai – not, however, before issuing a stark warning that, should Egypt ever again blockade the Straits of Tiran, they would regard it as a *casus belli* and launch war on Egypt.

The 1967 war

Imposing a blockade on the Straits of Tiran to all Israel-bound ships was precisely what President Nasser, a self-declared leader of the Arab world, did ten years later, on 23 May 1967. The blockade – along with other warlike Egyptian actions, such as removing UN observers from the Sinai, combined with bellicose rhetoric from Syria and Jordan – led to a significant escalation of tension in the Middle East. Feeling cornered, Israel decided to pre-empt any Arab attack and strike first.

Using almost all its aeroplanes, the Israeli Air Force (IAF), flying low to avoid Egyptian radar, came from behind Egyptian lines and in a massive three-hour attack destroyed almost the entire Egyptian air force (most of it still on the ground). Israeli ground forces then invaded the Sinai Peninsula and engaged the Egyptian army. Lacking any air support, the Egyptians stood little chance and retreated, chased by Israeli tanks and attacked intensely from the air. The Israelis again seized the Sinai Peninsula, reaching the Suez Canal; they also took the Gaza Strip, which had been under Egypt's control since 1948. The war quickly expanded to other fronts, where the IDF continued to inflict major defeats on Arab armies: from Jordan it took the West Bank and Jerusalem, and from Syria it captured the strategic Golan Heights. It was a dramatic Israeli victory in a short war – it became known as the 'Six-Day War' – that 'changed the face of the Middle East'.

The 1973 war

After the 1967 war, Israel made it clear that it was reluctant to return the captured lands. It embarked on a creeping annexation, building settlements in the seized territories and exploiting resources such as oil in the Sinai and water in the Gaza Strip and West Bank. This deeply upset the Arabs. What is more, the United States and USSR were enjoying an unusual period of détente and were reluctant to have their Middle Eastern clients ruin the improved atmosphere. Both, therefore, seemed to accept the new status quo and to ignore Israel's actions. Egypt and Syria, however, decided to launch a military attack on Israel, to liberate at least some of their lost land and perhaps force it into diplomatic negotiations over withdrawal from the rest.

'We were all silent, focused on the radar. Then the first brigade crossed the canal and put up the Egyptian flag on the other side. We all cheered.'
General Abdel Ghani el-Gamasy, Egypt's chief of operations, on the crossing of the Suez Canal, 1973

Egypt and Syria attacked on 6 October 1973, which was Yom Kippur, the holiest day in the Jewish calendar, thus catching Israel surprised and unprepared. The Arab offensive started with a massive Egyptian–Syrian air bombardment on Israeli targets in the Sinai and the Golan Heights. In the Sinai, soon after the air strike, Egyptian guns opened a tremendous bombardment along the Suez Canal; in the Golan, Syrian guns opened a similar barrage on Israeli positions. Back at the Suez Canal 4,000 Egyptian troops poured over the ramparts and slithered in disciplined lines down to the water's edge to begin crossing in small boats. In twenty-four hours, the Egyptians managed to land 100,000 men, 1,000 tanks and 13,500 vehicles on the Israeli side of the canal. Facing this invasion were a mere 505 Israeli troops, who could do little to stop the Egyptians. On the Golan Heights, in the meantime, a first wave of 500 Syrian tanks, closely followed by a further 300, crashed through the Israeli lines along the entire front and penetrated deep into the Golan Heights. At this point the Egyptian and Syrian success appeared to be as great as that of the Israelis in 1967, and the Arab world was jubilant, after six years of humiliation at the hands of the previously 'invincible' foe.

It took the Israelis some time to mobilize their reserves, which form the main bulk of the IDF. Their first priority was to contain the Syrian invasion on the Golan, where there was no strategic depth and Jewish settlements were close to the front line. The Israelis successfully halted the Syrian advance, but it would take a week before it was the Syrians who were on the defensive, as Israeli troops crossed east of the Golan towards Damascus. Back in the Sinai, on 8 October the IDF tried but failed to counter-attack. On 14 October they succeeded, inflicting heavy losses on the Egyptians, who made the mistake of moving away from their ground-to-air missile umbrella that so far had shielded them from the IAF (see box on p. 236). On the ground Major-General Ariel Sharon, a division commander, managed to cross the Suez Canal to form a bridgehead on the Egyptian side of the water; by 18 October, the IDF had a substantial force of three armoured brigades and an infantry brigade on the western bank of the canal. Then, in a daring manoeuvre,

Above Egyptian troops plant their flag on captured Israeli territory on the eastern bank of the Suez Canal, 1973. Crossing the canal during the conflict's initial phase was an impressive achievement for the Egyptian army.

Right The Yom Kippur War, 6–26 October 1973.

Opposite Major-General Ariel Sharon (right) confers with fellow general Haim Bar-Lev over a map of the Sinai Desert, 17 October 1973.

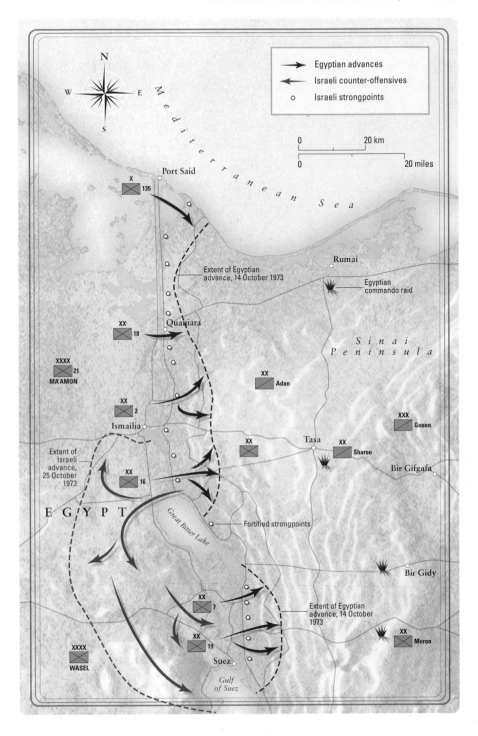

Sharon completely cut off the Third Egyptian army from the rear, isolating about 45,000 Egyptian troops and 250 tanks from the rest of the Egyptian forces. International pressure stopped the war, and the forces later disengaged. In military terms IDF performance in the 1973 war – the way it recovered from the initial surprise, mobilized and counter-attacked – was more impressive than its performance in the 1967 war. But in most people's minds, including those of many Israelis, in 1973 Egypt and Syria were the victors.

Surface-to-Air Missiles

In the 1960s, as was demonstrated during the 1967 war, the IAF enjoyed air superiority in the Middle East. Israel's opponents, particularly Egypt and Syria, concluded that the solution lay not in trying to match Israeli air power, but in creating an effective surface-to-air-missile (SAM) system as protection from IAF attacks. The Soviets supplied the missiles, and Arab air-defence planners created a thick, almost impenetrable, belt that included, among other missiles, the SAM-2. With its range of 45 km (30 miles) and altitude of 20,000 m (65,000 ft), the SAM-2 was guided by radio signals. Its warhead weighed 195 kg (430 lb), and it had a lethal radius of about 65 m (215 ft) at low altitudes and a wider radius of up to 250 m (820 ft) at higher altitudes.

During the initial phases of their October 1973 attack, Egyptian and Syrian forces operated under this missile umbrella (which also included the SAM-3 and other types of surface-to-air weapon). But so rapid was their advance, particularly on the Egyptian front, that no additional forward SAM belts were there for protection against the IAF. Thus, when the advancing Egyptian forces left the SAM cover, they exposed themselves to ferocious IAF strikes and were eventually stopped by the Israelis.

A SAM-2 surface-to-air missile providing cover for Egyptian forces during the Yom Kippur War, October 1973.

A young Lebanese girl undergoing military training to fight the Israeli enemy, Beirut, 1982.

The 1982 war in Lebanon

By 1982 General Sharon was Israeli defence minister. From the day of his appointment his attention was firmly focused on Lebanon, where he identified two main problems. The first was the presence of Syrian troops and their ground-to-air missile system in the Beka Valley, which hindered the IAF's freedom to fly over Lebanon; the second was the presence of the Palestine Liberation Organization (PLO), led by Yasser Arafat, whom Sharon suspected of wanting to take over Lebanon and turn it into a base from which to attack Israel. Sharon wished to strike at both the PLO and the Syrians in Lebanon.

The opportunity came on 3 June 1982, when gunmen of a dissident Palestinian faction, led by Abu Nidal, shot and seriously injured the Israeli ambassador to London. Despite the fact that Abu Nidal was a sworn enemy of Arafat, such was the mood in Israel following the assassination attempt that ministers were willing to accept the view of those who urged the attack on the PLO. On 4 June Israeli aircraft struck at nine PLO targets in Lebanon; the PLO hit back and for twenty-four hours shelled villages in northern Israel. On 5 June the Israeli Cabinet authorized an invasion of Lebanon, 'Operation Peace for Galilee'; it would later come to be known as the Lebanon War. The Cabinet gave the IDF the mission of 'freeing all the Galilee settlements from the range of fire of terrorists' and instructed that 'the Syrian army [stationed in Lebanon] should not be attacked unless it attacks our forces'. Defence Minister Sharon made it clear that the operation's objective was to remove the PLO from firing range of Israel's northern border, approximately 45 km (28 miles).

On 6 June 1982 the IDF invaded Lebanon. On the western sector along the Lebanese coast forces moved northwards, but rather than stopping 45 km from the international border as instructed by the Cabinet, Sharon ordered them to proceed up to Lebanon's capital, Beirut, in order to hunt down the PLO leader, Yasser Arafat. By 1 July, Beirut was encircled and under Israeli siege. On the eastern sector, after crossing the international border into Lebanon, troops advanced in the direction of the Syrians without firing at them. The Syrians, however, faced with Israeli tanks and troops moving in their direction, understandably opened fire. With his forces 'under attack', Sharon allowed them to return fire, sparking all-out war between Israeli and Syrian troops. Claiming that Syrian ground-to-air missiles in the Beka Valley hindered IAF efforts to support the ground forces, Sharon persuaded the Cabinet to allow him to destroy the Syrian missiles. The attack was delivered on 8 June by the IAF and knocked out nearly all the Syrian batteries (the remaining two were destroyed the next day). The Syrian air force intervened and lost ninety-six MiGs – Soviet-built fighters – without a single Israeli plane lost. This was a demonstration of how Israel's superior training and technology led to positive results on the battlefield.

In the meantime a massive Israeli bombardment against Beirut also produced results (and an international outcry), forcing the Lebanese government to demand that Arafat and the PLO leave the city. In less than a fortnight almost 15,000 Palestinian guerrillas were evacuated to other countries, including Yasser Arafat, who went to Tunis; 5,200 Syrian troops also left Beirut for Syria. Yet now the Israelis made what would prove to be a catastrophic mistake. They allowed a Lebanese Christian militia to enter the Palestinian refugee camps of Sabra and Shatilla between

16 and 18 September in order to remove the 2,000 armed PLO fighters who, according to Israeli intelligence, remained in the camps after the Palestinian evacuation. The Christian militia found no armed Palestinians, only women, children and the elderly: but they massacred hundreds of them anyway.

From a military point of view Sharon did manage to achieve at least some of his aims: the IDF pushed the PLO and Syrian forces out of Beirut, and the IAF destroyed the Syrian air defence in eastern Lebanon. But the price was high, as the war brought on Israel unprecedented international condemnation, particularly after the massacre in Sabra and Shatilla. Israeli troops remained in Lebanon for eighteen years, under constant harassment. Here was a lesson that the Israelis should have learned from the experience of others, notably from the Americans in Vietnam: that it is relatively easy to invade, but much more complicated to disengage. Armies can occupy territory in days, but getting out can take years.

The 1987 intifada

Until 1987 the Arab–Israeli conflict had mainly taken the form of an encounter between conventional armies, but this began to change when the IDF was confronted by an uprising in lands under its occupation. On 8 December 1987 an Israeli and a Palestinian vehicle collided, killing four Palestinians and injuring seven others. Rumours spread among the Palestinians that the car crash was somehow deliberate, and at the victims' funerals in the Jabalya refugee camp in Gaza angry Palestinians hurled stones at nearby Israeli army units. A soldier opened fire and killed a Palestinian, which led to riots. These quickly spread from Jabalya to refugee camps throughout the Gaza Strip, and then engulfed the more secular and affluent West Bank. These events were the beginnings of the *intifada* ('shaking off'), which saw the highly trained and well-equipped Israeli army come into conflict with loose gangs of Palestinians, often no more than children, often armed only with rocks. This asymmetry was to prove a major problem for the Israelis. By avoiding a classic guerrilla war, the Palestinians effectively neutralized Israel's vast military superiority.

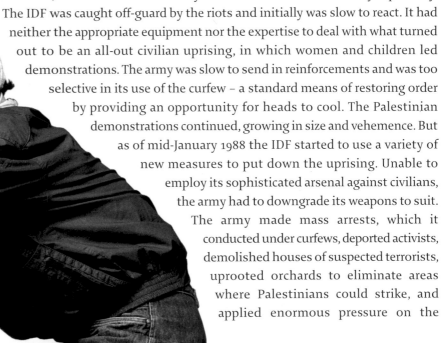

The IDF was caught off-guard by the riots and initially was slow to react. It had neither the appropriate equipment nor the expertise to deal with what turned out to be an all-out civilian uprising, in which women and children led demonstrations. The army was slow to send in reinforcements and was too selective in its use of the curfew – a standard means of restoring order by providing an opportunity for heads to cool. The Palestinian demonstrations continued, growing in size and vehemence. But as of mid-January 1988 the IDF started to use a variety of new measures to put down the uprising. Unable to employ its sophisticated arsenal against civilians, the army had to downgrade its weapons to suit. The army made mass arrests, which it conducted under curfews, deported activists, demolished houses of suspected terrorists, uprooted orchards to eliminate areas where Palestinians could strike, and applied enormous pressure on the

Palestinian population to submit. These measures made economic conditions in the occupied territories dire. Throughout the six years of the intifada the army managed to reduce the volume of Palestinian violence, but it was never able to declare an outright victory over the insurgents. On 13 September 1993 Israeli Prime Minister Yitzhak Rabin and Palestinian leader Yasser Arafat signed the Oslo Accords, which, among other things, put an end to the intifada. It was thus a political deal rather than military might that stopped the uprising.

THE IRAN–IRAQ WAR

In another corner of the Middle East the 1980s saw the long and bloody eight-year war between Iraq and Iran. Tensions between Iran and Iraq had been simmering for a long time before the outbreak of war, which focused mainly on a territorial dispute over the Shatt al-Arab. This strategically important river is formed by the confluence of the Euphrates and the Tigris, and at its southern end constitutes the border between Iraq and Iran before it discharges into the Persian Gulf.

In 1975 Iraq, which at that time was militarily weak in comparison with Iran (which under the shah enjoyed American patronage and had the fourth-largest army in the world), signed over to Iran partial control of the waterway, but continued to harbour desire for full control over it as a vital national interest. A religious divide between the countries did not help ease tensions; while both nations were Muslim, the leaders of Iraq came primarily from the Sunni branch, while the Iranians were mostly Shiite. This difference became more significant after the 1979 Iranian Revolution, when Ayatollah Ruhollah Khomeini, Iran's new leader, began encouraging Iraqis to overthrow Saddam Hussein, Iraq's leader, because his more secular regime was, as Khomeini put it, 'anti-Islamic'.

At this point Saddam Hussein believed Iran was vulnerable because its new leader had not yet solidified his power, and Iran's army, whose highest-ranking officers had all been executed by the new regime, was in disarray. He calculated that a surprise attack on Iran could gain him full control of the Shatt al-Arab, and possibly also Iran's oil fields in Khuzestan, and could also help establish him as the leader of the Arab world – particularly now that the traditional leadership of Egypt was out of favour following its signing of peace with Israel in March 1979.

On 1 April 1980 the Iranian-supported al-Dawah group attempted to assassinate Iraqi minister Tariq Aziz. In response Saddam Hussein ordered all al-Dawah members to be arrested and deported to Iran, together with thousands of Shias of Iranian origin. In June 1980 the two nations severed diplomatic relations, and that summer military clashes occurred along the Iraqi–Iranian border. On 17 September, Saddam Hussein declared the 1975 treaty over the Shatt al-Arab null and void.

The war begins

Saddam Hussein ordered the invasion of western Iran on 22 September 1980, beginning with a massive air attack. But this failed to destroy Iran's aircraft, which were protected in specially strengthened hangars. Simultaneously, seven Iraqi army divisions penetrated Iran on three fronts, with the main thrust of five divisions being in the direction of the Khuzestan province in western Iran, with the aim of capturing Khorramshahr and other cities. This would cut off Iranian reinforcement routes and

Opposite A Palestinian youth armed with a catapult during the first intifada, April 1988. Using such primitive arms was a clever tactic, forcing the well-equipped Israeli army to downgrade its own weapons.

Below Saddam Hussein, president of Iraq, gives a report on the state of the war with Iran, 5 July 1987. He had miscalculated, assuming that post-revolution Iran would be an easy target.

deliver to Iraq the Shatt al-Arab along with Khuzestan's vast oil fields. Since the majority of people in this province were ethnic Arabs rather than Persians, Saddam wrongly assumed that they would welcome the Iraqi troops, but instead they joined the Iranian forces.

The Iraqi army met its first serious opposition when it attempted to take Khorramshahr, and, with casualties mounting, Saddam ordered his army to surround the remaining cities and starve them out; Khorramshahr eventually fell on 10 November 1980. By that time, however, the Iraqi invasion had lost much of its momentum, and with winter closing in the troops had to dig in without achieving total control of Khuzestan. At this point Saddam hoped to force Khomeini to negotiate a deal that would leave the Shatt al-Arab in Iraqi hands.

But in mid-1981 Khomeini's forces counter-attacked, broke the Iraqi siege of Abadan and later recaptured Khorramshahr. By 29 November, Iran had resorted to human wave attacks, sending lines of children into the combat zones to detonate concealed mines and to open routes for assaulting forces, and by June 1982 Iraqi forces had been driven out of Iran completely. Khomeini rejected international calls to stop the war and launched a counter-invasion. But with neither side having enough self-propelled artillery or air power to support major offensives, the confrontation settled into a bloody trench war of attrition.

The war expands

In April 1984 Iraq attacked Iranian oil tankers in the Persian Gulf, as well as an oil terminal in Iran. Saddam Hussein was desperate to force Iran to negotiate a ceasefire, and hoped that the international community, fearful of disrupted oil supplies, would intervene. Iran struck back at Iraqi oil tankers, and thus began the 'tanker war'. In 1985 Khomeini's forces launched a massive offensive to cut the main highway between Baghdad and Basra; as many as 40,000 soldiers from both sides were killed.

Opposite An Iranian boy bids farewell as he volunteers to fight in the war against Iraq.

Above Iraqi troops constructing a bridge at Khorramshahr, south-western Iran, 1981. During this phase of the Iran Iraq War, the Iraqis were still achieving success and moving deeper into Iranian territory.

Above right Two dead Iraqi soldiers lie on a battlefield in Fao, Iraq, 23 February 1986. By this point of the conflict, successful Iranian counter-attacks had inflicted massive damage on the Iraqi army and caused many casualties.

Saddam again attempted to escalate the war in order to force Iran to negotiate. He dispatched his air force to attack Iran's capital, Tehran, and later started using Scud missiles against Iranian cities. But Iran retaliated by launching its own Scud missiles on Baghdad; in all, it is estimated that Iraq launched 520 Scuds against Iranian cities, and received 177 in exchange.

In 1986 and at the beginning of 1987, Iran continued to launch new offensives, the last reaching the outskirts of Basra before again getting bogged down. Iraq, in the meantime, escalated the tanker war in the Gulf, which led eventually to a growing involvement of the international community; Kuwait even transferred some of its tankers to American registry so that US warships could protect them. American ships sank eight Iranian craft and accidentally shot down a civilian Iranian airliner, believing it to be an attacking fighter jet. The United States also provided Iraq with weapons and access to satellite imagery of Iranian troop movements. By August 1988, realizing that it would be impossible to break the deadlock in the war, Ayatollah Khomeini finally agreed to a UN-mediated ceasefire.

Total casualties in the war are estimated at up to 1.5 million dead, a figure that puts this conflict in the same category as some of the bloodiest wars in human history. After eight years of fighting, neither side could claim an outright victory, and the border disputes were not resolved. Nevertheless, Iraq emerged from the war with roughly 1 million men under arms, 500 combat aircraft and 5,500 tanks – the nucleus of the force that would fight the UN-led coalition in the next Gulf War (see the following chapter).

13 A New World Order and the War on Terror

MICHAEL ROSE

Opposite US Marines returning from Operation Desert Storm take part in a victory parade, New York, June 1991.

At the end of the Cold War, US President George Bush senior told the American people the world had entered a period of great transition and great hope, and yet also of great uncertainty. He later expressed his wish for a new order in which the world would become a more stable, more peaceful place. But the explosion of violence and disorder that spread across the world following the fragmentation of the Soviet bloc undoubtedly destroyed all possibility that the end of the Cold War would bring about a safer world. Indeed, in the decade that followed the fall of the Berlin Wall, 5 million people were killed and over 35 million people were displaced from their homes.

Nevertheless, compared with the high level of violence that had occurred during the Cold War, the actual number of conflicts that took place in the 1990s declined by 30 per cent, and civilian casualties also fell by one third. This happened in spite of the far higher lethality of modern weapon systems. By the start of the 21st century, the major powers of the world were to find themselves in the midst of the longest uninterrupted period of peace that they had experienced in many centuries, and this continues to be the case today – notwithstanding the outbreak of what President George Bush junior called the 'global War on Terror'.

CIVIL WAR IN THE 1990S

Most of the wars of the 1990s were civil wars in which nation states were failing or had ceased to exist, as in Somalia or Yugoslavia. Of the 55 conflicts fought during that decade, 44 were civil wars. Ethnic and religious animosity rather than a desire for independence had become the chief cause of wars, and, because of the inevitably high level of human suffering caused by this type of conflict, the United Nations was increasingly drawn into peacekeeping and humanitarian missions. For the first time in its fifty-year history, NATO also became involved in operations outside its borders. Most importantly, as its troops were released from their principal task of helping to defend Europe, the United States was able to pursue an increasingly active interventionist policy whose goal was avowedly to spread freedom and democracy to the peoples of the world – and thereby bring about global peace and security. At the same time, of course, the US would be extending its influence and economic interests – especially in the Middle East, in order to gain unimpeded access to oil.

The technical nature of war was also being radically transformed by the rapid development of advanced surveillance systems, smart weapons and stealth technology. In particular, the use of unmanned aerial vehicles (UAVs: see box overleaf) had allowed the covert surveillance and targeting of insurgents by remote means,

Unmanned Aerial Vehicles

The ability to identify and instantly destroy targets from unmanned aerial vehicles has completely transformed counter-insurgency warfare in the 21st century, for it is now possible to identify, track and finally destroy the enemy covertly without deploying special forces on the ground. Predator, the first true generation of modern unmanned aerial vehicles, had its first flight in February 2001. It was powered by a turboprop engine and was designed as a long-endurance, high-altitude unmanned aircraft for reconnaissance, surveillance, targeting and weapons delivery, as well as for scientific research. Its technically advanced successor, Reaper, which carries a far greater payload and is much faster than the original Predator, is a true hunter/killer system. It has been in daily use in Iraq and Afghanistan, and has carried out many effective strikes against the Taliban and al-Qaeda leadership.

Above An MQ-9 Reaper prepares to land after a mission in Afghanistan. The Reaper can carry both precision-guided bombs and air-to-ground missiles.

Below US officers perform routine checks after launching an MQ-1B Predator at Balad air base, Iraq.

and this has transformed the tactics and doctrine of modern counter-insurgency warfare. By the end of the 20th century the US lead in military capability had become so great that no other power in the world could successfully confront US forces in conventional warfare because of their overwhelming conventional military superiority. After the Cold War their military advantage gave the United States a historically unique opportunity in which it was able to exercise its interventionist foreign policy.

INTERNATIONAL INTERVENTION VERSUS NATIONAL SOVEREIGNTY

From the early 1990s the response of the international community to the disintegration of nation states and the outbreaks of conflict was confused. On the one hand, in the United States and in NATO there was a belief that military force could be effectively used to resolve the sort of complex political and humanitarian emergencies that were taking place in the Balkans and in Africa. This belief was reinforced by a feeling that there was a moral duty to intervene where human rights abuses or extreme humanitarian emergencies were occurring – even if this meant ignoring national sovereignty.

On the other hand, there was an equally strong view, represented mainly in the United Nations, that the sovereignty of nations was paramount and that national consent was required before peacekeeping or humanitarian missions could be launched. Furthermore, it was firmly believed that peacekeepers should use only minimum levels of military force in self-defence or for the enforcement of a mandate.

The incompatibility between these two opposing views was dramatically exposed in Somalia in 1993, when a UN peacekeeping mission led by the United States began to pursue war-fighting goals. The disastrous consequences of going beyond the basic peacekeeping mandate resulted in the withdrawal of the UN mission, and this would directly influence the international community's approach to the wars in Bosnia and Rwanda a year later. However, the experience of the 1990s did not end

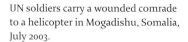

UN soldiers carry a wounded comrade to a helicopter in Mogadishu, Somalia, July 2003.

Rwandan Hutu refugees in Goma refugee camp, eastern Zaire, 1994. The Hutu-dominated regime in Rwanda had been defeated, and an estimated 2 million Hutus had streamed across the border into neighbouring Zaire.

the argument between those who held the two opposing points of view, and by the end of the century the statesmen of the West had still not worked out the nature of the conflict they were engaged in, what their military responses should be or, indeed, whether they should be involved at all.

Although the Balkan Wars of the 1990s attracted most media attention and international resources – the 23,000 peacekeepers deployed at the height of the conflict in Bosnia represented the largest and most expensive peacekeeping contingent that the UN had ever deployed – the civil wars in the Great Lakes area of Africa that took place during the same decade were in fact responsible for far more civilian deaths. They also created huge numbers of refugees. In 1994, while the Western world agonized over the siege of Sarajevo and the undoubted suffering of the Bosnian people caught up in a three-sided civil war, between 800,000 and 1 million people were being slaughtered in a terrible genocide that was taking place in Rwanda. This was nearly ten times the number of people killed in the Bosnian war. Yet little was done by the international community to halt the slaughter, in spite of urgent appeals by the UN commander on the ground, General Roméo Dallaire.

Rather than using the conflicts of the 1990s to develop clear viable strategies with which to respond to the coming challenges of the 21st century, lack of clarity and consistency of purpose ensured that the West would become the chief contributor to that very uncertainty that President Bush senior had predicted would characterize international affairs following the end of the Cold War.

THE BALKAN WARS

The declaration of independence by the republics of Slovenia and Croatia on 25 June 1991 signalled the start of the Balkan Wars of the 1990s. In Slovenia, after only ten days of fighting the largely Serb forces of the Yugoslav People's Army withdrew, and a de facto independence was granted to the country by President Milošević in Belgrade, who realized that it would be impossible to keep Slovenia as part of Yugoslavia. He saw that Yugoslavia needed to concentrate its military effort in Croatia and Bosnia if it was not to disintegrate completely. At that time both the United Nations and the US supported his view that regional security required that the national integrity of Yugoslavia should be preserved – with the exception of Slovenia.

The military situation in Croatia was complicated by the fact that Serbs occupied 30 per cent of the country and were located in the Krajina Serb enclaves that bordered Bosnia to the east and south. The clashes between the Croatian paramilitary groups and local Serb militias in these enclaves soon led to full-scale civil war, with thousands of civilians fleeing the fighting. Two major Croatian cities, Vukovar and Dubrovnik, came under sustained siege and suffered the largest artillery bombardment that Europe had witnessed since the end of World War II. The battle in Vukovar raged for eighty-seven days before the city finally fell to the Yugoslav army, supported by Serb militia, on 18 November 1991. Some 264 Croatian survivors of the battle were massacred, and the remaining Croats were forced to leave the ruins of their city. A ceasefire between the Croatian forces and those of Yugoslavia was finally agreed on 2 January 1992, and the Yugoslav army started to withdraw from Croatia; at the same time both sides agreed to the presence of a UN peacekeeping force to ensure the protection of the minority Serb communities in the Krajinas.

Dubrovnik under siege, November 1991. The Croatian city suffered intense bombardment of a kind not seen in Europe since the end of World War II.

But although Croatia had lost the battle for Vukovar, it proved to be a turning point in the Balkan Wars. The European Union and the United Nations, horrified by the brutal methods employed by the Yugoslav army and Serb militias, gave formal recognition to the independent state of Croatia on 15 January 1992.

On 25 September 1991, at the height of the fighting, the UN passed a resolution imposing a total arms embargo on Yugoslavia in an effort to reduce the level of conflict in the region. Further resolutions followed, including one establishing a no-fly zone over the country. However, these measures gave a considerable military advantage to the Bosnian Serbs, since they were already in possession of heavy artillery, tanks and other military equipment. Two years later the United States broke the arms embargo and breached the no-fly zone, bringing in weapons and equipment, and flying unmanned reconnaissance aircraft over Bosnia in order to tilt the military balance in favour of the Croatian and Bosnian forces. NATO, which was complicit in these violations, had been tasked by the UN with enforcing the arms embargo and no-fly zone. NATO air power was also available to support UN peacekeeping forces on the ground, but the engagement of NATO with an agenda that was incompatible with peacekeeping ultimately made the UN mission in Bosnia unworkable.

Armed conflict between Muslims, Serbs and Croats had already begun when Bosnia-Herzegovina declared independence on 6 April 1992. The withdrawal of the regular Yugoslav army from Croatia following the ceasefire and peace agreement resulted in an intensification of the fighting in Bosnia-Herzegovina. As a result of their superior military power, the Serbs were rapidly able to seize 70 per cent of the country. At that time almost half the population of Bosnia-Herzegovina was Muslim (44 per cent of 4.4 million people); the Serbs represented 31 per cent and the Croats 17 per cent. Each side immediately started to drive out opposing civilian populations from the areas that they controlled, through programmes of mass killings, the destruction of entire villages and widespread intimidation. The majority of

Right Tanks of the Yugoslav People's Army in action on a country road in Croatia, May 1991.

Opposite UN peacekeeping forces monitor the ceasefire in Sarajevo, February 1994.

'Any successful peacekeeping operation has to be based on some agreement between the hostile parties . . . [it] also requires parties to the conflict to respect the UN, its personnel and its mandate . . . and none of the parties there can claim to satisfy that condition.'

Boutros Boutros-Ghali, UN secretary-general, on peacekeeping in Bosnia-Herzegovina, 1992

this 'ethnic cleansing', as it came to be called, was carried out by the Serbs, although the Bosnians and Croats were also guilty of similar crimes against humanity.

During the fighting from 1992 to 1995, over 102,000 people died, of whom more than 55,000 were civilians. Millions of people fled their homes, and infrastructure was destroyed in what rapidly became a three-sided civil war. The western and southern districts of Sarajevo were captured by the Serbs, who put the remainder of the city under siege and subjected its citizens to intense bombardment. In 1993 a NATO ultimatum created a military exclusion zone on the highest mountain overlooking Sarajevo, Mount Igman, which allowed a trickle of supplies to reach the city. Nevertheless, the people of Sarajevo remained almost entirely reliant on UN aid for their survival. At the height of the war, 2.7 million people became dependent on UN aid, most of them living in non-Serb areas.

Because of the strong international belief that something had to be done to try
to bring an end to the war and to reduce the level of human suffering, on 8 June 1992
a mandate was agreed for a UN peacekeeping presence in Bosnia-Herzegovina. By
October 1993, forty-seven Security Council resolutions had been passed in response
to the deteriorating situation. However, there was no consensus over what should
be done. Those countries that had provided peacekeeping troops were largely against
military confrontation with the Serbs, while those, such as the United States, that
did not have troops on the ground supported a 'lift and strike' policy, whereby
the arms and no-fly embargo would be suspended, and an aerial bombardment
of the Serbs would be launched by NATO. Lacking consistent direction from the
UN, the peacekeeping mission in Bosnia-Herzegovina was obliged to determine its
own course.

One of the agreements reached in the UN came about as a result of a suggestion
by the International Committee of the Red Cross. Demilitarized 'safe areas' were
proposed, in which people would be able to live without fear of harassment, killing
or arrest. This would require the consent of the warring parties, for peacekeepers
are clearly not able to defend locations or populations using war-fighting means.
Peacekeepers are, however, by their presence able to deter attacks against safe areas
and to report any breaches of the agreement. On 18 April 1993 Srebrenica became
the first of six agreed safe areas; the others were Sarajevo, Zepa, Tuzla, Goražde and
Bihać. Yet the Bosnian government forces failed to demilitarize these areas and
continued to launch attacks against the surrounding Serb military installations and
villages. These attacks were sometimes, but not always, in response to the failure
of the Serbs to respect the integrity of the safe areas. A year after safe areas had been
established, the Serbs launched a major attack against Goražde that was halted only

Opposite A US Air Force F-15 takes off in preparation for a NATO air strike in Kosovo, 1999. Over the course of eleven weeks, NATO aircraft completed around 38,000 combat missions.

Above Refugees from Srebrenica arrive in Bosnian-held Tuzla, 16 July 1995.

by NATO air strikes – the first time in its history that NATO had taken live military action. The UN had estimated that it would require an additional 32,000 troops to reinforce the concept of the safe areas, but in the event none of the resolutions' sponsors was prepared to contribute these additional troops. It was thus left to the already overstretched peacekeeping force to implement the resolutions.

In February 1994 the governments of Croatia and Bosnia-Herzegovina agreed to cease hostilities and to form a federation against the Serbs. This agreement had to be implemented on the ground, and this was done by the UN. Although this placed an additional burden on the peacekeeping force, the situation around Sarajevo had been eased by an agreement between all parties to cease fighting and to withdraw their heavy weapons from a 20-km (12-mile) zone around the city. It was thereafter possible for commercial convoys of supplies to reach the beleaguered citizens and for electricity and water supplies to be repaired. A semblance of normality began to return to the city, but this development was deemed unacceptable to the government of Bosnia-Herzegovina and its US backers. They were determined that no UN-brokered peace deal should succeed if it in any way rewarded the aggressor Serbs. The politically acceptable solution would be a return to the full territorial integrity of the state. As a result, in September 1994 the Muslim army in Sarajevo launched a massive artillery and mortar attack against surrounding Serb positions. The UN-brokered cessation of hostilities that was agreed between the federation and the Serbs on 31 December 1994 broke down on 31 March 1995. Both sides were determined to resolve their dispute by military means and had spent the intervening months preparing for a return to war.

Following the massacre of 7,000 Muslims in the enclave of Srebrenica in July 1995, and the bombing of the Markale marketplace in Sarajevo on 28 August 1995 in which

'The Croatian offensive in the Krajina profoundly changed the nature of the Balkan game and thus the diplomatic offensive.'

Richard Holbrooke, former US peace negotiator, 1998

37 people were killed and 90 injured, NATO finally launched a series of air strikes against the Serbs. In the post-action battlefield damage assessment, NATO determined that many of the locations hit had been emptied of significant military content, as the Serbs had seen NATO practising on these targets for some time. In the report it was also accepted that NATO aircraft had frequently been asked to return to attack empty targets in order to sustain the political line that NATO was continuing to do something useful. The report concluded that, although there had been a temporary interruption of communications and some psychological damage to the morale of the Bosnian Serb army, the NATO bombing campaign had had little strategic military effect. It was only when Croatian and Bosnian troops of the newly formed federation swept into the Krajinas and the northern, Serb-held parts of Bosnia-Herzegovina that the Serbs finally agreed to halt their military campaign.

The Serb high command had at last realized that much of the territory in the west of Bosnia that they had wished to trade for peace on their terms was now being lost – and that to continue with the war would risk losing everything that they had fought for. In November 1995 they therefore accepted the terms of what became known as the Dayton Peace Agreement. Tragically for the people of Bosnia, what was agreed at Dayton was little different from what had been proposed by the UN in previous talks – but which had been rejected by the Bosnians at the behest of the Americans.

Above Ethnic Albanians leave the woods where they had been hiding from Serb shelling for three days, north-west Macedonia, March 1999.

Opposite Kosovo Liberation Army fighters in the village of Studencane during a standoff with Serb forces, February 1999.

Although there was a widespread belief in NATO that the early use of air strikes against the Serbs would have prevented the conflict in Bosnia-Herzegovina from developing, the real lesson to emerge from this war was that, if NATO had agreed to deploy its troops to Bosnia-Herzegovina in a preventative role when President Izetbegović had asked for such a deployment early in 1992, the civil war would never have happened. That such preventative action could be successful was demonstrated by the UN when it deployed into Macedonia in January 1993 to prevent war breaking out between Yugoslavia and Macedonia over border disputes. Prompt preventative action saved many lives from another Balkan bloodbath.

However, NATO developed an undue confidence in the ability of air power to solve humanitarian problems on the ground, and this led it to go to war in Kosovo in March 1999. Yet the use of air power alone proved insufficient. In the ensuing eleven weeks, in spite of the most intensive bombing campaign in the history of war hitherto, NATO failed to destroy the Serb military machine. As a result, 10,000 Kosovo civilians were killed and 1 million driven from their homes. (This failure notwithstanding, the belief that air power had been successful in Kosovo would be a major factor in President George W. Bush's strategic assumptions, and ultimately led to his decision to go to war in Iraq in 2003.)

The subsequent claim by NATO that it had ultimately been responsible for ending the tyranny of Slobodan Milošević, the Yugoslav president, is untenable. The elections that brought about this event occurred over eighteen months later, in October 2000, and were the result of a democratic decision by the Serb people, who had had enough of war. During the ensuing NATO mandate in Kosovo, over 100,000 Serbs were driven out and forced to settle either in Serbia or in the Republika Srpska in Bosnia.

For the UN, three somewhat different lessons emerged from the experience of peacekeeping during the Balkan Wars. First, traditional peacekeeping missions were ineffective where parties to a conflict were determined to continue fighting. UN peacekeeping capabilities therefore needed to be strengthened militarily. Second, in the context of intra-state conflicts, where one party to a peace agreement was violating human rights, impartiality of treatment of the warring parties by the UN was likely to result in ineffectiveness and might amount to complicity with evil. In a UN report issued after the Balkan Wars, it was assessed that no failure had done more to damage the standing and credibility of UN peacekeeping in the 1990s than its reluctance to distinguish victim from aggressor. Finally, national sovereignty could no longer be used as a shield by those who violated the rights and lives of their fellow human beings – and in the face of mass murder, armed intervention authorized by the Security Council would be a legitimate and necessary response. However, no military action could be taken unilaterally without the authority of the UN. Not surprisingly, NATO's decision to intervene unilaterally in Kosovo was used as a justification by Russia ten years later to intervene unilaterally in Georgia (see Chapter 14).

> '*Our objective is to prevent more human suffering and more repression and violence against the civilian population of Kosovo.*'
>
> Javier Solana, NATO secretary-general, press statement, 23 March 1999

AFRICAN WARS

Although thirty different conflicts took place across Africa during the 1990s, by far the most brutal were those that occurred in Somalia, Rwanda, the Democratic Republic of Congo and Sudan. Millions of people fled their countries or were internally displaced; deprivation and starvation were widespread. In terms of human suffering the African wars of the 1990s were among the most devastating in human history. The international community, however, limited its response to the delivery of aid, although in Somalia a brief effort was made to secure the delivery of aid by military means.

Somalia

Traditionally, Somalia had existed without central government from ancient times, and its people had relied on an egalitarian clan structure for rule. Although conflicts between the clans had arisen many times in the past, they were settled by the clan chiefs. When independence came in 1960, the country was not yet ready for unification or rule by central government. Within a decade, there was a military takeover led by Major General Siad Barre, who was backed by the Soviet Union.

In 1977 Siad Barre launched a war with neighbouring Ethiopia in an attempt to take back Somali territory that had been granted to Ethiopia by the former colonial powers. Although he was successful at first, outside help for Ethiopia came from the Soviet Union and Cuba, and the Somali army was totally defeated. The switch in Soviet policy was a key element in this defeat, which led to the collapse of the authority of the central Somali government. In revenge, Ethiopia immediately started to support resistance movements in Somalia based on clans opposed to Barre, and this finally led to civil war. In 1991 President Barre was ousted by a combined northern and southern clan-based force, all of which was backed by Ethiopia. But rather than work to unite the country, the victorious clan chiefs attempted to seize power for themselves. This led to further conflict and to a complete breakdown of the agricultural economy of the country. Somalia was soon facing famine caused by extreme drought and war.

In response to pressure from the international community, the UN deployed a peacekeeping operation, UNOSOM, in 1992. This proved largely inadequate in the face of continuing violence by the warring clans. Pressure grew on the US president, George Bush senior, to act in order to avoid complete humanitarian disaster. He therefore agreed to the deployment of US troops to support a revamped UN mission in the country. Yet rather than integrate the US contribution into the already existing UN mission, the US administration decided that a separate task force, UNITAF, would be created under the direct command of the US. This force would have the role of creating a secure environment in Somalia for the UN aid operations. Command relationships between the two forces were never clearly established – nor was a policy agreed regarding the extended use of military force.

At that time the dominant clan chief in the Somali capital, Mogadishu, was General

Above Children in Mogadishu look at an image of Mohamed Farrah Aidid, who opposed the presence of the UN mission and US troops in Somalia, October 1993.

Opposite A young clan fighter displays his machine gun, Mogadishu, February 1992.

Aidid. He regarded the arrival of US troops as a threat to his power, particularly when they sought to establish secure areas in Mogadishu. In June 1993 his militia attacked a Pakistani patrol, killing 24 peacekeepers and injuring many more. Fighting escalated until, in October 1993, 18 American troops and more than 1,000 Somalis were killed in a failed raid against Aidid's headquarters in Mogadishu. This led to the withdrawal of all US troops from Somalia and ultimately to the end of the UN mission in March 1995. The first military intervention in support of a peacekeeping mission to have taken place since the end of the Cold War had been a spectacular failure. This led to a reluctance by the United States to become involved in UN operations, which was soon to have disastrous consequences for the people of Rwanda and Bosnia.

Rwanda

The civil war in Rwanda arose out of animosity between the Hutu and Tutsi tribes that represented the majority of the country's population. In the space of four years two separate genocides took place. The first happened in October 1990, when Tutsi Rwandan Patriotic Front (RPF) troops, on their return from a war in Uganda, attacked Hutu civilians, and the second in April 1994, when the presidents of Rwanda and Burundi were killed in a plane crash while returning from peace talks in Tanzania. In response to what they believed to have been an assassination, Hutu militias killed 800,000 Tutsis and also a number of moderate Hutus.

'In their greatest hour of need, the world failed the people of Rwanda.'

Kofi Annan, UN secretary-general, addressing the Parliament of Rwanda, 7 May 1998

Prior to this genocide, a peacekeeping mission, the United Nations Assistance Mission for Rwanda (UNAMIR), had already deployed in the country to implement a peace agreement signed in August 1993 between the armed forces of the mainly Hutu government of Rwanda and the Tutsi-led RPF. A battalion of peacekeepers composed of contingents from Belgium and Bangladesh had deployed in December 1993, but the force had not reached its authorized strength of 2,548 when the genocide started in April 1994. Nevertheless, the UN sought to arrange a ceasefire, but without success. Its personnel came under attack, and ten Belgian peacekeepers were killed. As a result of these attacks, a number of countries unilaterally withdrew their contingents, and the Security Council reduced UNAMIR's strength in Rwanda from 2,548 troops to 270.

Although the UN subsequently adopted a resolution increasing UNAMIR numbers to 5,500, it took nearly six months for member states to provide the necessary troops, by which time the killings were largely over. The UNAMIR force commander, General Dallaire, believes that a rapid dispatch of 5,000 troops in April 1994 in response to events in Rwanda could have prevented the terrible slaughter. Four years after the genocide, President Clinton apologized to Rwanda for this failure of the international community.

Congo

The effects of the war in Rwanda were soon felt in neighbouring Zaire. In 1994, 2 million Hutus had fled Rwanda and had established refugee camps in eastern Zaire. Among them were elements of the Hutu militias that had perpetrated the genocide in Rwanda, and they soon started to launch attacks back into Rwanda and also against indigenous Zairian Tutsis called the Banyamulenge. President Mobutu of Zaire supported these attacks because he suspected that not only the Ugandans and Rwandans but also his own indigenous Tutsis were helping a rebel movement, the Alliance of Democratic Forces for the Liberation of Zaire (AFDL), which sought to overthrow him. This movement was led by Laurent Kabila. After a bloody and protracted conflict in which at least 60,000 people were killed, the AFDL succeeded in overthrowing the government of Mobutu in May 1997, and Kabila declared himself president. He also changed the name of the country to the Democratic Republic of Congo.

Within a year Kabila had turned against his Ugandan and Rwandan backers, accusing them of attempting to gain control of the valuable mineral deposits in his country and ordering them to leave. This led to a second, more devastating, war, which started in August 1998 and lasted until July 2003. The intensity of the conflict was greatly heightened by the dispatch of foreign troops into the DRC by Uganda, Rwanda and Burundi in support of the rebels, who as a result were able to make rapid progress against the forces of Kabila.

Opposite A survivor of the Rwandan genocide, with scars visible on her head, visits a memorial to the victims, April 2004.

Below A young boy watches a convoy of vehicles from the UN mission in the Democratic Republic of Congo, June 2003.

By the end of August 1998 the rebel forces were threatening Kinshasa, the capital city of the DRC, and it was only the sudden arrival of Zimbabwean forces that halted a rebel advance that had reached the city outskirts. Meanwhile, a number of neighbouring countries had offered their support to Kabila, including Namibia, Sudan, Angola and Chad, and they prevented the overthrow of the Kabila government. In spite of the enormous death toll caused by the war, it was not until the end of 1999 that the UN sent 90 observers to monitor the Lusaka ceasefire agreement, which had been signed in July that year. In February 2000 a larger UN mission numbering 5,537 personnel was authorized, with the somewhat vague mission of contributing to the pacification and general improvement of security in the country.

On 16 January 2001 an assassination attempt was made against Kabila, who died two days later. He was immediately succeeded by his son Joseph Kabila, who offered a greater prospect of peace. However, it was to be almost two years before all Ugandan and Rwandan troops finally left the country, facilitating a halt to the terrible civil war. In December 2003 all parties to the conflict in the republic agreed a plan for the holding of parliamentary and presidential elections within two years, but it was not until July 2006 that those elections took place and finally brought the war to an end. It has been estimated that 5.4 million people died during the conflict, mainly from disease and starvation, yet in the West it was largely ignored.

Sudan

The principal causes of Sudan's numerous and bloody civil wars can be traced back to the religious and ethnic divide between Arabs and Africans. The Khartoum government had failed to deliver on its promises that after independence, in 1956, it would create a federal system that would give a degree of autonomy to the south. Growing resentment against northern Muslim Arab domination among the southern, mainly African, tribes turned into a struggle for regional autonomy or secession from Sudan. However, the presence of oil fields in the south of the country, which contributed 70 per cent of Sudan's foreign earnings, meant that the

Khartoum government would never agree to the break-up of the country. Conflict became inevitable.

In 1983 the Sudan People's Liberation Army was formed under the leadership of John Garang to fight for the independence of the southern provinces of Sudan. Since then conflict has taken place not only with the government forces of the north, but also among competing rebel groups. The tactics of the northern government were to bomb and starve the civilian population into submission; it is also estimated that 200,000 women and children in the south were taken into slavery by the north. By the start of the 1990s, there was mass starvation in the south, and the international community began to deliver humanitarian aid in the rebel-held areas, with the reluctant acquiescence of the Khartoum government. In January 2005 in Nairobi a peace agreement between the south and north was finally signed, which granted autonomy to the south for six years, after which a referendum would be held regarding its future status. Oil revenues would be split equally between the north and south.

It has been estimated that almost 2 million people died and 4 million people were displaced during the 22-year war. Once again the international community limited its response to the delivery of humanitarian aid. It was not until the government of Sudan gave support to Saddam Hussein and to al-Qaeda that the West started to take limited military action against the country. Today Sudan continues its human rights abuses in Darfur (see Chapter 14).

THE GULF WARS AND THE RISE OF TERRORISM

First Gulf War

The major first war of the 1990s was a conventional one, and it arose when Iraq unexpectedly invaded and occupied Kuwait on 2 August 1990. In response, the UN immediately passed a Security Council resolution condemning the invasion and calling on Iraq to withdraw. At the same time the United States, supported by a

Opposite left A convoy of US Marines arrives in Saudi Arabia in preparation for the campaign against Iraqi forces in Kuwait, January 1991.

Opposite right A US helicopter flies over an oil well ignited by retreating Iraqi forces, Kuwait, March 1991.

Below Destroyed vehicles on a road leading out of Kuwait City. Iraqi forces were bombed by coalition forces as they retreated, February 1991.

'In the foreseeable future, armed conflict will not take the form of huge land armies facing each other across extended battle lines.'

General Norman Schwarzkopf, October 1992

coalition that included Arab states, began to deploy combat troops, ships and aircraft to neighbouring Saudi Arabia. Following an intensive air bombing campaign that began on 17 January 1991 and that largely destroyed Iraq's air power, command and control facilities, as well as its ability to manoeuvre its ground forces freely, the coalition forces crossed into Kuwait. Within 100 hours they had driven out all Iraqi troops. It had been a brilliant lightning victory that was accomplished with few coalition force casualties, and it demonstrated beyond all doubt the unique superiority of US military power.

Potential enemies of the United States were henceforth forced to adopt the unconventional strategies of insurgency warfare, of which terrorism – even at the level practised by al-Qaeda ('The Base'), the most prominent Islamic terrorist organization – is merely a subclass. The long experience of insurgency warfare gained by the peoples of the developing world in fighting colonialism would be employed during the 1990s by Islamic extremists who were opposed to global domination by the United States and its Western allies. These ideologues were able to find ready supporters within the many oppressed and dispossessed populations of the Muslim world.

Al-Qaeda

Al-Qaeda was founded by Osama Bin Laden to fight the Soviet occupation of Afghanistan. Following the Soviet withdrawal in 1989, Bin Laden determined to extend the Islamic struggle worldwide against those he deemed to be the enemies of Islam. He was outraged by the continuing presence of US troops in Saudi Arabia following the end of the First Gulf War in 1991, and in 1996 he declared a *jihad*

Opposite A US television channel broadcasts news of the terrorist attacks on the World Trade Center, New York, 11 September 2001.

Right Muslim demonstrators in Jakarta, Indonesia, protest against the US-led war in Afghanistan, 19 November 2001.

('struggle') with the aim of driving all foreigners from traditional Muslim lands. Subsequently al-Qaeda sought any opportunity to attack US installations, and during the next five years al-Qaeda attacks against Americans included the bombing of the Khobar Towers in Saudi Arabia in 1996, the bombing of the US embassies in Tanzania and Kenya in 1998, and the attack against the USS *Cole* in Aden in 2000. After a brief sojourn in Sudan, Bin Laden established his headquarters and training camp in Afghanistan, which had by then come under the rule of the Taliban, who offered his organization both support and protection. It was from Afghanistan that he authorized the notorious aerial attacks on 11 September 2001 against the World Trade Center in New York, the Pentagon in Washington, D.C., and one other unconfirmed target (probably the Capitol Building in Washington, D.C.).

'*Containment is no longer possible when unbalanced dictators with weapons of mass destruction can deliver those weapons on missiles or secretly provide them to terrorist allies . . . we must take the battle to the enemy.*'
US President George W. Bush, 1 June 2002

The attacks on the eastern seaboard of the United States, which came to be known as 9/11, resulted in the deaths of almost 3,000 people and brought about a significant change in US foreign and security policy strategy. From now on, as part of the global War on Terror, not only the terrorists themselves, but also the regimes that harboured them would be regarded as hostile. In a lightning campaign that began on 7 October 2001, the United States invaded Afghanistan, in concert with the Northern Alliance, which was the only effective indigenous resistance movement still operating against the Taliban. Al-Qaeda training camps were rapidly destroyed, and the Taliban government was overthrown. At home, the US dramatically increased the size of its military budget to ensure that the new foreign interventionist policy could be backed effectively by military force.

Second Gulf War

By the end of the 1990s the powerful new US strategic dynamic had been shaping international relations, but it was soon to lose direction and momentum in Iraq. For the political and military imperatives of fighting a war on terror are not those of conventional warfare but of insurgency – and yet the Americans had chosen to limit their response to conventional war. Their victory over Saddam Hussein in the spring of 2003 may go down as one of the most brilliant military campaigns ever fought in the history of warfare, but it will also be seen as a political disaster.

In spite of an expenditure of $1 trillion, the loss of over 3,000 US servicemen and -women, and injuries to many thousands more, the United States had failed in its three strategic aims of bringing good governance, security and reconstruction to Iraq. Far from becoming the beacon of democracy and peace that President Bush had hoped would shine throughout the Middle East, Iraq had been destroyed as a functioning state. Some 2 million people had fled the country and another 2 million had become internally displaced. Up to 600,000 Iraqis had been killed or injured. The economy was in ruins and the country had been brought to the verge of civil war. Most importantly, winning the global war on terror had been made an almost impossible goal to achieve because its prosecution had alienated the Muslim people

'Iraq is going to go down in history as the greatest disaster in American foreign policy.'

Madeleine Albright, former US secretary of state, 27 March 2008

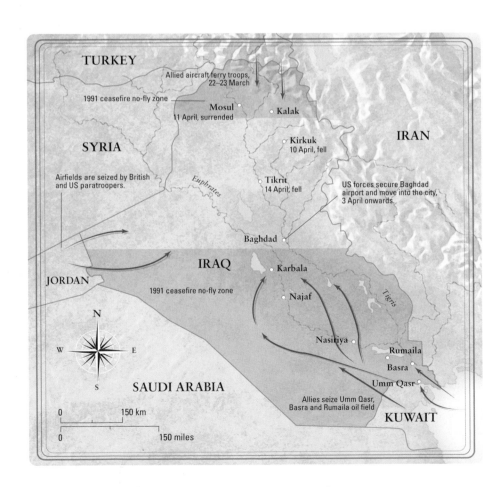

of the world – the very people whose support would be essential in any war against global terror.

In the summer of 2007 President Bush sent an additional 20,000 troops to Iraq, and within three months there had been a dramatic reduction in the level of violence – particularly in the Sunni areas, where many of the attacks against the coalition forces had formerly occurred. This was claimed by many as proof that the US strategy was finally working. However, the significant fall in the number of attacks owed far more to the Americans' having changed sides than to the increase in troop numbers. For the US administration had finally understood that, by pursuing the goal of democracy in Iraq, they had alienated the Sunni, who had been the traditional rulers of that country and who were predominantly behind the insurgency. Furthermore, the Americans realized that by guaranteeing political power to the majority Shia, they would be giving Iran undue influence in Iraq. The Americans therefore made a secret arrangement with the Sunni that they would rearm them in return for a cessation of Sunni attacks against the coalition forces, and that together they would eliminate the al-Qaeda terrorists whom the Sunni had brought into Iraq to help them regain power. In the year following the adoption of this new strategy, nearly 100,000 Sunni civilians had been trained and equipped by the Americans. The fact that, when the Americans finally left Iraq, the Sunni would be in a sufficiently strong position to seize political power from the Shia by military means was left unstated. It is clear that President Bush's 'surge' had provided the camouflage for a fundamental change of US strategy – and that long-term hopes for the establishment of democracy in Iraq would remain remote.

> '*This is not the sort of struggle where you take a hill, plant the flag and go home to a victory parade.*'
>
> General David Petraeus on Iraq, September 2008

CONCLUSION

Although the start of the period under discussion was marked by a conventional war in which a US-led coalition successfully expelled Saddam Hussein's forces from Kuwait, the First Gulf War was not characteristic of the form of conflict that would predominate during the 1990s, which was mostly civil war. The failure of the international community to deal effectively with these civil wars determined Western leaders not to allow such lapses to happen again. An interventionist approach, backed by military force, would now become the preferred strategy of foreign policy. In combination with the declaration of the 'global War on Terror' by the United States in September 2001, this approach ensured that the first decade of the 21st century would be no more peaceful than its predecessor.

Opposite Allied operations in Iraq, 2003.

Below A ceremony to mark the formal withdrawal of US combat troops from Iraqi towns and cities, 29 June 2009.

14 War in the 21st Century

JEREMY BLACK

Opposite A young Liberian rebel sits in an abandoned classroom. Four years of civil war left the country's infrastructure severely damaged.

If we consider the early years of the 21st century, it is readily apparent that the central narrative of military history that has been dominant for so long, which focused on 'high-tempo' symmetrical warfare, is inappropriate. Alongside the continued threat of such conflict we must devote more attention not only to 'little wars', but also to issues such as counter-insurgency and even civil control.

AFRICA

Africa has been the continent where in recent years, as in the 1990s, warfare has been most common. Many of the causes of conflict remain those of the late 20th century, including ethnic violence and the chaos associated with 'failed states'. In the latter – for example in Liberia and Sierra Leone, in both of which rebellions led to the collapse of civil society – political objectives beyond the capture of power have been hazy, and 'wars' have benefited from the large-scale availability of small arms, financed primarily by criminal operations and extortion. There have been no chains of command, nor often even uniforms that distinguished 'troops' from each other, or from other fighters. Politically, these conflicts are examples of a more widespread process in which warlords moved from being rebels to presidents, or vice versa.

Struggles over resources have complicated the situation in Africa, with land and water – traditional areas of dispute – being accompanied by issues of government expenditure, employment and access to raw materials, especially oil. These tensions have interacted with the issue of central control over tribal groups and peripheral areas, leading to conflict, for example in Sudan. Indeed, the problems there have been symptomatic of wider currents in violence. Control over oil has helped drive governmental determination to suppress secessionism in the south, while the government also faced a serious rebellion in the west.

Dating to the 1970s, but breaking out with greater intensity in 2003, this rebellion, mounted by the Sudan People's Liberation Army based in the Darfur region, was directed against the oppression of non-Arabs by the government. In response, from 2004 the government used its regular forces, including aircraft and infantry moved in trucks, to support an Arab militia, the Janjaweed (many of whom ride on horses and camels), in order to slaughter the Fur, Masalit and, in particular, Zaghawa native tribes in Darfur. Alongside large-scale slaughter, especially of men and boys (even very young boys), and the systematic rape and mutilation of women, natives were driven away, their cattle and therefore livelihood seized, the wells poisoned with corpses, and dams, pumps and buildings destroyed. The government was assisted by serious divisions among the opposition in Darfur, not least over negotiations and also over whether the goal was partition or a different Sudan. Militarily, the government benefited from its control over the central point of the capital, Khartoum; from the funds gained from resource exploitation, especially of oil, which enabled it to buy Chinese and Russian arms; and from its use of air power and artillery. The conflict in Sudan spilled over into neighbouring states, especially Chad and the Central African Republic. Chad accused Sudan of backing rebels and, in response, Chadian forces crossed the border into Darfur in April 2007 and fought Sudanese troops.

The means of waging war have been far removed from those discussed by commentators, especially in the United States, who had discerned from the 1990s what they termed a 'Revolution in Military Affairs' – one largely defined in terms of modern information-led weapons systems. Thus, in the Democratic Republic of Congo, much of the killing has been done with machetes, and bows and arrows and shotguns have been employed alongside the frequent use of mortars and submachine guns. Conflict there has led to cannibalism and to the use of child warriors, who are also seen in West Africa, Uganda and Nepal, and in Afghanistan under the Taliban. Other aspects of African conflict distant from Western warfare have included the use of traditional charms and spirit mediums. As in the former Yugoslavia in the 1990s, violence has often been brutal and symbolic. In the Katanga region of Congo in 2004, insurgents reputedly cut off the genitals of victims and drank their blood.

More generally, rivalries between states became intertwined with insurrections and other civil conflicts elsewhere. Thus warfare between Eritrea and Ethiopia, which involved large-scale fighting of a conventional type, spilled over into internal conflicts in Somalia. In November 2006 Meles Zenawi, prime minister of Ethiopia, called Islamists in Somalia a 'clear and present danger' to Ethiopia, a Christian state, claiming that they were being armed by Eritrea. In turn, the Somali Islamists, the Islamic Courts Union, met at Mogadishu and declared that they would defend Somalia against a 'reckless and war-thirsty' Ethiopia. Both Eritrea and Ethiopia sent troops into Somalia.

Local struggles such as this have been interpreted by outside powers in terms of alleged wider alignments, not only regional but also global, such as the struggle between the US and Muslim fundamentalists. Thus, in Somalia in 2006, warlord resistance to the fundamentalist attempt to capture Mogadishu was covertly supported by the US. In the event, though, the capital fell that June to the Islamic Courts Union, and the forces of the latter pressed on to attack the Somali transitional government that had taken refuge in the town of Baidoa. In turn, the US government encouraged the Ethiopian invasion that overthrew the Union and captured Mogadishu in the winter of 2006–7. For the US, this was a welcome opportunity to benefit from regional animosities and to leave the military work on the ground to local forces, although the Americans did provide some air support, a strong ground-attack capability that Ethiopians lacked. Subsequently, opposition in Somalia to the Ethiopian-backed transitional government of Abdullahi Yusuf continued and became more clearly

A Janjaweed militiaman on horseback, Darfur, 2004. The Janjaweed (loosely translated as 'devils on horseback') have been targeting the native tribes of Darfur since 2003.

'All the high-tech weapons in the world won't transform the US armed forces unless we also transform the way we think, train, exercise, and fight.'
Donald Rumsfeld, US secretary of defense, 2002

Ethiopian troops, engaged in a long-running border conflict with Eritrea, 2000. The Ethiopians benefited from superior airpower, better armour and greater numbers, but the Eritreans fought well, taking advantage of the terrain.

linked to fundamentalists, notably to al-Shabab ('the young men'), who sought to overthrow it. Al-Shabab were a continuation of the militias that had supported the Union, and al-Qaeda also played a role. At the same time, the opposition in Somalia lacked the benefits enjoyed by the Taliban in Afghanistan, notably a largely safe haven in neighbouring Pakistan and the experience gained by several years of relatively constant conflict.

A CLASH OF CIVILIZATIONS

The problem of relating all conflicts to a supposed clash of civilizations – an idea advanced from the 1990s, initially in terms of Islam and Christendom – has also been demonstrated in the far south of Thailand, where Muslim separatists have been seen as resisting a pro-Western government. There are certainly cultural elements to a conflict that has continued since 2004, but other issues are involved. The cultural factors are more complex than allowed by the thesis of a clash of civilizations, and have included the problems of absorbing a largely Malay-speaking Muslim people annexed in 1902 by a Thai-speaking Buddhist state. Moreover, the 'cultural' issues have often been made concrete by issues of military brutality, which played a major role in the upsurge of tension in late 2004 in which troops fired on

267

Thai Muslim protestors raise their fists and shout the slogan 'God is great' during a demonstration at the Central Mosque, Pattani, 4 June 2007. Many disturbances around the world have centred on religiously significant sites.

demonstrators, as well as by exploitation of potential conflicts by politicians and drug barons seeking their own local advantages.

Similarly, in Uzbekistan, the regime of Islam Karimov claimed that opposition was led by Muslim terrorists, a view that neglects the extent to which the dictatorship has faced opposition for a number of reasons. (In 2005 in the Uzbek city of Andijan troops fired on a crowd demonstrating against the poor economic situation.) Yet religion has undeniably been a key lightning rod for tensions. In 2007 Pakistani forces stormed the Lal Masjd ('Red Mosque'), a centre of opposition by radical Muslim clergy, in the capital, Islamabad. In response, attacks on the security forces increased. The issues that have led to violence might seem trivial, but the tensions have often been serious, as in 2002 in Kaduna, Nigeria, where Muslim anger about the planned staging of the Miss World competition in the federal capital, Abuja, led to riots in which many were killed.

INTERNAL DISORDER AND FOREIGN INTERVENTION

Disputes linked to sectarianism are not the only ones to have been portrayed in terms of wider concerns, nor, therefore, the sole disputes to have been internationalized. More widely, foreign assistance has been sought and, if necessary, hired to help resist insurrections. Thus, between 1993 and 2003, Ange-Félix Patassé, president of the Central African Republic, survived seven coup attempts, including one in 2002 by General François Bozizé, one-time head of the army, that involved serious street fighting in the capital, Bangui. Patassé turned for support to Libya, which provided backing until 2002, and then to a Congolese rebel group, but in March 2003 Bozizé, at the head of 1,000 men, overran Bangui. The unpaid army was unwilling to resist. Instability in the Central African Republic reflected the knock-on effects of war elsewhere, for conflict in Congo hit its trade links down the Congo River.

Coups and the possibility of such plots have continued to play a major role in military history, underlining the central role of military concerns in a military history that is not restricted to war. In 2000 American and Brazilian pressure on Paraguayan military leaders led them to thwart an attempted coup, and that year the army eventually suppressed an attempted coup on the Pacific island of Fiji. An attempted military coup in Chad failed in 2003. There were also military coups in Fiji and Thailand in 2006, although the Thai army was unable to sustain the political order it sought to create. In Fiji the coups reflected bitter and persistent ethnic conflict between the Indian and Fijian populations.

In Zimbabwe in 2008 the military-dominated Joint Operations Command in effect gained control from the weakened Robert Mugabe and organized the use of force in order to keep him in power against popular pressure and democratic methods.

> *'I can still punch.'*
>
> Robert Mugabe, president of Zimbabwe, 2003

The armed forces, whose members and former members gained assets and government posts, were linked to violent gangs in brutalizing opponents. Such violence, combined with economic problems, compelled large numbers to flee to neighbouring states, such as Botswana, South Africa and Zambia; but the economic competition they presented in a situation of high unemployment in turn led to violence against refugees in South Africa.

The role of the military in politics is usually considered in terms of the Third World, but that may well underplay its importance elsewhere. If it is judged in terms of tanks in the street, there has been scant sign of this role, but nevertheless it is relevant in three respects. First and most obviously, the armed forces play a role in military policy that is often greater than the constitutional situation would allow, and with civilian oversight circumvented. Second, reliance on the military is important in giving security to government as well as an ability to implement particular policies. Third, the military may well have greater political influence in specific contexts. As an example, the military has had great influence in Israel in recent decades, not only with former generals playing a major role as politicians, but also with the serving military being important in terms of policy such as settlements in the occupied territories and relations with other states. In some states, it is unclear how far the military is under the control of the government or how far it is in effect autonomous. This question is particularly relevant in China, where it appears far more autonomous than in Japan or India, and some Chinese units are identified with particular regions.

Illegal immigrants from Zimbabwe cross the border into South Africa, March 2007. Politically authoritarian and economically incompetent, Zimbabwe relied on force to control its impoverished people.

POWER PROJECTION BY THE MAJOR STATES

The relationship between violence within countries and external intervention offers a way to consider not only conflict across the Third World, but also those specific conflicts in which Western powers have committed troops, for example France in the Ivory Coast. At the same time, this situation poses a difficulty for Western intervention, highlighting the extent to which civil conflict is frequent – if not (in some countries) constant. This approach calls into question the analysis that sees violence largely in terms of resistance to Western powers. Instead, it is appropriate to note the high levels of civil violence in many states, for example Afghanistan and Iraq (in the second of which the insurgents have particularly disparate goals). Moreover, this violence cannot readily be contained by Western intervention or by sustained fighting against insurgents.

While problems in Afghanistan and Iraq have suggested that Western approaches to understanding (as well as winning) war have important limits, it is also notable that the Iraqi insurgents, like the Taliban in Afghanistan, have found that their ideas and practices have brought less success than had been expected. This failure contributed to the general inability of war-making in 2001–8 to achieve the results

A US construction battalion arrives at an airfield in western Iraq to support operations in al-Anbar, 22 September 2008. By 2007, the US was spending $43 billion annually on military operations in Iraq.

desired by both sides. In Afghanistan the problems of creating a stable political solution, and thus of making the results of military intervention durable, have been fully demonstrated. The government of Hamid Karzai, established as a result of the American intervention in 2001, proved very vulnerable from 2005 to a Taliban resurgence, and this led to intervention by NATO. The fighting, however, has indicated the potential of insurrectionary forces, especially when backed by a relatively secure foreign base, in this case the North West Frontier Province of Pakistan. The Taliban have not been short of fighters, and have also benefited from the extent to which they were able to take the initiative. As far as tactics are concerned, NATO and Afghan government forces have been based in settlements whose walls and orchards have provided cover for Taliban assailants. Taliban ambushes of road links have led to NATO's being dependent on helicopters for mobility and logistics, with firepower also provided by fixed-wing aircraft; but there has been only so much air power and only so much it could achieve – especially, but not only, in bad flying conditions. As a result,

'Either you are with us or you are with the terrorists.'
US President George W. Bush, 2001

'We have the possibility of regional instability and also failed states . . . We do not see or expect a regional power or a peer competitor for the next 10 or 15 years, but we have to prepare for that possibility certainly in the years beyond.'

William Cohen, US secretary of defense, 1997

NATO and Afghan government forces have frequently seemed reactive and unable to protect potential allies, which has increased the political impact of the Taliban.

The Russian invasion of Georgia in 2008 underlined the problem of gauging military success. The Russians rapidly defeated the Georgian army, thus ending its forcible attempt to suppress secessionism in South Ossetia, but at the same time the invasion revealed serious deficiencies in the Russian military, not least in achieving air superiority and in night fighting, while it was unclear whether the local success merited the subsequent loss of international support. To that extent, there was a parallel with the American invasion of Iraq in 2003, although the Russian action cost far less and could be more readily afforded thanks to the buoyant state of the oil-rich Russian revenues. Both invasions, however, highlighted the contrast between the successful operational application of greater power and the more problematic wider strategic context. As far as Georgia was concerned, Russia's idea of its own sphere of influence and power had been reasserted, especially in the divided region of the Caucasus; this was accompanied by America's tacit recognition that even its power does not extend militarily to Georgia, and NATO's weakness there was apparent.

In the aftermath of the American invasion of Iraq, the key elements have proved to be not the situation in that country, but rather the regional consequences of greater relative Iranian power (now that the Iraqi counterweight has been removed); the terrible fiscal consequences of the invasion, which have weakened the United States and increased its dependence on foreign capital inflows, especially from East Asia and from oil-rich states; and the strategic rapprochement of China and Russia, which has undone the advantages the United States had gained from the Sino-Soviet rift in 1960.

Above Taliban militants armed with rocket launchers and AK-47s in an undisclosed location in Afghanistan, January 2009. Using deadly improvised explosive devices, the Taliban were able to put considerable pressure on NATO forces.

Opposite A Georgian man squats in the rubble of a street destroyed by Russian air strikes, Gori, 11 August 2008.

CONCLUSIONS

In the first decade of the new century, military commentators did not generally think in terms of such strategic dimensions, but they did underline the unexpected consequences and hazards of going to war, as well as the extent to which the technological triumphalism of the US 'Revolution in Military Affairs' was totally misplaced. The latter point looks to the future, not least to the way in which possible developments in military capability – robotic or cloned soldiers, for example, or genetic engineering to improve effectiveness, or weapons systems such as aircraft capable of flying anywhere in the world in two hours – will offer little guidance where 'tasking' (the setting of goals for the military) is concerned. These goals may well revolve around international struggles, especially over scarce resources, but it is also likely that conflict within countries will become more prominent as systems of social cohesion and control are placed under greater pressure, not least as a result of population growth and its impact on resource competition.

There is a contrast here between warfare and military capability, since some major and second-rank powers either did not engage in war (China, Japan, Brazil) or

'The great struggles of the twentieth century between liberty and totalitarianism ended with a decisive victory for the forces of freedom . . . We will extend the peace by encouraging free and open societies on every continent.'

National Security Strategy issued by US government, September 2002

did so with only a fraction of their forces (India in Kashmir). Warfare has involved some poor states, but not all of them. Ethnic division led to serious civil conflict in some countries, such as Sri Lanka, where a long-lasting Tamil insurrection was suppressed only in 2009, but not in others. Issues surrounding resources have increased tensions, but competition for water and energy has not as yet led to the large-scale breakdowns that have been predicted. These points serve as a reminder of the unpredictability of war – an unpredictability that remains a constant factor as governments and militaries seek to plan and train for future contingencies.

Further Reading

Chapter 1

Beckett, I. F. W. *Victorians at War* (London, 2003)

Erickson, E. J. *Defeat in Detail: The Ottoman Army in the Balkans, 1912–1913* (Westport, Conn., and London, 2003)

Hall, R. *The Balkan Wars, 1912–1913: Prelude to the First World War* (London, 2000)

Herrmann, D. G. *The Arming of Europe and the Making of the First World War* (Princeton, N.J., and Chichester, 1996)

Judd, D. and K. Surridge. *The Boer War* (London, 2003)

Kowner, R. (ed.). *The Impact of the Russo-Japanese War* (London, 2007)

Menning, B. W. *Bayonets before Bullets: The Imperial Russian Army, 1861–1914* (Bloomington, Ind., 1992)

Miller, S. *Volunteers on the Veld: Britain's Citizen-Soldiers and the South African War, 1899–1902* (Norman, Okla., 2007)

Patrikeeff, F. and H. Shukman. *Railways and the Russo-Japanese War* (London and New York, 2007)

Sakurai, T. *Human Bullets: A Soldier's Story of Port Arthur* (1907; repr. Lincoln, Nebr., 1999)

Scholtz, L. *Why the Boers Lost the War* (Basingstoke, 2005)

Steinberg, J. W. and D. Wolff (eds). *The Russo-Japanese War in Global Perspective: World War Zero*, 2 vols (Leiden, 2005–7)

Stevenson, D. *Armaments and the Coming of War: Europe, 1904–1914* (Oxford, 1996)

Stone, J. and E. A. Schmidl. *The Boer War and Military Reforms* (Lanham, Md., and London, 1988)

Westwood, J. N. *Russia against Japan, 1904–05* (Basingstoke, 1986)

Wilson, K. (ed.). *The International Impact of the Boer War* (New York, 2001)

Chapter 2

Astore, W. and D. Showalter. *Hindenburg: Icon of German Militarism* (Dulles, Va., 2005)

Chickering, R. *Imperial Germany and the Great War, 1914–1918* (Cambridge, 1998)

Chickering, R. and S. Förster (eds). *Great War, Total War: Combat and Mobilization on the Western Front, 1914–1918* (Cambridge, 2000)

Clayton, A. *Paths of Glory: The French Army, 1914–1918* (London, 2003)

Doughty, R. A. *Pyrrhic Victory: French Strategy and Operations in the Great War* (Cambridge, Mass., 2005)

Ellis, J. *Eye Deep in Hell: Trench Warfare in World War I* (Baltimore, Md., 1976)

Ferguson, N. *The Pity of War* (New York, 1999)

Herwig, H. H. *The First World War: Germany and Austria-Hungary, 1914–1918* (London, 1997)

Horne, A. *The Price of Glory: Verdun, 1916* (London, 1962)

Jünger, E. *Storm of Steel* (New York, 2004)

Keegan, J. *The First World War* (New York, 1999)

Manning, F. *Her Privates We* (London, 1986)

Neiberg, M. S. *Foch: Supreme Allied Commander in the Great War* (Washington, D.C., 2003)

——*Fighting the Great War: A Global History* (Cambridge, Mass., 2005)

Sheffield, G. *Forgotten Victory: The First World War Myths and Realities* (London, 2001)

——*The Somme* (London, 2003)

Showalter, D. *Tannenberg: Clash of Empires* (Dulles, Va., 2004)

Smith, L., S. Audoin-Rouzeau and A. Becker. *France and the Great War, 1914–1918* (Cambridge, 2003)

Stevenson, D. *Cataclysm: The First World War as Political Tragedy* (New York, 2004)

Strachan, H. *The First World War, Vol. 1: To Arms* (Oxford, 2001)

Wiest, A. *Haig: The Evolution of a Commander* (Dulles, Va., 2005)

Chapter 3

Asprey, R. B. *The German High Command at War: Hindenburg and Ludendorff Conduct World War I* (New York, 1991)

Chickering, R. *Imperial Germany and the Great War, 1914–1918* (Cambridge, 1998)

Clayton, A. *Paths of Glory: The French Army, 1914–1918* (London, 2003)

Cornish, N. *The Russian Army and the First World War* (Stroud, 2006)

Doughty, R. A. *Pyrrhic Victory: French Strategy and Operations in the Great War* (Cambridge, Mass., 2005)

Grotelueschen, M. *The AEF Way of War: The American Army and Combat in World War I* (Cambridge, 2007)

Gudmundsson, B. I. *Stormtroop Tactics: Innovation in the German Army, 1914–1918* (New York, 1989)

Harris, J. P., with N. Barr. *Amiens to the Armistice: The BEF in the Hundred Days' Campaign* (London, 1998)

Hart, P. *Aces Falling: War above the Trenches, 1918* (London, 2007)

Herwig, H. H. *The First World War: Germany and Austria-Hungary, 1914–1918* (London, 1997)

Hughes, M. *Allenby and British Strategy in the Middle East, 1917–1919* (London, 1999)

Kocka, J. *Facing Total War: German Society, 1914–1918* (Leamington Spa, 1984)

Neiberg, M. S. *Foch: Supreme Allied Commander in the Great War* (Washington, D.C., 2003)

Offer, A. *The First World War: An Agrarian Interpretation* (Oxford, 1989)

Passingham, I. *The German Offensives of 1918: The Last Desperate Gamble* (Barnsley, 2008)

Prior, R. and T. Wilson. *Passchendaele: The Untold Story* (London, 1996)

Schreiber, S. B. *The Shock Army of the British Empire: The Canadian Corps in the Last 100 Days of the Great War* (Westport, Conn., 1997)

Smith, L., S. Audoin-Rouzeau and A. Becker. *France and the Great War, 1914–1918* (Cambridge, 2003)

Zabecki, D. T. *Steel Wind: Colonel Georg Bruchmüller and the Birth of Modern Artillery* (Westport, Conn., 1994)

—— *The German 1918 Offensives: A Case Study in the Operational Level of War*, Strategy and History (New York, 2006)

Chapter 4

Balfour, S. *Deadly Embrace: Morocco and the Road to the Spanish Civil War* (Oxford, 2002)

Davies, N. *White Eagle, Red Star: The Russo-Polish War, 1919–1920, and 'The Miracle on the Vistula'* (London, 2003)

Fromkin, D. *A Peace to End All Peace: The Fall of the Ottoman Empire and the Creation of the Modern Middle East* (New York, 2001)

Mawdsley, E. *The Russian Civil War* (London, 2001)

Moreman, T. *The Army in India and the Development of Frontier Warfare, 1849–1947* (London, 1998)

Omnisi, D. *Air Power and Colonial Control: The Royal Air Force, 1919–1939* (Manchester, 1990)

Waldron, A. *From War to Nationalism: China's Turning Point, 1924–1925* (Cambridge, 2003)

Chapter 5

Barnhart, M. A. *Japan Prepares for Total War: The Search for Economic Security, 1919–1941* (Ithaca, N.Y., 1987)

Benton, G. *Mountain Fires: The Red Army's Three Year War in South China* (Berkeley, Calif., 1992)

Chickering, R. and S. Förster (eds). *The Shadows of Total War: Europe, East Asia and the United States, 1919–1939* (New York, 2003)

Corum, J. S. *The Roots of Blitzkrieg* (Lawrence, Kans., 1992)

Glantz, D. M. *Stumbling Colossus: The Red Army on the Eve of World War II* (Lawrence, Kans., 1998)

Murray, W. and A. R. Millett (eds). *Military Innovation in the Interwar Period* (Cambridge, 1996)

Van de Ven, H. *Warfare and Nationalism in China, 1925–1945* (London, 2003)

Chapter 6

Dear, I. C. B. and M. R. D. Foot (eds). *The Oxford Companion to World War II* (Oxford, 1995)

Glantz, D. and J. House. *When Titans Clashed: How the Red Army Stopped Hitler* (Lawrence, Kans., 1998)

Hastings, M. *Armageddon* (New York, 2006)

——*Retribution* (New York, 2008)

Keegan, J. *The Second World War* (New York, 1990)

Murray, W. and A. Millett. *A War to be Won* (Cambridge, Mass., 2001)

Overy, R. *The Air War, 1939–1945* (New York, 1980)

——*Why the Allies Won* (London, 2006)

Porch, D. *The Path to Victory: The Mediterranean Theater in World War II* (New York, 2004)

Spector, R. H. *Eagle against the Sun: The American War with Japan* (New York, 1985)

——*At War at Sea: Sailors and Naval Combat in the Twentieth Century* (New York, 2001)

Weinberg, G. *A World in Arms* (Cambridge, 1994)

Chapter 7

Auer, J. E. *Who Was Responsible? From Marco Polo Bridge to Pearl Harbor* (Tokyo, 2006)

Bix, H. P. *Hirohito and the Making of Modern Japan* (New York, 2000)

Callahan, R. *Burma, 1942–1945* (London, 1978)

Dower, J. W. *War without Mercy: Race and Power in the Pacific War* (New York, 1986)

Drea, E. J. *MacArthur's ULTRA: Code Breaking and the War against Japan, 1942–1945* (Lawrence, Kans., 1992)

Dunnigan, J. J. and A. A. Nofi. *Victory at Sea: World War II in the Pacific* (New York, 1995)

Evans, D. C. (ed.). *The Japanese Navy in World War II* (Annapolis, Md., 1969)

Evans, D. C. and M. R. Peattie. *Kaigun: Strategy, Tactics, and Technology in the Imperial Navy, 1887–1941* (Annapolis, Md., 1997)

Frank, R. *Downfall: The End of the Imperial Japanese Empire* (New York, 1999)

Hayes, G. and M. R. Peattie. *The History of the Joint Chiefs of Staff in World War II: The War against Japan* (Annapolis, Md., 1982)

Horner, D. *The Second World War, Vol. 1: The Pacific* (Oxford, 2002)

Ienaga, S. *The Pacific War: World War II and the Japanese, 1931–1945* (New York, 1978)

Marston, D. (ed.). *The Pacific War Companion* (Oxford, 2005)

Prados, J. *Combined Fleet Decoded: The Secret History of American Intelligence and the Japanese Navy in World War II* (New York, 1991)

Spector, R. H. *Eagle against the Sun: The American War with Japan* (New York, 1985)

Thorne, C. *The Issue of War: States, Societies and the Far East Conflict* (London, 1985)

Toland, J. *The Rising Sun: The Decline and Fall of the Japanese Empire* (New York, 1970)

Van der Vat, D. *The Pacific Campaign: The U.S.–Japanese Naval War, 1941–1945* (New York, 1991)

Willmott, H. P. *The Second World War in the Far East* (London, 1999)

Wilson, D. *When Tigers Fight: The Story of the Sino-Japanese War, 1937–1945* (New York, 1982)

Chapter 8

Baer, G. W. *One Hundred Years of Sea Power: The US Navy, 1890–1990* (Stanford, Calif., 1994)

Barnett, C. *Engage the Enemy More Closely: The Royal Navy in the Second World War* (New York, 1991)

Bell, C. *The Royal Navy: Sea Power and Strategy between the Wars* (Stanford, Calif., 2000)

Corbett, J. *Some Principles of Maritime Strategy* (London, 1911)

Epkenhans, M. *Tirpitz: Architect of the German High Seas Fleet* (Washington, D.C., 2008)

Friedman, N. *Sea Power as Strategy: Navies and National Interests* (Annapolis, Md., 2001)

Gordon, A. *The Rules of the Game: Jutland and British Naval Command* (London, 1996)

Grove, E. *The Future of Sea Power* (London, 1990)

Herwig, H. H. *'Luxury' Fleet: The Imperial German Navy, 1888–1918* (London, 1980)

Hobson, R. *Imperialism at Sea: Naval Strategic Thought, the Ideology of Sea Power and the Tirpitz Plan, 1875–1914* (Boston, Mass., 2002)

Keegan, J. *The Price of Admiralty* (London and New York, 1988)

Kennedy, P. M. *The Rise and Fall of British Naval Mastery* (London and New York, 1976)

Lambi, I. N. *The Navy and German Power Politics, 1862–1914* (Boston, Mass., and London, 1984)

Rodger, N. A. M. (ed.). *Naval Power in the Twentieth Century* (Basingstoke, 1996)

Rüger, J. *The Great Naval Game: Britain and Germany in the Age of Empire* (Cambridge, 2007)

Sondhaus, L. *Naval Warfare, 1815–1914* (London, 2001)
———*Navies in Modern World History* (London, 2004)
Sumida, J. T. *In Defence of Naval Supremacy: Finance, Technology, and the British Naval Policy* (Boston, Mass., and London, 1989)
Till, G. *Seapower: A Guide for the Twenty-First Century* (London, 2006)

Chapter 9
Biddle, T. D. *Rhetoric and Reality in Air Warfare* (Princeton, N.J., 2002)
Buckley, J. *Air Power in the Age of Total War* (London, 1999)
Corum, J. S. and W. R. Johnson. *Airpower in Small Wars* (Lawrence, Kans., 2003)
Douhet, G. *The Command of the Air* (1921 and 1927; London, 1942)
Gooch, J. (ed.). *Airpower: Theory and Practice* (London, 1995)
Gray, P. W. (ed.). *Air Power 21: Challenges for the New Century* (London, 2000)
Gray, P. W. and S. Cox (eds). *Air Power History: Turning Points from Kitty Hawk to Kosovo* (London, 2002)
Grayling, A. C. *Among the Dead Cities* (London, 2006)
Hallion, R. *Strike from the Sky: The History of Battlefield Air Attack* (Washington, D.C., 1989)
———*Air Power Confronts an Unstable World* (London, 1997)
Kennett, L. *The First Air War, 1914–1918* (New York, 1990)
Mason, T. *Airpower: A Centennial Appraisal* (London, 1995)
Meilinger, P. S. *Airwar: Theory and Practice* (London, 2003)
Morrow, J. H. *The Great War in the Air: Military Aviation from 1909 to 1921* (New York, 1993)
Murray, W. *Luftwaffe: Strategy for Defeat* (Washington, D.C., 1985)
Olsen, J. A. *John Warden and the Renaissance in American Air Power* (New York, 2007)
Overy, R. *The Air War, 1939–45* (London, 1980)
Pape, R. *Bombing to Win: Air Power and Coercion in War* (New York, 1996)
Paris, M. *Winged Warfare: Literature and Theory of Aerial Warfare in Britain* (Manchester, 1992)
Warden, J. *The Air Campaign: Planning for Combat* (Washington, D.C., 1989)
Wells, H. G. *The War in the Air* (London, 1908)

Chapter 10
Bayly, C. and T. Harper. *Forgotten Wars: Freedom and Revolution in South-East Asia* (Cambridge, Mass., 2007)
Best, A. *The International History of East Asia, 1900–1968* (London, 2008)
Black, J. *Rethinking Military History* (London, 2004)
———*The Age of Total War, 1860–1945* (Westport, Conn., 2006)
Bregman, A. *Israel's Wars: A History since 1947* (London, 2002)
Duara, P. (ed.). *Decolonization: Perspectives from Now and Then* (London, 2003)
Dufour, J.-L. and M. Vaïsse. *La Guerre au XXe siècle* (Paris, 1993)
Galula, D. *Counterinsurgency Warfare* (Westport, Conn., 2006)
Lapping, B. *End of Empire* (London, 1989)
Lawrence, M. A. and F. Logevall (eds). *The First Vietnam War: Colonial Conflict and Cold War Crisis* (Cambridge, Mass., and London, 2007)
Lynch, M. *Mao* (London, 2004)

Trinquier, R. *Modern Warfare: A French View of Counterinsurgency* (Westport, Conn., 2006)

Chapter 11
Andrew, C. and V. Mitrokhin. *The World Was Going Our Way: The KGB and the Battle for the Third World* (New York, 2005)
Beisner, R. L. *Dean Acheson: A Life in the Cold War* (New York, 2006)
Brodie, B. *War and Politics* (New York, 1973)
Brown, A. *Seven Years That Changed the World: Perestroika in Perspective* (Oxford, 2007)
Brzezinski, Z. K. *The Soviet Bloc: Unity and Conflict* (New York, 1961)
Gaddis, J. L. *The Cold War: A New History* (New York, 2005)
Garthoff, R. L. *Détente and Confrontation: American–Soviet Relations from Nixon to Reagan* (Washington, D.C., 1994)
Gati, C. *Failed Illusions: Moscow, Washington, Budapest, and the 1956 Hungarian Revolt* (Stanford, Calif., 2006)
Hoopes, T. *The Limits of Intervention* (New York, 1969)
Hough, J. F. *The Struggle for the Third World: Soviet Debates and American Options* (Washington, D.C., 1986)
Jones, R. A. *The Soviet Concept of 'Limited Sovereignty' from Lenin to Gorbachev: The Brezhnev Doctrine* (Basingstoke, 1990)
Kubálková, V. and A. A. Cruickshank. *Marxism-Leninism and Theory of International Relations* (London, 1980)
Kuniholm, B. R. *The Origins of the Cold War in the Near East: Great Power Conflict and Diplomacy in Iran, Turkey, and Greece* (Princeton, N.J., 1980)
Larres, K. *Churchill's Cold War: The Politics of Personal Diplomacy* (New Haven, Conn., 2002)
Lewy, G. *America in Vietnam* (New York, 1978)
Lüthi, L. M. *The Sino-Soviet Split: Cold War in the Communist World* (Princeton, N.J., 2008)
MacFarquhar, R. and M. Schoenhals. *Mao's Last Revolution* (Cambridge, 2006)
Maley, W. *The Afghanistan Wars* (New York, 2009)
Meray, T. *Thirteen Days That Shook the Kremlin: Imre Nagy and the Hungarian Revolution* (New York, 1959)
Stueck, W. *The Korean War: An International History* (Princeton, N.J., 1995)
Taubman, W. *Khrushchev: The Man and His Era* (New York, 2003)
Valenta, J. *Soviet Intervention in Czechoslovakia, 1968: Anatomy of a Decision* (Baltimore, Md., 1991)
Westad, O. A. *The Global Cold War: Third World Interventions and the Making of our Times* (Cambridge, 2005)

Chapter 12
Bar, J. U. *The Watchman Fell Asleep: The Surprise of the Yom Kippur War and Its Sources* (New York, 2005)
Bregman, A. *Israel's Wars: A History since 1947* (London, 2002)
Cordesman, A. and A. Wagner. *The Lesson of Modern War, Vol. 2: The Iran–Iraq War* (Boulder, Colo., 1990)
Heikal, M. *The Road to Ramadan: The Inside Story of How the Arabs Prepared for and Almost Won the October War of 1973* (London, 1975)
Khalid, R. *Under Siege: P.L.O. Decision-Making during the 1982 War* (New York, 1985)
Mansfield, A. *A History of the Middle East* (London, 1992)
Morris, B. *1948: A History of the First Arab–Israeli War* (London, 2008)

Oren, M. *Six Days of War: June 1967 and the Making of the Modern Middle East* (Oxford, 2002)

Schiff, Z. and E. Ya'ari. *Israel's Lebanon War* (London, 1984)

Shalev, A. *The Intifada: Causes and Effects* (London, 1991)

Shazly, S. *The Crossing of Suez: The October War (1973)* (London, 1980)

Chapter 13

Allard, K. *Somalia Operations: Lessons Learned* (Washington, D.C., 1995)

Bacevich, A. J. and E. Cohen (eds). *War over Kosovo* (New York and Chichester, 2002)

Bacevich, A. J. and E. Inbar (eds). *The Gulf War of 1991 Reconsidered* (London, 2003)

Burg, S. L. and P. S. Shoup. *The War in Bosnia-Herzegovina* (Armonk, N.Y., and London, 1999)

Scales, R. H. *Certain Victory: The U.S. Army in the Gulf War* (Washington, D.C., 1993)

Smith, S. *Allah's Mountains: The Battle for Chechnya* (London, 2001)

Chapter 14

Biddle, S. *Afghanistan and the Future of Warfare* (Carlisle, Pa., 2002)

Bobbitt, P. *The Shield of Achilles: War, Peace and the Course of History* (London, 2002)

Clark, J. F. (ed.). *The African Stakes of the Congo War* (Basingstoke, 2002)

Coker, C. *Waging War without Warriors?* (Boulder, Colo., and London, 2002)

Giustozzi, A. *Koran, Kalashnikov and Laptop: The Neo-Taliban Insurgency in Afghanistan* (London, 2007)

Murray, W. and R. H. Scales. *The Iraq War* (Cambridge, Mass., 2003)

Ricks, T. E. *Fiasco: The American Military Adventure in Iraq* (New York and London, 2006)

Woodward, B. *Plan of Attack* (New York and London, 2004)

List of Contributors

Jeremy Black is Professor of History at the University of Exeter and the author or editor of over seventy books, including *The Cambridge Illustrated Atlas of Warfare: Renaissance to Revolution, 1492–1792*, *World War Two: A Military History* and, for Thames & Hudson, *The Seventy Great Battles of All Time* and *Great Military Leaders and Their Campaigns*.

John Bourne was Director of the Centre for First World War Studies at Birmingham University from 2002 until his retirement in 2009. His research focuses on the British Army during the Great War. He is the author of *Britain and the Great War 1914–1918*, *Who's Who in the First World War* and (with Gary Sheffield) *Douglas Haig: War Diaries and Letters 1914–1918*.

Ahron (Ronnie) Bregman was born in Israel in 1958. After six years of army service, during which he took part in the 1982 Lebanon war and reached the rank of captain, he left the army to work at the Knesset as a parliamentary assistant. He studied in Jerusalem and London, completing a doctorate in War Studies at King's College London in 1994. He is author of *The Fifty Years War: Israel and the Arabs* (with Jihan el-Tahri), *Elusive Peace: How the Holy Land Defeated America*, *Israel's Wars: A History since 1947* and *A History of Israel*. He is currently teaching at the Department of War Studies, King's College London.

John Buckley is Professor of Military History at the University of Wolverhampton. His research has concentrated on air power, the Battle of the Atlantic, the Northwest European Campaign 1944–45 and British armoured forces in World War II. He is the author of *The RAF and Trade Defence 1919–1945*, *Air Power in the Age of Total War* and *British Armour in the Normandy Campaign, 1944*.

François Cochet is Professor of Contemporary History at Metz University. His research focuses on prisoners of war and on the fighting experience in wars from the middle of 19th century to today. He is the author of *Soldats sans armes: La captivité de guerre*, *Les Soldats de la drôle de guerre* and *Survivre au front: Les poilus entre contrainte et consentement*. He is, with Colonel Rémy Porte, the editor of the *Dictionnaire de la Grande Guerre* and is currently working on a dictionary on the First Indochina War. In English he has published 'World War I: 1914–1918: Daily Life in Western Societies' in *Daily Lives of Civilians in Wartime Twentieth-Century Europe* (ed. N. Atkin).

Michael Epkenhans is Director of Historical Research at the German Armed Forces Historical Research Office in Potsdam, Germany, and Professor at the History Department of Hamburg University. His research concentrates on German military history. In addition to numerous articles on 19th- and 20th-century German history, he is the author of *Tirpitz: Architect of the German High Seas Fleet* (2008) and of a biography of Vice-Admiral Albert Hopman.

John Ferris is a Professor of History at the University of Calgary, Honorary Professor in the Department of International Politics, the University of Wales, Aberystwyth, and Adjunct Professor in

War Studies at the Royal Military College of Canada. He writes widely on strategic, international and intelligence history and on strategic studies, with a focus on the 19th and 20th centuries. Among his publications are *Men, Money and Diplomacy: The Evolution of British Strategic Policy, 1919–26*, *The British Army and Signals Intelligence in the First World War*, *A World History of Warfare* (co-authored) and *Intelligence and Strategy: Selected Essays*.

William Maley is Professor and Director of the Asia–Pacific College of Diplomacy at the Australian National University, Canberra, and has also taught at the Russian Diplomatic Academy and at the University of Oxford. He is author of *Rescuing Afghanistan* and *The Afghanistan Wars*, and co-edited *The Soviet Withdrawal from Afghanistan*, *The Transition from Socialism: State and Civil Society in the USSR* and *Russia in Search of its Future*.

Allan R. Millett is the Stephen Ambrose Professor of History and Director at the Eisenhower Center, University of New Orleans, as well as senior military advisor at the National World War II Museum, also in New Orleans. He has written about the Pacific War in a history of the US Marine Corps, a general history of the military experience of the United States, a biography of General Gerald C. Thomas, and in *A War to be Won: Fighting the Second World War* (with Williamson Murray).

Williamson Murray is Professor Emeritus at The Ohio State University and the author and editor of a number of books, including *A War to be Won: Fighting the Second World War* (with Allan Millett) and *The Making of Peace: Rulers, States, and the Aftermath of War* (co-edited with Jim Lacey). At present he is working as a defence consultant in Washington, D.C.

Michael Neiberg is Professor of History and Co-Director of the Center for the Study of War and Society at the University of Southern Mississippi. He is the author or editor of twelve published and forthcoming books, as well as many articles and book reviews. He specializes in World War I and the global dimensions of the history of warfare. His most recent books include *Fighting the Great War: A Global History* and *Soldiers' Daily Lives: The Nineteenth Century*. He is currently serving on the US Department of the Army Historical Advisory Committee.

Michael Rose studied at the Sorbonne and at Oxford University. He joined the British Army in 1964 and served with the Coldstream Guards and Special Air Service Regiment, becoming Adjutant General and a member of the Army Board before retiring in 1997. He is the author of *Fighting for Peace*, which gives an account of the United Nations' experience of peacekeeping in Bosnia in 1994, and of *Washington's War*, which compares Britain's strategic failures during the American War of Independence with those of the United States in Iraq in 2003.

Dennis Showalter is Professor of History at Colorado College and a past president of the Society for Military History. The joint editor of *War in History*, he specializes in comparative military history. His recent monographs include *The Wars of German Unification* (2004), *Patton and Rommel: Men of War in the Twentieth Century* (2005.) and *Hitler's Panzers* (2009).

Lawrence Sondhaus is Professor of History at the University of Indianapolis, where he directs the Institute for the Study of War and Diplomacy. He specializes in strategy and policy, with a focus on military and naval topics. He is author of eleven books, including, most recently, *Strategic Culture and Ways of War* and *World War I: The Global Revolution, 1914–1919*.

Sources of Quotations

8 From an address to Allied artillery officers in Germany, 27 June 1945; **11** Floor statement to the US Senate, 18 January 2007; **16** Quoted in V. Halperin, *Lord Milner and the Empire: The Evolution of British Imperialism* (London, 1952), 122; **19** Tadayoshi Sakurai, *Human Bullets: A Soldier's Story of Port Arthur*, ed. A. M. Bacon, trans. Masujiro Honda (Lincoln, Neb., 1999); **21** Quoted in D. C. Evans and M. R. Peattie, *Kaigun: Strategy, Tactics, and Technology in the Imperial Japanese Navy, 1887–1941* (Annapolis, Md., 1997), 118; **27** The Tirpitz Memorandum of June 1897, quoted in J. Steinberg, *Yesterday's Deterrent: Tirpitz and the Birth of the German Battle Fleet* (London, 1965), 209; **28** Fisher to the Prince of Wales, 23 October 1906, quoted in A. J. Marder (ed.), *Fear God and Dread Nought*, vol. 2 (1956), 102–5; **29** L. Trotsky, *The War Correspondence of Leon Trotsky: The Balkan Wars, 1912–13*, trans. B. Pearce, ed. G. Weissman and D. Williams (New York, 1980), 366; **33** Quoted in J. Terraine, *White Heat: The New Warfare, 1914–18* (London, 1982), 209; **35** T. M. Kettle, *The Ways of War* (London, 1917); **36** Quoted in R. Asprey, *The First Battle of the Marne* (New York, 1962), 153; **37** Quoted in S. Williamson, *The Politics of Grand Strategy* (Cambridge, 1969), vii; **42** P. Witkop, *German Students' War Letters*, ed. and trans. A. F. Wedd (Philadelphia, 2002), 67; **45** Quoted in E. J. Erickson, *Ordered to Die* (New York, 2002); **46** Quoted in D. E. Omissi, *The Sepoy and the Raj: The Indian Army, 1860–1940* (London, 1998), 117–18; **47** *The Note-Book of an Attaché* (New York, 1915); **53** *The Battles of the Somme* (London, 1917); **54** *The World Crisis* (London, 1923 31), vol. 2; **59** Quoted in D. T. Zabecki, *The German 1918 Offensives: A Case Study in the Operational Level of War*, Strategy and History (New York, 2006), 113; **62** *The Military Correspondence of Field-Marshal Sir William Robertson ... December 1915–February 1918*, ed. D. R. Woodward (London, 1989), 197; **64** Quoted in J. Sheldon, *The German Army at Passchendaele* (Barnsley, 2005), 195; **70** Quoted in J. Hampden Jackson, *Clemenceau and the Third Republic* (London, 1946), 179; **72** *Douglas Haig: War Diaries and Letters, 1914–1918*, ed. G. Sheffield and J. Bourne (London, 2005), 448; **73** F. Lockwood, 'War Diary, 1916–18', West Yorkshire Archive Service: Kirklees, Huddersfield Central Library; **77** Report, quoted in a letter from the Air Officer Commanding, Iraq, 6 March 1924, National Archives, PRO, AIR 5/338; **83** L. Trotsky, *The Military Writings and Speeches of Leon Trotsky*, ed. and trans. B. Pearce, vol. 3: *The Year 1920* (London, 1981), 84; **84** Quoted in N. Davies, *Europe: A History* (Oxford, 1996), 935; **87** Quoted in M. Gilbert, *Churchill and America* (New York and London, 2005), 336; **89** M. Knox, *To the Threshold of Power, 1922/33: Origins and Dynamics of the Fascist and National Socialist Dictatorships*, vol. 1 (Cambridge, 2007), 361, citing *Hitler: Reden, Schriften, Anordnungen: Februar 1925 bis Januar 1933* (Munich, 1992–2003); **90** Quoted in M. Gilbert, *Winston S. Churchill, 1874–1965*, vol. 5 (London, 1976), 550; **96** Quoted in W. Murray, *The Change in the European Balance of Power, 1938–1939: The Path to Ruin* (Princeton, N.J., 1984), 61–62; **97** W. S. Churchill, *The Gathering Storm* (London, 1948), 327; **98** Churchill, *The Gathering Storm*, 347; **100** Allied Military Committee, 'The Major Strategy of the War, Note by the French Delegation', Kew, The National Archives, PRO, CAB 85/16, M.R. (J)(40)(s) 2, 11 April 1940; **115** Quoted in R. Lewin, *Slim, The Standardbearer* (London, 1976), 71; **123** Quoted in M. Miller, *The Far Shore* (New York, 1945); **139** Field Marshal the Viscount Slim, *Defeat into Victory* (New York, 1961), 448; **142**

Quoted in F. Gibney, *Senso: The Japanese Remember the Pacific War* (Armonk, N.Y., 1995), 132; **143** Quoted in B. Alcine, *Yank* (14 April 1944), 3; **146** Quoted in J. H. Alexander, *Utmost Savagery: The Three Days of Tarawa* (Annapolis, Md., 1995), 105; **147** U. Matome, *Fading Victory: The Diary of Admiral Matome Ugaki, 1941–1945*, ed. D. M. Goldstein and K. V. Dillon, trans. C. Masataka (Annapolis, Md., 2008), 416; **150** T. G. Gallant, *The Friendly Dead* (1981), 61; **154** Quoted in F. Gibney, *Senso: The Japanese Remember the Pacific War* (Armonk, N.Y., 1995), 204; **158** Quoted in G. Till, *Sea Power: A Guide for the Twenty-First Century* (London, 2004), 17; **160** Cited in A. von Tirpitz, *My Memoirs* (London, 1919), vol. 2, 456; **161** Quoted in H. H. Herwig, '*Luxury' Fleet: The Imperial German Navy, 1888–1918* (London, 1980), 188; **162** Quoted in Till, *Sea Power*, 63; **167** Quoted in P. M. Kennedy, *The Rise and Fall of British Naval Mastery* (London, 1992), 281; **169** Quoted in W. Rahn, 'German Naval Power in the First and Second World Wars', in N. A. M. Rodger (ed.), *Naval Power in the Twentieth Century* (Houndmills, 1996), 94; **170** Quoted in G. Till, *Seapower: A Guide for the 21st Century* (2nd edn, London, 2009), 149; **171** Quoted in Till, *Seapower*, 198; **173** Quoted in Till, *Seapower*, 57; **176** Letter to C. M. Hitchcock, 21 June 1917; **178** Quoted in Giulio Douhet, *The Command of the Air*, ed. Joseph P. Harahan and Richard H. Kohn (Washington, D.C., 1983); **179** Quoted in K. Middlemas and J. Barnes, *Baldwin: A Biography* (London, 1969), 735; **180** A. Harris, *Bomber Offensive* (London, 2005), 52; **184** Quoted in W. H. Morrison, *Fortress Without a Roof* (New York, 1982); **185t** Lothar Metzger, 'The Fire-Bombing of Dresden: An Eyewitness Account' (1999), *Timewitnesses* [website], http://timewitnesses.org/english/~lothar.html (accessed 1 March 2010); **185b** Quoted in J. Samuel Walker, *Prompt and Utter Destruction: Truman and the Use of Atomic Bombs Against Japan* (Chapel Hill, N.C., 1997); **186** C. E. LeMay with M. Kantor, *Mission with LeMay: My Story* (Garden City, N.Y., 1965), 565; **189** Oval Office meeting, 13 September 2001; **192** Quoted in the *Daily Mirror*, 23 August 1978, after his death; **193** *Time* magazine, 15 December 1952; **199** Quoted in M. Vaïsse (ed.), *L'Armée française dans la guerre d'Indochine* (Brussels, 2000); **200** Quoted in Lam Quang Thi, *The Twenty-Five Year Century* (Denton, Tex., 2001); **201** P. Journaud and H. Tertrais, *Paroles de Dien Bien Phu: les survivants témoignent* (Paris, 2004); **204** Quoted in Y. Courrière, *Le Temps des léopards* (Paris, 1969), 357–58; **210** *Winston S. Churchill: His Complete Speeches, 1897–1963*, ed. R. R. James (New York, 1983), vol. 7, 124; **216** Quoted in C. Gati, *Failed Illusions: Moscow, Washington, Budapest, and the 1956 Hungarian Revolt* (Stanford, Calif., 2006), 198; **217** B. MacArthur (ed.), *The Penguin Book of Twentieth Century Speeches* (London, 1999), 323; **218** Quoted in R. L. Beisner, *Dean Acheson: A Life in the Cold War* (New York, 2006), 336; **224** Quoted in A. S. Grossman, 'Sekretnye dokumenty iz osobykh papok: Afganistan', *Voprosy istorii*, 1993, no. 3, 25; **227** M. J. Cohen and J. Major, *History in Quotations* (London, 2004), 888; **231** Statement to the House of Commons, 4 November 1956; **249** Report to the UN Security Council, 12 May 1992, quoted in Report of the Secretary-General pursuant to General Assembly resolution 53/35: The fall of Srebrenica, 15 November 1999, http://www.unhchr.ch/Huridocda/Huridoca.nsf/TestFrame/4e8fe0c73ec7e4cc80256839003eeb04?Op endocument (accessed 2 March 2010); **252** Nato press release

(1999)040, 23 March 1999; **256** Address to the Parliament of Rwanda, Kigali, 7 May 1998, http://www.un.org/News/Press/docs/1998/19980506.SGSM6552.html (accessed 2 March 2010); **260** H. N. Schwarzkopf with P. Petre, *General H. Norman Schwarzkopf, the Autobiography: It Doesn't Take a Hero* (New York, 1992), 502; **261** Office of the Press Secretary, The White House, Washington, D.C., 'President Bush Delivers Graduation Speech at West Point', 1 June 2002; **262** Interview in *Newsweek International*, 24 July 2006; **263** Interview with BBC, 11 September 2008, http://news.bbc.co.uk/1/hi/world/middle_east/7610405.stm (accessed 2 March 2010); **266** D. H. Rumsfeld, 'Transforming the Military', *Foreign Affairs*, May/June 2002, 29; **269** Interview with SABC, broadcast 8 June 2003; **271** Address to a Joint Session of Congress, 20 September 2001, http://georgewbush-whitehouse.archives.gov/news/releases/2001/09/print/20010920-8.html (accessed 2 March 2001); **272** US Department of Defense News Briefing, 19 May 1997, http://www.fas.org/man/docs/qdr/t051997_t0519qdr.html (accessed 2 March 2010); **273** National Security Strategy of the United States, issued 17 September 2002.

Sources of Illustrations

The illustrations are identified by their page numbers in **bold**.
t: top, b: bottom, l: left, r: right, c: centre

AWM: Australian War Memorial, Canberra; LoC: Library of Congress, Washington, D.C.; NARA: the US National Archives and Records Administration, Maryland; NHF: Naval Historical Foundation, Washington, D.C.; USNI: US Naval Institute, Maryland

1 David Rubinger/Corbis; **2–3** Tim Page/Corbis; **4–5** Michael Hanson/Aurora Photos/Corbis; **6** Interfoto/Lebrecht Collection; **7cl** Harry S. Mueller/LoC; **7tr** Bettmann/Corbis; **8** Hiroshima Peace Memorial Museum; **9** akg-images; **10** Paul Lowe/Panos Pictures; **11** Dylan Martinez/Reuters/Corbis; **12** Kasai Torajiro/LoC; **14** Cartoon of Paul Kruger (1825–1904), President of the Transvaal Republic of South Africa, *Vanity Fair* (1899); **15t** AWM (A04341); **15b** akg-images; **16** AWM (P05667.003); **17** AWM (ART19820); **18** Dagli Orti/The Art Archive; **19tl, 19tr** Museum of Fine Arts, Boston; **20, 22** Underwood & Underwood, New York/LoC; **23tc** akg-images; **23br, 24–25, 26t, 26cl** George Grantham Bain Collection/LoC; **28** K. Koch/National Archives/Time Life Pictures/Getty Images **30cl** National Portrait Gallery, London; **30br** John Batchelor; **31** George Grantham Bain Collection/LoC; **32** E.C.P.A., Ivry/The Art Archive; **34–35** Hulton Archive/Getty Images; **36t** Henry Guttmann/Getty Images; **36bl** Edward Penfield/LoC; **38cl** Musée des Deux Guerres Mondiales, Paris/White Images/Photo Scala; **38bl** George Grantham Bain Collection/LoC; **40** LoC; **42** Hulton-Deutsch Collection/Corbis; **43tl** Ernest Brooks/AWM (G00205); **43tr** Ernest Brooks/AWM (G00599); **44tr** R. McGeehan/AWM (P06493.001); **44b** Canadian War Museum, Ottawa; **45** Imperial War Museum, London; **46** akg-images; **47** AWM (H10344); **48t** AWM (E04851); **48b** AWM (RELAWM04523.005); **49** LoC **50** Fred Spear/LoC; **52** Ernest Brooks/AWM (H15924); **53** Erich Lessing/akg-images; **54–55** Imperial War Museum, London/AWM (H15925); **56** Hans Rudi Erdt/LoC; **58** LoC; **59** Hulton Archive/Getty Images; **60, 61** Imperial War Museum, London/The Art Archive; **62** AWM (A00573); **63** AWM (H09212); **64** Library and Archives Canada, Ottawa; **66tl** AWM (E02877); **66–67b** AWM (RELAWM05040.001); **67tl** Imperial War Museum, London/AWM (H15948); **67tr** LoC; **69t** AWM (E01917); **69b** French Government/AWM (H04640); **71** Pictorial Press/Alamy; **73, 74** Bettmann/Corbis; **76** Photos 12/Alamy; **77** Mary Evans Picture Library/Alamy; **78** Authenticated News/Getty Images; **79** Hulton-Deutsch Collection/Corbis; **81t, 81b, 82–83, 85tr** Bettmann/Corbis; **85cl** Russian Revolutionary poster, 1919; **86, 88** Bettmann/Corbis; **90** Lordprice Collection/Alamy; **91** George Grantham Bain Collection/LoC; **92, 93** Mary Evans Picture Library/Alamy; **94** Bettmann/Corbis; **96** Imperial War Museum, London; **97** NARA; **98** Bettmann/Corbis; **99tr** The Art Archive; **99b** John Batchelor; **100** NARA; **101** RIA Novosti/Alamy; **102** Laski Diffusion/Getty Images; **104** Bettmann/Corbis; **105c** AWM (REL30993); **105tr** E. Bullock/AWM (P03438.003); **105bl** AWM (020368); **106** M. Johnson/AWM (P01112.001); **107** Hulton-Deutsch Collection/Corbis; **108** Lordprice Collection/Alamy; **110bl** LoC; **110br** Imperial War Museum, London; **111** Photos 12/Alamy; **112**

Index